The Cape Breton Fiddler

Allister MacGillivray

Our book is dedicated to Mike MacDougall (1928-1981) —
gifted, vital, determined, kind and unforgettable.

This publication was made possible with assistance from the Explorations Division of the Canada Council, The Cape Breton Development Corporation, The Cape Breton Fiddlers' Association and The Beaton Institute.

COPYRIGHT © 1997
SEA-CAPE MUSIC LTD.

All rights reserved. No part of this book may be reproduced or transmitted in any form or by any means, electronic or mechanical, including photography, recording, or any information storage and retrieval system, without permission in writing from the publisher.

FIRST REPRINT
Published 1997 by
SEA-CAPE MUSIC LIMITED
1011 Hillside Mira
RR #2 Marion Bridge, Cape Breton Island
Nova Scotia, CANADA
B0A 1P0
(902) 562-3433

Canadian Cataloguing in Publication Data

MacGillivray, Allister 1948 -
    The Cape Breton Fiddler

ISBN 0-920336-12-4

1. Violinist, Violoncellists, etc. - Nova Scotia - Cape Breton Island - Biography.   2. Country musicians Nova Scotia - Cape Breton Island - Biography.   3. Folk music, Canadian - Nova Scotia - Cape Breton Island - Biography.   I. Title.

ML398.M24   787.1'092'2   C81-094766-8.

Printed by
CITY PRINTERS LTD.
Sydney, Nova Scotia

Consulting and Contributing Personnel

ARCHIE NEIL CHISHOLM

FR. JOHN ANGUS RANKIN

DOUG MacPHEE

FRANK MacINNIS

JOEY BEATON

BEVERLY MacGILLIVRAY

Preface

THE CAPE BRETON FIDDLER is a many-faceted creature, being at once an elderly man with a Sunday suit and tunes that have no names; a young lady, a smile in her eyes and Gaelic in her bow; a little boy clutching candy in one hand, rosin in the other - as motley a mosaic as ever you'd hope to find. Yet, from Donald Campbell (b. 1789) to Dougie MacDonald (b. 1968), the individuals presented herein share one obvious characteristic - a consuming love for the music of the Celt; the joyous music which has soared in the face of oppression, starvation, tempest, disease and separation; the expressive music which has reflected every attitude but surrender; the complex music which has always demanded the most of its performers.

I have not **written** a book on Cape Breton fiddling; I have merely co-ordinated the contributions of others, all the while monitoring the pulse of the community at large. However, it is upon **my** shoulders that the ultimate editorial responsibility must lie, and, not wishing to offend, I have chosen my subjects on the basis of much more than sheer musical ability; I have taken into consideration such factors as the personality, originality and accessibility of each person. The result, I feel, is a work which gives an indication of the rich tableau yet to be explored, and must not be mistaken as a "top 100" rating of our most talented violinists.

This morning, as I closed the manuscript of "The Cape Breton Fiddler" for the last time, a momentary sadness swept over me. A stream of memories paraded forth of warm country kitchens, lively conversations, spontaneous music and bottomless pots of tea - all of which I have experienced in abundance during the last two years of concentrated research. I sincerely hope that this publication will prove entertaining to the hundreds of fiddlers and fans of fiddling who have made my project so pleasurable.

In closing, I would like to quote violinist-composer-philosopher, the late Dan R. MacDonald of Judique, who, in conversation with Ron MacInnis, once said something which in its simplicity rings of truth, and perhaps incapsulates the creed of our beloved fiddlers: "The Devil won't do nothing to me because I played music all my life and was enjoying people!"

Allister MacGillivray
Breton Cove
May 1/81

Contents

The Cape Breton Scot and His Music	1
Cape Breton Fiddling Techniques	5

THE PAST
Feature Articles	7
Assorted Photos of Past Players	72

THE PRESENT
Feature Articles	79
Assorted Photos of Present Players	167

THE FUTURE
Assorted Photos	177

A Partial Directory of Cape Breton Violinists	179
Some Prominent Accompanists - Past and Present	188
Short Titles	190
Footnotes	191
Photographic Credits	192
Art Credits	193
Acknowledgements	193

The Cape Breton Fiddler

The Cape Breton Scot and His Music

"There is a legend about the origin of the violin. A man's wife, named Viola, died and he said 'I will make her image; it will sing and cry but will not speak.' If you examine the violin, you will see it has a woman's form."

— Joe Kennedy
Inverside, Cape Breton

The story of traditional Scottish violin playing began in the late 1600's when the instrument, as we know it today, became popular in Scotland. Evidence seems to suggest that the Highlands, which at that time, included the mountainous mainland area of Scotland as well as the Islands, contributed a great deal to the emergence of the Scottish fiddling style of the 1700's. This was largely due to the principal composers and collectors of fiddle music being from this area. Some of the more well-known were: - Niel Gow (1727-1807), Nathaniel Gow (1763-1831), Robert "Red Rob" MacIntosh (a. 1745-1807), William Marshall (1748-1833) and Captain Simon Fraser (1773-1852) as well as McGlashen, Bremner, Anderson and Malcolm McDonald.

The "Golden Age" of the Arts in Scotland flourished throughout the eighteenth century and witnessed the evolution of Gaelic-speaking fiddler-composers. The style of music favoured by these Gaels was influenced by the sound of the bagpipes. It was during this era that most of the evacuation of Scots took place; the event that largely precipitated this move was the Highland Clearances. Following the Battle of Culloden in 1746, the domination of England, as well as their own destitution, led the despairing Celts to seek a home in the forests of the New World.

The first shipload of emigrants arrived in Pictou, Nova Scotia on September 15, 1773 aboard the "Hector". Some two hundred men, women and children, their trunks filled with the cherished articles banned from usage at home, were determined to forge a home in this new land. The wave of emigration to Canada had begun and by 1851 approximately 55,000 emigrants had come to Nova Scotia, of which 12,000 were Scots to Cape Breton. Parts of this Island became reconstructions of entire districts of Scotland.

The stoic forbearance of these Highland Scots served them well in coping with a pioneer life that was hard and lonely. Comforts were few. The rural communities the settlers had left behind had had little in the way of material means, and, as a result of this, their expansive Gaelic aural traditions were the principal source of entertainment. Not surprisingly, this continued to be the case in their new homes. The isolation of the pioneer families inspired them once again to find companionship in their pipes and violins and to play from the large store of tunes that had arrived with them. "A violin would be a fairly common possession, though there'd be a minority of note-readers; you'd have more people remembering the tunes by singing than by use of books." - Father John Angus Rankin. The melodies were thus transmitted correctly and absorbed some inflection of Gaelic speech. "When Mama was spinning or rocking one of the kids to sleep, she never let up singing Gaelic verses or humming pieces of fiddle music. Those tunes were as correct as if they were taken from the book - we found that out years later." - Archie Neil Chisholm, Margaree Forks.

The settlers usually reserved Sunday afternoons for violin music, and, particularly during the winter months when there was not as much outside work to be done, old tunes were exchanged and new ones written in the comforting warmth of a wood fire. "The music was the antidote for the hard times, and it seems it achieved its greatest and most sensitive expression where survival was the most difficult."[2] Nothing could arouse a lonely, low-spirited emigrant like the music of his native country.

In time, each settlement had its own fiddler and piper. At most get-togethers - be they weddings, frolics, kitchen rackets (informal house parties) or ceilidhs - dancing took place, and the fiddle was as ubiquitous at these gatherings as were the people themselves. This music was "universally popular, immediately understandable and functionally related to the settlers' way of life."[3]

Some of the early Cape Breton clergy held to the ancient superstition that fiddles and pipes were "instruments of the devil". As in Scotland, these zealous churchmen tried to stamp out the music and all activities that went with it. The most well-known case of this occurred during the pastorship of Father Kenneth MacDonald (1865-94), who gathered up all the violins in his Mabou-West Lake Ainslie parish and destroyed them in the hope of banishing the demonical atmosphere which he felt centered around them. Despite odds such as these, the music flourished, and in the late 1800's a new social event came into prominence - the parish picnic. Sanctioned by the Church, this fund-raising event was usually held over a two-day period. It consisted of suppers, sporting events, fiddling and dancing. Bough-covered platforms were erected to accommodate the solo dancing (eg. "Flowers of Edinburgh" and "Whistle O'er the Lave O't") and "Scotch Fours", with the musicians often playing on into the morning. Bagpipes were becoming comparatively rare at this time, being expensive and difficult to construct; a fiddle could be carved, however, at no cost from a tree or an old piece of wood.

When no particular social occasion presented itself, the spontaneous joy the music created in the people soon led to the establishment of school-house dances and eventually to the construction of dance halls.

Cape Breton was becoming an Island of Fiddlers with a style that was, now, uniquely its own. The music of Scotland's "Golden Age" with its affinity to the sound of the pipes, seasoned with the flavour of the Gaelic and animated by the rhythms of dancing feet, had crossed the ocean with the emigrants and had remained unchanged amidst the hills and valleys of this "New Scotland". It manifested joy to the listener - a joy in the freedom from oppression. It was, indeed, a music stronger than the opposition to it!

There existed isolated pockets of music - such as Mabou, Iona, Queensville and Margaree - and the poor conditions of early roads prevented much communication between these villages. Thus, until the early part of this century, each region preserved a pure strain of ancient Highland Gaelic, piping and fiddling. Overseas, however, the old ways were becoming altered due to many outside influences, and the folk dancing, so integral to the lively renditions of tunes, was lost.

The Cape Breton fiddling community now had heroes of its own. There were prominent musical families who not only composed and played well, but also, through additions and improvisations, changed and improved the old tunes. There arose distinctive Cape Breton variants; for example, "Christy Campbell", "Flora MacDonald", "The Braes of Mar", "The Duke of Gordon's Birthday" and "Farewell to Whisky".

This strong attraction to Scottish music was felt among the French and in the Micmac villages as well. Many fine Highland-style Cape Breton fiddlers were produced by these ethnic groups.

Due to impoverished conditions in most of the settlements, there were few keyboard instruments to accompany the early fiddlers. Players would often team up, and, to gain more volume, would occasionally use (1) special tunings, such as "high counter and bass" and "low bass", and (2) a technique called "first and second violin" in which one fiddler utilized the back strings while another concentrated on the front to create octave harmonies around the melody line. Sometimes a woman would tap her knitting needles on the neck or body of the violin to provide a rhythm, and some men played along with spoons, jew's harps or merely "kept bass" with their voices by humming through cupped hands, thus creating a novel form of chording. As the pump organ became more common, it was used to provide a bagpipe-like drone behind the fiddling, and it was not unusual to see a wagon or sleigh transporting these heavy instruments to a dance. In time, the piano replaced the organ and the accompaniment became more elaborate. The piano stylings became as distinctive as the violin playing, with special bass runs and doubling of the melody being characteristic.

The twentieth century slipped unobtrusively into Cape Breton, but the old way of life was already showing signs of decline. As early as the 1800's, the lure of the urban centres had taken its toll on the population of farming communities. Young people, in steadily increasing numbers, continued moving to Sydney, and then farther afield to Halifax, Upper Canada and the "Boston States" to seek their fortunes. The harmful effects of this exodus from country to city on the music and language was somewhat counter-balanced by metropolitan radio shows such as "The Cape Breton Ceilidh", "Kismuil Castle", and "Cotter's Saturday Night". The first "78's" came out in the early thirties and among Cape Breton's premier recording artists were Angus Chisholm (on Decca and Celtic), Dan J. Campbell, Angus Allan Gillis (on Celtic) and "Alick" Gillis and His Inverness Serenaders (on Decca). A lesser-known group called The Columbia Scotch Band (sometimes referred to as The Caledonia Scotch Band), led by Charlie MacKinnon also released a few discs on the Columbia label. The transition of Cape Breton music from living-room to recording studio was accompanied by certain misgivings. Here, Angus Allan Gillis of Margaree offers a candid description of his experience in Montreal in 1935: "We were stuck in a sound-proof room and a fellow told us we had to be fifteen feet exactly from the piano! When the first light came on, you were supposed to start playing. There was no talking or any damned thing!"[4]

In 1940, Gordon MacQuarrie, with much help from his friend Joe Beaton, published the first collection of Cape Breton compositions. This celebrated work featured not only MacQuarrie's music, but that of Dan R. MacDonald, Dan Hughie MacEachern, "Big" Ronald MacLellan, Sandy MacLean, Alex "The Piper" MacDonald and others.

The era of the parish picnic by now had begun to wane and Scottish concerts, which required less organization, took their place. Father Mike MacAdam and Father John Hugh MacEachern were among the first Cape Breton clergymen to vigorously promote such gatherings. In time, during the summer months, many parishes such as Broad Cove and Big Pond held these annual events. However, television, "pop" music and the ever-urgent trend towards modernity continued to overpower traditional pastimes. New and diverse activities took the emphasis off "ceilidh-ing" and live music. Young people migrated westward and southward in droves and, by the 1950's and '60's, it appeared imminent that, like the Gaelic, the Cape Breton fiddler was to become but a memory of a by-gone age.

In 1971, the CBC radio and television program entitled "The Vanishing Cape Breton Fiddler", produced by Ron MacInnis, predicted that unless more children took an interest in the music, it would, in fact, vanish! It pointed out that the older generation was dying, and with it was going a legacy of tunes and techniques. The immediate result of this show was an aroused Cape Breton public and the formation of the Cape Breton Fiddlers' Association. This group, including stalwart clergymen, was determined to disprove the myth of the "vanishing fiddler".

In July of 1973, the first Glendale Fiddling Festival was held. This extremely successful endeavour featured over 130 players, cheered on by approximately 10,000 fervent fans. Cape Breton music was revived! It was rejuvenated and revitalized! Soon old men, whose violins had been gathering dust, took them up again. Young people, who formerly thought the music "dated", joined newly-established fiddle classes and sought out these elder players for advice and tunes. CBC produced the popular network television show "Ceilidh" which incorporated the talents of some of the Island's finest fiddlers. The Scottish concerts flourished and every week-end, all summer long, expatriate Cape Bretoners returned home to attend and perform. A number of new Lp's were recorded and these sold successfully. It was as if the very soul of this venerable music had found a fresh expression.

In an age where people are searching for their roots, their link with the past and, ultimately, their own identity, Cape Breton's fiddling tradition appears, once again, to be strong and secure.

"The music comes from the fiddler's heart,
through his strings and straight into **your** heart."
-Father John Angus Rankin

Cape Breton Fiddling Techniques

Though slight variations in the following characteristics have been noted in different areas of the Island (e.g. Margaree, Ingonish, Iona and Mabou), the basic Cape Breton "sound" is unmistakable.

The local terms "lift" and "lively bow" are generally used to describe that aspect of a fiddler's playing which encourages dancing. With the up-stroke bowing of most players being as powerful as the down-stroke, the result is an effective execution of figures such as the "Scotch snap", the signature of the strathspey. The overall flavour suggests the inflections of piping and Gaelic music, such as puirt-a-beul and canntaireachd.

A fiddler's left hand contributes the wide array of grace notes and embellishments typical of Island playing, while the right hand supplies the all-important "cuts" (called bow shakes or "gearraidhean"). These consist of rapid and successive notes of the same pitch, which are usually employed at the discretion of the player in an attempt to add a degree of complexity to simpler aspects of the melody line. A three-note cut may be bowed in either of two methods: (1) with alternating up-and-down strokes of the bow, or (2) with one stroke in a single direction. The most adept fiddlers can cut as effortlessly bowing downward as they can upward. The best cuts result from the wrist action of the player, not the shoulder motion, and they are generally applied to only to the march, strathspey and reel. A number of tunes can be ornamented with "double cuttings", that is, two cut-clusters in immediate succession.

Another common feature of Cape Breton fiddling is the semi-improvisational application of drone notes both above and below the melody, which creates a rich, polyphonic texture. Derived from the era of solo playing, when the violinist had to supply more volume as well as his own accompaniment, this method at times recalls the hum of a bagpipe. The drone effect can also be achieved by employing an old tuning called "high bass and counter (tenor)" in which the G string is brought up in pitch to sound the note A, and the D string is raised to sound E; this results in an A/E/A/E setup when bowing the four strings open from bass to treble. The tuning is designed for the key of A, and adds increased volume and resonance to pieces performed in this manner. There exists a fairly large repertoire of tunes suitable for this scordatura tuning, but it is mostly the older violinists who seem to specialize in them. Additional tunings include "high bass" (i.e., adjusting the G string only) and "low bass" (dropping the G string to either F or E, for use in the keys of F major and E minor respectively).

Many players use another technique which is referred to as "doubling" or "unisons". Here, with the little finger of his left hand, the fiddler duplicates the note of an open string by depressing the next lowest string on the violin at the appropriate position, sounding the two equal notes simultaneously. Moreover, some Cape Breton violinists avoid using the mere open string whenever possible, even in reels. Doubling adds a new dimension to both tone and volume, and allows for some special effects, especially on the "old music".

The bow is held in the most comfortable fashion, as a rule, with little emphasis being placed on the classical grip. The fiddle is occasionally supported against the upper chest instead of under the chin. Both of these habits interfere with some forms of positional playing, but do not seem to hinder the use of the first position where most of the tunes are primarily situated. A recent theory, which is gaining popularity, suggests that the Cape Breton method of holding the bow, in fact, facilitates accurate renditions of traditional-flavoured pieces.

Some violinists incorporate a complicated foot-tapping pattern into their playing style. One variation, which combines a heel-and-toe beat on one foot with a syncopated tap on the other, results in a clever rhythm that can serve to complement unaccompanied playing. Some fiddlers rely on foot-tapping as an aid to keeping strict time.

As a medley of tunes progresses through the sequence of march, slow strathspey, "dance" strathspey and reel, there occurs a marked sensation of growing anticipation and excitement. During the repeat of the second turn of the last strathspey, which precedes "breaking into" the reel, the beat often accelerates so that the final transition into reel tempo is quite smooth. If a dancer is involved, the interplay between the two artists can result in a thrilling experience for the onlooker.

The final and most crucial ingredient is joy! The theory has been proposed that because the Cape Breton settlers had escaped from the oppression in their mother country, the overriding new mood of the old music was a blend of defiance and exhilaration. The fact that the slow air and lament have not enjoyed the same popularity on this side of the Atlantic as they have in Scotland seems to support that theory. Whatever the case, on comparing the fiddle music of Cape Breton with that of the "auld country", one discovers a definite difference in basic spirit.

The Past

Alexander J. Beaton

Dates: born May 28, 1837 at Mabou Coal Mines; date of death unknown
Parents: Squire John Beaton (Iain MacFhionnlaidh, 1794-1865) and Mary MacDonald
(Mairi Aonghuis Thullaich, 1795-1880)

Alexander J., the youngest of eight children, was known in Gaelic as "Alasdair MacIain 'ic Fhionnlaidh". His grandfather, Finlay Beaton (b. 1766), was from Glen Spean in Scotland and became a pioneer settler of the Mabou Coal Mines area, having arrived on June 16, 1809.

Although Alexander's musical heritage could be traced all the way back to Alexander of Skye, who was his great-great grandfather and a known fiddler[5], it was from closer relatives that he received firsthand exposure to Highland music. His mother, Mary, had been a distinguished dancer in Scotland and, after emigrating to Cape Breton, set up a school near MacKinnon's Brook for the purpose of teaching that skill. Alexander's older brother, Angus, was also a stepdance teacher, and his first cousin, Archibald Beaton, was a brilliant piper.

While in the prime of life, Alexander excelled as both a violinist and a dancer. Sometimes he played his fiddle with the choir in the Mabou church. As an older man of about seventy years, he used to make winter visits to the home of Alexander R. Beaton Sr. of MacKinnon's Brook, and on these occasions he would tutor the daughters, Mary and Jessie, on the violin. After the lessons, which were held twice a week, "Old" Alex would spend additional time showing Mrs. Peggy Beaton, the mother, dance steps which she did not know. The aforementioned Mary (now referred to as Mairi Alasdair Raonuill), having absorbed those dance techniques as well as the tunes, in time became a legendary figure in Cape Breton's fiddling community, with much credit going to Alexander J., an important link in the Island's Celtic-music chain[6].

Alexander lived on the old homestead at the Coal Mines, on the section called "Cul na Beinne" meaning "back of the mountain". He married Margaret MacDonald, daughter of "Raonull Diolladair", and they were blessed with eleven children.

Danny Beaton

Dates: 1894-1950, a native of Mabou Coal Mines
Parents: Johnny Ranald Beaton (1862-1928) and
Catherine Anne Campbell

On October 31, 1894, the very day that the notorious Fr. Kenneth MacDonald resigned as pastor of Mabou parish, Danny "Johnny Ranald" was born. Fr. Kenneth, in his religious fanaticism, had tried to stifle the sound of the violin in Mabou; Danny, on the other hand, was to dedicate his life to the glory of Highland music.

With his father and three uncles on the Beaton side supplying the inspiration, Danny displayed a passionate interest in the music while still a child. Around 1904-05, he was rewarded with a little tin fiddle at Christmas; however, Johnny Ranald soon granted his son the use of the family violin, which had once belonged to Danny's uncle, "Little" Sandy Beaton.

Since a seed of music was readily nurtured in his home, by age fourteen Danny was providing the fiddling at community dances. His mother, a pianist with some knowledge of notation, contributed a degree of preciseness to Danny's learning of melodies, he being an "ear player". His cousin, Donald Angus Beaton, says, "Danny didn't **have** to have the notes. He was one of those fiddlers that, when he played with a note-reader, you couldn't tell the difference!" At age sixteen, he performed at a picnic in Brook Village, and in 1914, with money he had earned in the Inverness Mine, Danny provided himself with a new violin.

During his service in the mines, Danny received a serious head injury which plagued him throughout the rest of his life, though it never affected his playing. Donald Angus continues, "He was a very good set player. We teamed up at dances at Port Hood, Judique, Mabou, et cetera. He also used to entertain at the Glencoe picnics." Besides the piano playing of his mother, Danny often utilized the talents of the late Neil Finn of Mabou, especially when appearing at Earl's Hall in Port Hood. His arrangements of "Big John MacNeil", "Lord MacDonald's Reel", "King George the Fourth Strathspey" and "Christy Campbell" were powerful. In addition, he mastered scores of nameless traditional tunes, and, during their delivery, often displayed spirited gestures as he became totally engrossed in his own music.

Known to travel the roads and visit neighbours, even in the middle of the night, Danny's arrival was always met with enthusiasm, for he'd usually produce the violin immediately. "He often called at the home of John Alex MacDonell, whose sister played the piano. You could hear the music two or three houses away!" says Donald Angus.

Donald John "the Tailor" Beaton

Dates: 1856-1919, a native of Mabou Coal Mines
Parents: John Beaton (Iain Alasdair an Taillear) and Isabel MacDonald

Donald John n the Tailor", called "Domhnull Iain an Taillear" in Gaelic, was the grandson of Alexander Beaton, a pioneer of the Mabou Coal Mines area who settled in 1809. The youngest of ten children, he took to the violin as a small boy, for his father wanted all the children to play. Donald's niece, Sr. Sara Anne Beaton, relates the following story: "Allan Cameron, a professor with a degree from a college in Edinburgh, was tutoring Domhnull Iain's older brother (nicknamed Donald 'the Miller') on the violin. Domhnull Iain was only seven years old at the time, and he was looking on. When the lesson was over, he stole away to his secret place behind the chimney on the second floor of the house, where he practiced in private. Then one day, Domhnull Iain said to Mr. Cameron, 'If I were playing that tune, I'd put in this note', and he demonstrated. The tutor was so shocked that he answered, 'You're the one who will be a great player!'" Immediately following this episode, Allan Cameron began teaching Donald John musical theory.

Using the family violin, Donald John practiced diligently, seeming to know that music was his calling. He possessed the hands of a born musician, having long, slender fingers. Known as a light, smooth and very listenable fiddler, he did not do much advanced position work, though his first-position playing was universally regarded as "terrific".

Every hall in Inverness County knew the ring of Donald's violin, for he was a very popular and dependable performer. The legendary "Little" Jack MacDonald is supposed to have made this comment about "The Tailor": "I'd walk anywhere in the county when I heard he was playing!" Of her own home, Sr. Sara says, "We were never a night without music, and Domhnull Iain usually supplied it. He was a nice, Christian gentleman and a favourite of the family. He didn't show off in any way, yet he wasn't afraid to play in front of anyone - he had that confidence! Both of his hands were talented, so that his left was as thrilling as his right." Lauded far and wide for his excellent musicianship, letters to Domhnull Iain were often addressed: "Donald the Fiddler".

Through the years, Donald accumulated a fine collection of old and valuable fiddle-tune books. He possessed both a phenomenal memory for tunes, as well as the ability to notate them with ease. These talents are demonstrated in the following story, told by his grand-niece, Anna MacInnis: "Uncle Donald came to visit us in Margaree. When he arrived, late at night, my mother offered him something to eat, but he said, 'No thank you. I heard a tune on the train coming down and I'm going to write it down when I get up tomorrow, so I'll go straight to bed.'" Apparently he believed that if he paused for a meal before sleeping, it might cause him to forget a portion of the new tune overnight.

Sometimes, Donald would walk the long road to Paddy Gillis' place in Margaree Forks. Such was the great fiddler's reputation that the house would quickly fill with people as soon as word of his visit leaked out into the community.

In 1919, while playing for servicemen in Antigonish, Donald John took sick. Fr. Rory MacNeil, a relative and close friend, was instrumental in getting him to the hospital and stayed to comfort him. On Christmas Eve, the fading giant requested a violin and, with his remaining strength, appropriately played "Cuir 's a' Chiste Mhóir Mi" ("Put Me in the Big Chest"); moments later, he was dead. It is interesting to note that in certain parts of Inverness County, the Cape Breton variant of "Cuir 's a' Chiste Mhóir Mi" is now referred to by the title "Beaton's Last" in honour of Donald John.

On January 8, 1920, an Antigonish paper called "The Casket" carried this item:

"DIED:

In St. Martha's Hospital, on Christmas Eve, Donald Beaton, a native of Mabou, C.B., 63 years of age. He had a wide circle of friends who will deeply regret his departure from their midst. He was a welcomed visitor wherever he went, for his was a master hand at the violin, and capable judges pronounced him the best player of Scottish music in these parts. He was withal most gentle in his manners, unobtrusive and modest in his demeanor, and faithful in the practice of his duties to God and man. He received the grace of a good Christian death. Rev. R. McNeil, P.P. Georgeville and Dr. A.J. McNeil, Mabou, C.B., are nephews of the deceased. May his soul rest in peace." He was unmarried.

During the last one hundred years, which takes in Donald Beaton's prime as well as the long period since his death, the prevalent opinion has endured that he was one of the greatest musicians to bless the Island of Cape Breton.

Johnny "Ranald" Beaton

Dates: 1862-1928, a native of Mabou Coal Mines, Inverness County
Parents: Ranald Beaton (Raonull MacAlasdair Bhàin) and Jessie Rankin

Johnny Ranald, the great-grandson of Mabou Coal Mines pioneer Alexander Beaton (Alasdair an Taillear), was one of nine musical children. Of that family, the following four boys could skillfully handle the violin: Angus (Aonghas Raonuill), "Young" Donald, Alexander Jr. and Johnny himself. His uncle, John "Sandy" Beaton (Iain Alasdair Bhàin), was a fine violinist and stepdancer.

Johnny Ranald married Katie Anne Campbell, the sister of fiddler John Campbell (Iain Ruadh Aonghais Iain) of Glenora Falls. Donald Angus Beaton says, "My uncle, Johnny Ranald was a set player and played quite correctly. His wife, Katie Anne, was a note reader for piano; he got his correctness from her. He played some hard stuff on B-flat and F - all the flats. One tune I remember him playing was 'Mary Walker's Reel' on B-flat. He'd play in pretty near any key!" It is well worth mentioning here that Donald Angus' own fiddling is supposed to resemble Johnny Ranald's very much.

In spite of the zealous attempts of Fr. Kenneth MacDonald to silence all the violins in his Mabou parish in the late 1800's, the home of Mr. & Mrs. Johnny Ranald Beaton became famous for hospitality and music, and visitors would travel long distances by horse and wagon to share in the Gaelic humour, piping, fiddling and stepdancing.[8] "Fr. Kenneth came looking for fiddles to destroy," says Donald Angus. "Johnny had two, and so he gave Fr. Kenneth the worst one and secretly kept the other." However, the priest got wind of the ruse and eventually tore the violin right from Johnny Ranald's hands and smashed it.

Though Johnny worked hard at home as a farmer and a blacksmith, he maintained a generosity with his music. Often, he would leave his chores at the forge and lead the customer up to the house to entertain him royally with Mabou Coal Mines fiddling while Katie Anne provided organ accompaniment. Johnny's powerful hands, soiled from the day's labour, could charm the richest Celtic strains from the strings of his violin.[9] The music of the Coal Mines, rooted in Scotland's distant past, smacked of the Gaelic and resounded with the hum of the "high bass" and the tang of saucy "cuts", well placed and timed.

In 1897, five years after the pastorate of Fr. Kenneth had ended, Johnny participated in the first Mabou parish picnic; his brother Angus, and his uncle, John, contributed as well. In addition to his musical involvement in the community, Johnny R. served for several years as municipal councillor of his district.

Through the sheer love of Highland melody, this branch of the Beaton family tree has done more than its share in preserving a special brand of Cape Breton fiddling. Of Johnny Ranald's six children, four leaned heavily towards the violin: Danny (1894-1950), Jessie (1901-1972), Ronald Dan (1898-1974) and Johnny (1906-1980). Another son, Angus (1895-1971), was an exceptional piper.

Malcolm Beaton

Dates: born April 4, 1912 at Strathiorne, Inverness County, and died October 1, 1951
Parents: John A. Beaton (Iain MacAonghais 'ic Iain 'ic Fhionnlaidh) and Maggie Belle MacLellan
(Nighean Niall 'ic Ghilleasbuig 'ic Fhearchair)

"He is a gifted violinist and plays Scottish music with much expression and beauty." These words, describing Malcolm, were written in 1943-44 by Joe MacInnis for the publication "Eilean Cheap Breatann".[0] The twelfth of fourteen children, Malcolm was the grandson of Angus Beaton, who was a violinist and stepdance teacher and the brother of noted fiddler Alexander J. Beaton.

Malcolm was sixteen when his older brother, Neil Archie, purchased a violin at McNutt's Store in Inverness. Neil A. claims the violin was only a ten or twelve-dollar model, though it served the purpose admirably. Soon the elder brother mastered a tune, and Malcolm wasn't too far behind. After only a few months had passed, it was obvious to all that the Beaton boys were born to play. Instruction in music theory came from cousin Neil MacDonald of Inverness Corner and Allan Gillis of Foot Cape. They ordered collections from Scotland, Antigonish and Vancouver, and soon possessed Lowe's, The Skye, Marshall's, Gow's (I and II) and Glen's, to name but a few.

While only in his twenties, Malcolm's musical talent, coupled with his winning personality, earned him a far-reaching popularity. Besides performing at scores of schoolhouse dances and weddings, he and his brother were involved in a popular Antigonish-based radio show. Along with the two Beatons, poet and producer Kenneth Leslie of Halifax recruited Angus Allan Gillis and Dan J. Campbell to be featured on "Kismuil Castle". The first two programs were done at the CNBA Hall in Inverness with Jessie Maggie MacLellan as pianist. Neil A. recalls that they were connected to Sydney via telephone for broadcast throughout Cape Breton. Then, possibly due to the existence of better facilities, the show was moved to Antigonish and Neil A. remembers that period well: "We used to go across on the ferry about once a week for seven or eight weeks and we'd do the show 'live' in a part of the college. Mrs. Willie Hector MacDonald was our accompanist and we'd go to her home to practice before we'd do the show."

Though Malcolm had a slight preference for traditional strathspeys, his remarkable bow arm was evident in most of the tunes he played, especially those requiring high bass and counter tuning, a fine example being "Greig's Pipes Reel". Other selections he delivered with great virtuosity included

"The Balkan Hills", "Rothiemurchus Rant", "MacMillan's Lament" and "Cecil MacKenzie's Strathspey". Father Hugh A. MacDonald, who was a former classmate and close friend of Malcolm's, has the following recollections: "When he played, he went into another world. I've seen him, his eyes closed, his soul emersed in the music! He would become oblivious to everything around him. I saw him play often at the old Immaculata Hall at Mount St. Bernard in Antigonish around 1937 or '38." Violinists with whom Malcolm associated included Sandy MacLean, "Curly" Sandy Beaton, Angus Chisholm and Donald Angus Beaton.

Malcolm was a gentleman in the truest sense of the word. His kindness and Christian outlook endeared him to everyone. His stories, often laced with humour, could bring tears or laughter.

Francis MacKinnon, another friend and admirer of this singular violinist and poet, has written these words in his honour: "Malcolm Beaton was an eminently lovable man. The vicissitudes of fate dealt with him so harshly that only the resiliency of a great soul prevented him from becoming bitter and cynical. I first met Malcolm in a tuberculosis hospital, an institution to which he was forced to dedicate the best years of his life, and, like all others, immediately fell under the spell of his wit and humour. Almost belligerently Scottish, in another age he might have been a renowned bard or a great Highland chieftain.

"His most outstanding trait," Francis adds, "was a deep and abiding love of all things beautiful, coupled with a virile and unabashed sentimentality obvious in his poems. The rhythmic flow of his poetry, the cadence-like rise and fall of his words, betray the soul of a musician, and he **was** an excellent musician, a fine violinist."

Malcolm died on October 1, 1951 at only thirty-nine years of age. Donald Angus Beaton spoke for Cape Breton's fiddling community in these words: "When Malcolm Beaton passed away, not only did I lose a very good friend, but so did all Scottish music lovers.'"[11] Father Hugh A. adds a positive note: "Malcolm Beaton will never die. His memory will always be a benediction. May his kind words, music and Christian spirit endure in the hearts of us all.'"[12]

". . . When my soul shall take flight to the regions of light,
Away from strife, sorrow and sin,
I'll hear you again in the land of the blessed,
My sweet-voiced old violin."

-Malcolm Beaton, October 22, 1950

Colin J. Boyd

Dates: 1891-1975, a native of West Lakevale, Antigonish County
Parents: Alan R. Boyd and Eunice MacGillivray

"He learned his first fiddle tunes," says his daughter, Mary, "in his West Lakevale home where he listened to his uncle, Hughie MacGillivray, entertaining during frequent visits." Even as a three-year old, Colie positioned himself as close to his uncle as possible and listened with fascination. "One story is told," Mary continues, "that when he was still very young (about age six), he decided that a branch of a tree, which shaded the family well, looked like a violin and might well fulfill his desire for one of his very own. With that in mind, he climbed the tree to gain his prize, only to lose his footing and end up in the well. Fortunately, there was a member of the family nearby to fish him out."

When his uncle Hughie passed away, Colie, now twelve, inherited the violin which had originally stirred his love for music. By ear, he learned his first tune, "My Love She's But A Lassie Yet", which he often heard performed as a polka by his neighbour, Hugh A. MacDonald.

1909 found Colie in Cobalt, Ontario, taking part in the silver boom; bringing his fiddle, he often entertained in the mining camps. He spent the years 1911-16 in Boston, where he learned to read music. Taking instruction from two violin teachers, Colie expanded his love of the instrument to include classical music. A collection of theory books given to him by friend John Fraser further enhanced his music-reading skills. His specialty became hornpipes and, in private, slow airs.

In 1911 in Boston, Colie met a carpenter called Dan "the Ridge" MacDonald, formerly of Mabou and Antigonish. It was Colie's opinion that Dan was the finest violin player he had ever heard. Starting with an old Scottish tune Dan taught him, Colie made a few adaptations and came up with an original piece entitled "The Little Burnt Potato", a tune which has gained enormous popularity.

On March 18, 1932, Colie made the first known recording of Scottish violin music in Canada, and released it on the Brunswick label. Within a period of four or five years, he recorded two 78's for Brunswick, three for Columbia and two for Celtic Records.

A fluent Gaelic speaker, Colie's musical comrades included piper Sandy Boyd and Dan Rory MacDonald. "While my father milked the cows," says Mary, "Dan R. played the fiddle in the pasture. They discussed tunes and music while hay was being made or while my father attended to bugs on the potato plants."

In 1965, at age seventy-two, Colie made his only long-playing record. He passed away on June 17, 1975.

Dan J. Campbell

Dates: 1895-1981, a native of Glenora Falls, Inverness County
Parents: John A. Campbell (Iain Ruadh 'ic Aonghais Iain,
1855-1919) and Ann MacDonald

In the 1970's, in conversation with Archie Neil Chisholm, Dan J. revealed the following information about himself and his family: "My great-grandfather (John 'the Bear' Campbell) came from Scotland. He styled himself a Lochaber man, but he came from a place in Argyll. He came out here in 1816 and built a log cabin that same year, not very far from my place here.

"My grandmother was a MacInnis, and she had an uncle - he was John MacInnis; he came from Scotland and settled in this country at Mabou Ridge. I heard my father talking about John MacInnis, that he was the best player that came from Scotland. Then, there was my grand uncle, Ronald MacInnis. This Ronald was a good player, a real good player, a player that you'd like his style - the old style of playing and the old tunes! 'Raonul Aonghuis an Taillear', they called him in Gaelic.

"When I started to play, I was around ten years old. There was a fiddle in the old home, and an organ. My father was a fiddler, and my Uncle Donald (b. 1858) was pretty well advanced in music - he was a choir master at Mabou. My father was a note player and an old-time player, and he told us a few things, you know, about playing a fiddle and the style we'd have to take - and especially to play by the book!

"But, besides that, I used to listen to good fiddlers coming to the home and talking about music. Old Donald Beaton was one - 'Domhnull Iain an Taillear', as they say; I would say he was the best I heard. And, there was a MacDougall that used to call at the house and he lived most of his time in Glenville. I used to hear them saying that his brother was a master player - a fellow by the name of Ronald MacDougall; he was an exceptionally good player. And, there was a John Beaton at the Coal Mines.

"I heard this talk about music, and I heard some good fiddlers - if they didn't play absolutely out of the book, they had a genuine style of playing that would please you. There was a MacLellan in Glenville who was good - Donald Allan, they used to call him - and a few others. My brother was listening to the same talk; they called him Angus - he died young (1892-1922). He was a better player, I know, than I was. And, my sister (Catherine) took up music in Antigonish at Mount St. Bernard. She played by the book. She gave us a good push on how to read music, and Angus was pretty sharp on that business. That's how we started - talking to the good fiddlers.

"My father was always on the watch out for some good collections. There were some old books written - Niel Gow's Collection especially, and Marshall's. My father was out to get the best books he could on

Scottish music. And, this is the thing that goes with music - if you don't have a good judgement and know how to select good stuff, well, you're not going to leave much impression behind, I think!''

Dan J. was one of the first Cape Breton fiddlers to record a 78 rpm in Canada, having done so along with Angus Chisholm and Angus Allan Gillis in the mid-thirties for Celtic Records. The Sydney Post-Record, on Thursday, December 19, 1935, carried the following news item: ''Daniel J. Campbell, well known violinist of Glenora Falls, returned home Friday from Montreal where he had been for the past week having his music reproduced on records. Music lovers in this county and throughout the province are anxiously awaiting his records to be on display.'' Among the 78's released at that time were:

1. **CELTIC RECORDS 006** - Dan J. Campbell accompanied on piano by Bess Siddall MacDonald, Side A: ''Mrs. Dingwall of Brockley's'', ''Mist Over Cape Mabou'' and ''Carnie's Canter'', Side B: ''The Road to St. Rose'' and ''Song of the Water-mill'' (Hornpipes)

2. **CELTIC RECORDS 010** - Dan J. Campbell accompanied on piano by Bess Siddall MacDonald, Side A: ''Daintie Davie'', ''Cameronian Rant'', and ''Miss Grant'', Side B: ''Flee As a Bird'' (Clog Medley).

Though he played very well by note, Dan J. was also known for his extensive and impeccable interpretation of Scottish traditional music - that is, tunes which are not to be found in books, but which have been handed down through successive generations. Dan J.'s son, John, once described his father's playing in these words: ''He had the 'old sound', which has been lost in Scotland. He put in certain grace notes to give his fiddling a very special type of expression. My father played book music too, using that old kind of bowing.'' In 1943, Sydney writer Joe MacInnis referred to Dan J. as ''undoubtedly one of Inverness's best violin players. He possesses a very correct ear and is a very pleasing performer of Scottish national melodies and dance music.''[13]

Of his children, four daughters have contributed fine piano music to Celtic gatherings on the Island, and two sons, Donald and John, are highly respected for their abilities on the violin. In summary, it appears that Dan J. Campbell and his family have fully exemplified the old adage ''Far am bith Caimbeulach, bith ceòl'' - ''where there is a Campbell, there is music!''

Donald Campbell

Dates: 1789?-1878, a native of Scotland who emigrated to Lynch's River Cape Breton

Belief in the "daoine beaga" or "little men" was common among pioneer Cape Bretoners. The fairies, as they were often called, were associated with certain activities, such as the braiding of horses' manes and the making of enchanting music. Some folk believed that a human could be abducted into a fairy hill ("sithean"), only to be released one year later with an almost magical control of the violin or pipes; it was widely believed that Donald Campbell (Bàn) had an experience similar to this.

"Some say he had a fairy bow," says Joe Neil MacNeil of Big Pond. "He (or his father) was supposed to have been coming from playing all night at a wedding. As he came across the country at the break of day, he met a fairy woman milking a cow. If he told the owners what he saw, they might use a charm to harm the fairies, so she begged him to keep her secret. If he would agree, he would never he beaten at fiddling; and, the spell would carry through three generations.

"I was told," continues Joe Neil, "that Donald Campbell played for dancing and for listening. He had a unique tuning for the violin, and he always played according to that tuning; it wasn't 'high bass' - it was unique! He'd never hand you the violin while it had that tuning - he would deliberately put it out of tune first, so you could never catch on to it."

Steve "John S." MacNeil of Glengarry Road adds, "Rory MacIsaac (fiddler), whom we called 'Ruairidh Shim', once walked from Big Pond to St. Peters to hear him play, and, though Donald Campbell was old at the time, he played wonderful music. Old Campbell would lend you his fiddle, but never let you handle his bow - the fairies were supposed to have given it to him in Scotland."

Peter MacKenzie Campbell, a Red Islands historian, relates the following: "A good many years ago there lived at Lynch's River, near St. Peters, a man by the name of Campbell who apparently was an exceptionally good violinist. I don't know whether he was personally responsible for the impression that went abroad among the people to the effect that he had been taught by the fairies, or whether the people simply concluded that it was impossible to be so proficient unless he had received such instructions. In any case, some of the very aged with whom I came into contact in my early years believed implicitly that the fairies were responsible for the sweetness of the music which Campbell had taken out of his violin."[14]

An Antigonish paper called "The Casket" made this report on May 9, 1878:

"DIED:

At St. Peter's, C. Breton, on the 28th, ult. Donald Campbell (fiddler) in the 89th year of his age. Consoled by the last rites of the Church, he died in the full hope of meeting his reward. R.I.P."

James P. Campbell

Dates: 1863-1942, a native of Red Islands, Johnstown Parish
Parents: Peter Campbell and Annie MacDonald

James P. was the grandson of Hector Campbell, a pioneer settler of Red Islands (Na h-Eileannan Dearga) who first "raised smoke" around 1807. While he was still a young man, James spent fifteen years in the United States sailing on the "grand bankers" out of Boston and Gloucester. During this period, a fiddler from Prince Edward Island named Captain John Hugh McMullin taught him the art of the violin.

On finally returning home, James settled on part of the old homestead. Soon he secured a government subsidy to ferry people by sailboat across the lake to Grand Narrows. Until he relinquished this service in 1918, he was known locally as "The Ferryman".

James P. was an enthusiastic fiddler and associated with the following players: Murdoch MacMillan of Johnstown who was also a piper, and who used to sail with James to St. Peters to entertain at dances; Jack MacKenzie of Hay Cove; Hugh Jackson of St. Peters; "Little" Rory MacDonald of Inverness County; and Simon Cremo of Barra Head, the son of Captain Peter Cremo.

James was an "ear" player with a graceful style. Considered one of the leading fiddlers in the district, he was called upon to supply music for réiteich (engagement rites), jamborees, dances of many varieties and ceilidhs. These latter gatherings featured ghost stories, Gaelic singing, stepdancing, piping and fiddling. James would contribute by recounting his adventures at sea, but then, as his son Peter MacKenzie Campbell recalls, "During a lull in the conversation, my father would produce his violin and proceed to regale the audience with tunes he had learned during his years in the 'States'. He would play 'Pigeon on the Gate', 'Drowsy Maggie', 'Miller's Reel', 'Green Fields of America' and many others, but he always ended up with 'Miss MacLeod's Reel', and if anyone in the group could step to this lively tune, so much the better!"[15] James' repertoire consisted of Highland tunes as well as the Irish-flavoured reels he had picked up in his travels through America.

In 1926, James entered a violin competition in North Sydney and earned second place, just behind champion fiddler Mick MacInnis of Terra Nova.

Of the children of James P. and Mary Jessie Campbell, two boys gravitated to the violin - Alex A. and Michael. The aforementioned son, Peter, became an author and noted historian on the Red Islands community.

Tena Campbell

Dates: 1899-1949, a native of Salmon River Road, Grand Mira Parish
Parents: Joseph Campbell (Eosaiph MacAonghais) and Mary MacIntyre (Nighean Iain Aonghais 'ic Eachainn)

Though her father and brothers only "scratched away" at the violin, Tena was destined to make music her career. She first tried her hand at the fiddle at age seven, encouraged by such visitors to her house as Rory MacDonald and John Stephen Currie of the Mira area. Eventually, she left home to attend school in Sydney, a place where she was to remain.

Having been tutored in violin by Professors MacDonald and Chisholm of Cape Breton, Tena's ability and popularity grew in leaps and bounds. On July 25, 1932, she took first place in a contest in Glace Bay sponsored by the Fire Department. During this era, she could be heard on local radio as often as six nights a week, and, in the late 1930's, supplied the fiddle music for "Celtic Ceilidh" and "Cotter's Saturday Night" on the trans-Canada hook-up: the latter program had a fantastic network run.

Every weekend for years, Tena performed at East Bay parish, and, during the War, she travelled on a circuit of dancehalls from Antigonish to Glace Bay. For these engagements, she usually teamed up with noted pianist Beattie Wallace, who claimed that they had a wonderful time though the pay was small ($4.00) and the bus trips were usually long. "Tena was a great person - we never had a cross word!"[16] Beattie once remarked. In the 1940's, on occasion, the duo was joined by banjoist Ed MacGillivray and fiddler Sandy MacInnis at the Carpenter's Hall.

During her career, Tena captured a championship in Maritime competition, and she was often invited to perform in Boston. Her music was characterized by a driving rhythm which inspired dancing, and she loved to play the old standards such as "The Inverness Gathering" and "Lord MacDonald's Reel". Though tiny in stature, Tena delivered her tunes with great ferocity - so much so that it is said her fingertips left a deep and indelible impression on the fingerboard of her violin.

In her honour, a song was once composed entitled "Tena Campbell, Queen of the Bow", and J.J. MacInnis, in the 1943-44 edition of "Eilean Cheap Breatann", remarked that she played "with great skill and dexterity."[17]

Angus Chisholm

Dates: 1908-1979, a native of Margaree Forks, Cape Breton
Parents: Archie Chisholm and Isabel MacLennan (Nighean Ruairidh Iain 'ic Ruairidh)

"I was born in Margaree Forks-I remember the day!" Angus once said in jest during a taped interview with Frank MacInnis of Creignish. "My father didn't play; my mother's people played." Here, Angus was referring to his grand-uncle Angus MacLennan, and his uncle, also named Angus MacLennan. "I never heard either of them," he remarked.

It is commonly believed that Donald Beaton (ie. Domhnull Iain an Taillear) was one of the finest Cape Breton musicians of all time. When that man used to visit East Margaree, Angus' father would hitch up the horse and wagon and drive the five miles to hear him play. Though only a toddler at the time, Angus shared and retained one of those experiences: "I remember **that** was my first knowledge of a violin. I was wondering what, in the name of God, was coming out of it! He was playing the fiddle - 'Old' Dan Beaton. Of course, I was too young to realize who was a good player and who wasn't; I was only about two or three!"

It was around the age of eight that Angus' remarkable career as a violinist really began. "There was a fellow in the house, and I want to make mention of his name. He could play a little, and he was the first man who taught me how to play a tune - Johnny White, Johnny Stephen, from Margaree. I was watching him trying to teach my brother (Danny), who was older than I was. They sat down to dinner, so I took the fiddle." Mr. White became understandably excited when he heard the younger Chisholm's efforts, and spent the rest of the day with the boy. By the conclusion of this initial lesson, Angus could play "The Cock of the North".

Learning by ear in the beginning, Angus compiled a modest repertoire of tunes by mastering the ones which his sisters used to "jig" for him. "The first dance I ever went to play, I remember, was at Peter Coady's in Margaree, and I was so young that I had to go with my sister by the hand.

"I played by ear till I was about fourteen. Then, there was a fellow that stayed at our place for about a year." The man in question was Jimmy MacInnis of Big Pond, who was accomplished in two extraordinarily diverse fields, as Angus explained: "He learned classical music up in Maine, and he was a champion boxer - welter-weight ('Kid Carroll'). He gave me more pointers, you know, like changing positions and that sort of stuff. Those were the best pointers that I ever got. He taught me how to read; the first tune I learned by note was 'Stack of Barley'.

"My first violin was one that my brother, Willie D., bought from a horse trader - for fifteen dollars! The horse trader had it in his wagon; it might have been a trade, part of a deal for a horse. It wasn't worth any more than fifteen dollars either - I wouldn't give fifteen cents for it! But, it was the one that I learned on; I had to start somewhere!"

As he improved, which he did at an amazing pace, Angus was kept busy entertaining at wood frolics, "kitchen rackets", house dances and schoolhouse dances in the vicinity of Margaree. Archie Chisholm, however, was determined that his children would be well educated - Angus, though obviously gifted musically, was no exception.

After becoming a school teacher, Angus spent six years serving in various Cape Breton communities. Through his music, he eventually befriended the Island's most talented fiddlers; people such as Malcolm Beaton, Angus Allan Gillis, Dan J. Campbell, "Big" Ronald MacLellan, Donald Angus Beaton et cetera. When discussing great players, he always made a special mention of Mary MacDonald and her exquisite "cuttings".

While Angus was developing his own unique approach to Scottish fiddling, he became enthralled with the technique of another Margaree man: "What I was enthused about was watching Angus Allan Gillis' style of bowing. I used to like to sit behind him and watch him - he didn't know it."

Angus was among the first Cape Bretoners to make a 78 rpm recording of Scottish violin music, as verified in the following article taken from the December 18th, 1935 edition of the Sydney Post-Record: "Angus Chisholm, noted violin player of Margaree Forks, has gone to Montreal to make some violin recordings for the Brunswick Recording Company. While visiting in the United States last year, he played for a recording company and the records can now be purchased from music stores."

The following are numbered among Angus' earliest recordings:

DECCA 14004 (A) "Moonlight Clog" and "Hennessey's Hornpipe" (B) "Rothermurches Rant", "Braes of Auchertyre" and "Braes of Glencoe" with Elizabeth Mallett on piano (recorded in America).
CELTIC 007 (A) "Mr Murray", "The Ten Pound Fiddle" and "The Baker". (B) "Miss Minnie Foster" and "Fred Wilson's Clog" with Bess Siddall MacDonald on the piano (recorded in Montreal).
CELTIC 009 (A) "Glengarry's Dirk", "Bonnie Lass O'Fisher-row" and "Bird's Nest" (B) "Newcastle Hornpipe" and "President Grant".
CELTIC 015 (A) "Miss Lyall" and "Brother's Letter" (B) "Medley of Inverness Jigs".

While working in Cape Breton as a warden in the National Park, Angus introduced his fellow Islanders to music, the likes of which they had never heard before. Known more for his dazzling displays at concerts and private homes than for his dance playing, he attracted huge crowds wherever he travelled. Fr. John Angus Rankin of Glendale Parish remembers the night in Antigonish that Angus executed a sparkling one-hour medley with the underlying intention of impressing a local Scottish-music enthusiast.

During the years that he spent in central Canada and the United States, fiddling buffs beseiged Angus, awe struck by the virtuosity of both his bowing and fingering. By now, he had won so many competitions that promoters barred him from entering further ones. His love grew for the music of the famous Scottish composers like Skinner and Marshall, and he played their arrangements brilliantly. Often he would perform "The Tullochgorum" and "The East Neuk of Fife" back-to-back, usually at a speed which defied belief.

Though his precision-like technique was evident on every piece which he attempted, Angus had a preference for hornpipes and clogs. "I love to play clogs - they offer a challenge," he once admitted.

In his later years, Angus made the Boston area his home. There, he joined forces with Bill Lamey, John Campbell and Joe Cormier in providing Massachusetts with a rich sampling of Cape Breton culture, one of the most popular locales being the Orange Hall in Brookline.

Angus returned to Canada often to take part in scores of concerts and television programs, some hosted by John Allan Cameron, Tommy Makem and other prominent entertainers. The Chisholm clan had by now become a major musical force, led by Angus, his brother Archie Neil, his nephew Cameron Chisholm, and his nieces Margaret Chisholm MacDonald and Maybelle Chisholm - all outstanding instrumentalists.

In 1979, Angus Chisholm passed away in America, but was laid to rest in his native Margaree. His early 78 rpm records have been re-released in a long-playing album, but fans of Cape Breton fiddling should seek the private tapes upon which his true mastery of the Scottish violin has been captured.

"Little" Simon Fraser

Dates: 1897-1972, a native of Meat Cove
Parents: Simon Fraser and Christy MacLellan

The pioneer Frasers originally settled in Inverness County, but, in time, made their way to Lowland Cove on the tip of northern Cape Breton. Dan Fraser, "Little" Simon's brother, says, "If there's any background music in your family, you're sure to pick it up. There were thirteen children (eight boys and five girls), and all the boys except one played the fiddle. 'Little' Simon learned from a relative, Ronald Fraser. As soon as Ronald heard him trying to play, he showed Simon a lot of what he knew, like the tunes and how to handle the bow. Ronald was an old-time Scottish player.

"Simon used our father's fiddle first," Dan recalls. "The next one, he bought from a Gillis man in Glace Bay. The next one, he got from Fr. Angus Bryden; Simon used to play at the three-day picnics for nothing, so Fr. Bryden gave him the fiddle - a Steiner - for a present."

Simon began toying with the violin at about age six, and in two years had played his first dance set, all with the encouragement of neighbour Angus "Mossy" MacKinnon. As a teenager, he performed at picnics in communities like Bay St. Lawrence, Ingonish, Cheticamp and Dingwall. He entertained at weddings and wood frolics, and even held the occasional impromptu dance on the wooden bridge at Pleasant Bay. "He had million-dollar fingers!" says Dan. "After he played, I wouldn't touch the violin for three days! There were so many good fiddlers down north in those times," he continues, " - Hector MacDonald and his son, Angus MacDougall and his sons, 'Old' Mike MacDougall and his sons, the MacKinnons of Meat Cove and John R. Fraser, our cousin." One could add to this list Peter and James Willie MacKinnon of Smelt Brook, Artie Gwynn of Aspy Bay, the Fitzgeralds of White Point and John Angus Stephen MacKinnon of Bay St. Lawrence. Simon also maintained a friendship with Angus Chisholm who, for a time, was working at the National Park.

Though he was a fisherman and a farmer, "Little" Simon worked as a miner in Glace Bay for a few years. After contact with a music teacher, he became interested in "the flats" and in playing slow airs. "He was a very sweet player," says Margaret, his daughter. "He'd bring tears to your eyes with his music, especially on tunes like 'The Bonnie Lass of Bon-Accord', 'Highland Queen', 'Hector the Hero', 'The Bonnie Lass of Headlake' and 'The Little Heather'."

In ailing health, Simon spent over ten of his last years in Ontario, staying with his daughter. Never quite content away, he came back to Cape Breton around 1969, where he died a few years later.

Alex Gillis

Dates: 1900-1974, a native of South West Margaree
Parents: Malcolm H. Gillis ("The Bard") and Margaret MacFarlane

The son of one of Cape Breton's most gifted individuals, Alex always had a deep love for the violin, as did his brothers Jack, Jimmy, Ambrose, Bernie, John Joe and Dougall. A sister, Winnie, could also play, while a further brother named Malcolm was a medal-winning piper. Their father, Malcolm H., gave the children some fiddling instruction and would stroll behind them as they practiced, always listening attentively. Alex, a traditional-style player, absorbed a great many of his father's tunes, several of which incorporated the "high bass" technique of tuning.

An avid fan of all things Celtic, Alex loved to relate the tale of the time that he and John Gillis (son of "dancing master" Allan Gillis) were storm-stayed indoors together for six days. They apparently passed the entire time by fiddling and stepdancing, and during their confinement Alex learned a half-dozen new steps from his very capable friend.

In search of employment, Alex and his brother Jack spent a period of time in Glace Bay, always filling their evenings with dance playing when possible. In 1922, like so many Cape Bretoners before them, they left for Massachusetts, settling temporarily in New Bedford. Musically, Alex took advantage of the situation by studying with a violinist and teacher named Jones.

In a few years, the boys moved into Boston and found the city well populated with sons and daughters of Nova Scotia. An organization called The Cape Breton Club had been formed, and it was doing its best to promote formal and informal gatherings. With a number of dances scheduled every Saturday

night, the Gillis brothers lost no time in taking their place among the performers, earning a fee of about $5.00 each per night in those early years. On Sunday afternoons, the transplanted Cape Bretoners held lively "ceilidhs" where stories, dancing, Gaelic singing and violin playing reigned supreme. Not long after his arrival, Alex Gillis became the unofficial "dean" of the local Scottish music scene.

During the early 1930's, Alex took advantage of the large store of talent in the Boston area when he formed the group called "The Inverness Serenaders". Among the instrumentalists associated with that musical ensemble were: Alcide Aucoin and Alex Gillis (violins), Betty Maillet and Malcolm Gillis (piano), Jim Aucoin (accordion), Paul Aucoin (guitar and banjo) and Hughie Young (clappers). The music of the Serenaders was recorded by Decca, and these discs represent some of the earliest ever released featuring Cape Breton fiddling:

DECCA 12020 (A) "Go to the Devil and Shake Yourself" and "Margaree's Fancy" (B) "Irish-American Reel", "Clydeside Lassies" and "Norton's Reel" (side "B" features Alex's solo violin)

DECCA 12021 (A) "Great Western Clog" (includes tap dancing by Hugh Young) (B) "Key West" and "Corporal" - hornpipes (side "B" features Alcide's solo violin)

DECCA 14023 (A) "The Marchioness of Tullybardine" (B) "Money Musk", "Yon Toon" and "Go About Your Business"

DECCA 14024 (A) "King George", "King George the Fourth", "King's" and "Lochiel's" reels (B) "Joe's Favourite", "MacKinnon's Rant", "Pidgeon on the Gate" and "The Broken Wheel" (both sides feature Alex's solo violin)

On one occasion, Alex, Alcide and a few of their friends made contact with the folks at home in Cape Breton by recording one of their informal sessions, complete with greetings, conversation in Gaelic and English, and, of course, their beloved fiddling. This treasured 78 rpm record is now in the possession of Mary "Jack" Gillis of S.W. Margaree.

In addition to group and solo recordings, Alex promoted Cape Breton culture in the Boston area by organizing dances for ten years at the St. Croix and Intercolonial Halls. He received further exposure through radio station WHDH which broadcast a fiddle-music program every Saturday evening. This latter show could be received quite clearly in various sections of Cape Breton.

Whenever Alex returned to Cape Breton for a visit, he would head immediately for the home of Angus Allan Gillis and spend his entire holiday making music. Around 1946, he and his brothers Bernie and Malcolm came home for a few weeks following a seven-year absence on account of the war, and appeared at a large concert in Margaree.

Alex's new home, however, was the "Boston States", and it was there that he remained until his death in 1974. Like Angus Chisholm, "Big" Dan Hughie MacEachern, Rannie Graham, Agnes Campbell and so many others, Alex's contribution to the fiddling culture of the Boston area will long be remembered.

Angus Allan Gillis

Dates: 1897-1978, a native of Upper Margaree
Parents: Alexander Gillis and Catherine Gillis

Alexander Gillis of Upper Margaree had an extensive farm with a large sawmill. He had been a fiddler but lost a finger while working with a shingling machine at the mill; this abruptly put an end to the man's playing career. However, three of his sons - James A., Hughie, and the youngest boy, Angus Allan - were determined to maintain music in the home.

Following Angus Allan's first year of attendance, the South West Margaree school burned down. The nearest "seat of learning" being at Broad Cove Banks, he spent a year or two there, staying all the while with his married sister, Bella, whose father-in-law gave the little boy his first violin. Angus Allan, who was seven years old at the time, soon befriended another talented lad, Sandy MacLean of Foot Cape. Their teacher, Mr. Lauchlin MacLean was very sympathetic to a youngster's recreational needs and often used to clear the classroom floor and allow the children to dance while Angus Allan and Sandy provided fiddle music. After classes, the two boys would usually make their way to Sandy's home to practice. Surprisingly enough, Sandy's father failed to recognize the musical genius of either child, and he once offered them this prediction: "Neither of you fellows will ever make a fiddler!" - Mr. MacLean could not have been more incorrect.

In time, Angus Allan and Sandy made the acquaintance of a young girl named Lila MacIsaac. Lila's family owned an organ, and she began to accompany their playing. This trio, whose members shared a wonderful rapport, sustained the friendship and the music for ever after.

Following the erection of a new school in Margaree, Angus Allan returned home. Staying with the family at this point was his father's first cousin, the famous James D. Gillis, a brilliant and eccentric man. Jimmy "Dhu", as he was often called, could supply sweet music on the violin and was an accomplished note reader. Whenever he was available, he donated his time towards the development of Angus Allan's violin playing.

The years that ensued brought a rapid improvement in Angus Allan's fiddling as he deftly acquired old settings for the Highland music so popular in his area. Soon he became acclaimed for his remarkable "cuts", irresistible drive and strict timing, and these are the trademarks of an outstanding dance player.

Though a local priest had once placed a strict ban on dancing in the area, mainly due to abuses of liquor, by the time Angus Allan was in his twenties the mood had begun to change. Soon, dances enjoyed a period of renewed popularity and improved respectability. Among Angus Allan's most successful dances were those held at Glenville (with Buddy MacMaster), Brook Village, Kenloch and South West Margaree. His musical friendships expanded to include Dan J. Campbell, Angus Chisholm, Jack, Jimmy, Ambrose and Malcolm Gillis, and Allan "Black Angus" MacFarlane - the latter two being noted pipers.

By about age twenty-five, Angus Allan had inherited the family farm; however, hard days of labour in the fields never diminished his wit or his ability to provide lively music. His niece, Annie Dixon, says, "He had a wonderful personality, and he was very humourous. Often he'd exaggerate his stories to provide lighthearted entertainment; and, he was very gracious, willing to take out the violin and perform for company at all times." His daughter, Allison, recalls, "One tune he loved and played often was 'The Athole Highlanders' Farewell to Loch Katrine' from The Scottish Violinist. Another was called 'The Thunderbolt Reel', which was christened by Jack 'Malcolm' Gillis; it's on the 'high bass' - I don't think it's written in any book."

In 1933 in the company of Father J.H. Nicholson of New Waterford, Angus Allan travelled to Alexandria, Ontario where he took part in a competition during centenary celebrations. Edging out fellow finalist John Leo MacDonald of Ontario, Angus Allan won the St. Finnian's Cup, largely on the strength of his classic version of "Johnny Cope". Also in the early thirties, he journeyed to Boston where he played at a series of dances with Alex Gillis and The Inverness Serenaders.

In 1935, in response to an offer by Bernie MacIsaac of Celtic Records in Antigonish, Angus Allan made a historic trip to Montreal where he recorded three 78 rpm's (CX 005, 008, and 014) - his friends Dan J. Campbell and Angus Chisholm did likewise. Also released was an additional 78 (CX 011) featuring Angus Allan and Dan J. playing the "Old Time Wedding Reels".

Throughout the rest of his life, Angus Allan continued to bring happiness to all with whom he came in contact. Even while in his late seventies he could extract exciting music from his violin.

On October 12, 1978, Angus Allan Gillis went to his final reward. The funeral Mass included a performance by fifty fiddlers under the baton of Father John Angus Rankin.

> "A master of music has laid down his bow
> And silently passed to the realms of light;
> Like rests in the music, his departure unheard,
> So softly he left us and homeward took flight.
> Long may his memory linger amongst us,
> And long may his music with joy be recalled;
> And long may the name 'Angus Allan' be whispered
> By hearts that are fondly with music enthralled."
>   -Rev. Hugh A. MacDonald

Malcolm H. Gillis

Dates: 1856-1929, a native of South West Margaree
Parents: Hugh Gillis and Mary Gillis

A descendant of the Gillises of Morar, Scotland, Malcolm H. displayed many astounding talents during his lifetime. At the age of four, he composed his first rhyme, and only a year or so later took the family violin off the wall for his initial attempt at making music.

Besides local schooling, he received valuable instruction at Broad Cove Marsh, where a noted scholar named Malcolm MacLellan taught the Classics. This Scottish gentleman had studied in Edinburgh and then, emigrating to Canada, settled in Cape Breton. The knowledge he imparted to Malcolm H. gave him a firm foundation for what lay ahead. After completing his studies, Malcolm H. entered the teaching profession and served at various schools throughout Inverness County over the next thirty-nine years.

A romantic man through and through, Malcolm began writing poetry and songs in earnest while in his early twenties, inspired by the pastoral beauty and lifestyle in his native Margaree. Meanwhile, his versatility as a musician was astonishing, for he was able to perform on the violin, bagpipes, accordion, piano, organ and Irish pipes, as well as sing, stepdance and direct the local church choir.

As a fiddler, he was in great demand at picnics, and, in 1897, played at the first one ever held in Mabou parish. About ninety years ago, he earned a first-place trophy in a competition near Glendale, and, in 1926, he won a large, silver cup at a Boston contest. In Margaree, his fiddling companions included Joe MacFarlane, Allan Gillis, Allan MacFarlane (piper and fiddler), John Grant MacFarlane and Ronald MacDougall. In his "History of Inverness", J.L. MacDougall makes the following statement: "Malcolm Gillis, teacher, and the late Ronald MacDougall, Angus' son, were two of the best violin players in eastern Nova Scotia. Many were the sad old hearts they made light and glad."[18]

As a dancer, Malcolm was equally outstanding. His daughter-in-law, Mary "Jack" Gillis, relates the following information: "There were old 'dancing masters' around here then - Allan Gillis and

Alexander MacDonnell. The young people used to congregate at their homes - that was the recreation during the winter; and, there was no fee! In those days, if you could play or dance, you'd be only too glad to show the youngsters how to do it. The dancing then was very neat and graceful and 'close to the floor'." Malcolm received his skills via the above mentioned masters. His love and knowledge of dancing contributed to his ability to supply good, lively music at "kitchen rackets" and weddings. In 1927, at a picnic in Judique, he shared the judging of the stepdancing competition with the famous Dr. Kennedy of Mabou.

It has been said by Gaelic scholars that the "Bard", Malcolm H. Gillis, was among the best poets of his time. His song "Am Braighe" was recorded by Neil Steele, and by Finlay Campbell of Australia. Another song, "Nigh'n Donn a' Chuil Réidh", composed for an early sweetheart, gained great popularity in Scotland, and this was verified by the late Cape Breton politician, Angus L. MacDonald, who was very proud of Malcolm's accomplishments. In 1939, ten years after "The Bard's" death, a book containing a selection of his poetry was published entitled "Smèorach nan Cnoc 's nan Gleann" ("The Songster of the Hills and Glens"). This edition features a photograph of Malcolm with his beloved violin.

With Malcolm's assistance, many of his children became fiddlers, namely Alex, Jack, Jimmy, Ambrose, Bernie, John Joe, Dougall and Minnie. Another son, Malcolm, was a prize-winning piper.

In 1929, Cape Breton lost her Gaelic champion. Remarking on his talent and generosity, Angus Allan Gillis once said, "He was the greatest character who ever lived around here, and time meant nothing to him!"

On July 28, 1979, a cairn, originally proposed by Dr. Moses Coady in the 1950's, was erected in Malcolm's honour on the old homestead in South West Margaree. It boldly displays his full name in the language of his heart; CALUM EOGHAIN 'IC AONGHAIS 'IC CHALUIM 'IC DHOMHNAILL 'IC DHONNCHAIDH.

Ronald Kennedy

Dates: 1870-1958, a native of Broad Cove Chapel
Parents: Archie Kennedy and Margaret Beaton

Ronald Kennedy was known throughout Cape Breton as a great traditional fiddler with a powerful sound. One of the rare breed of left-handed players, he took encouragement from his father who was a violinist as well as a stepdance teacher. It was said of Ronald that "music flowed through his veins" for he conquered the violin with the greatest of ease.

By means of a rapid musical development, at the age of nineteen he had become a regular feature at the "big" weddings, events during which the Scottish music was sustained for days on end.

Ronald's fiddling style bore two distinctive traits - it served for dancing **and** for listening. "His playing was like singing," an old friend once remarked. As a dance player, his engagements stretched from Lower River Inhabitants to Cheticamp.

Ronald's circle of friends comprised the most accomplished Inverness fiddlers, men such as Joe, Jim and Ronald Smith, Johnny "MacVarish" MacDonald, Dan A. "Red John" MacLellan, Gordon MacQuarrie, Vincent MacLellan and Donald John "The Tailor" Beaton. Regarding this latter violinist, Ronald's son, Joe, has remarked, "Domhnull Iain used to come to stay at haymaking time. My father got a lot of music from him!"

Ronald employed two types of fiddle tunings other than standard: (1) the "high bass", common among the earlier players, and (2) the "low bass", a very rare tuning useful in the key of F, which he learned from Donald John "The Tailor". Ronald could also imitate bagpipe music with the violin by using the technique of continually sounding the E string while playing the melody.

Besides being an outstanding fiddler, Ronald was a piper and a talented stepdancer, having originally acquired the latter skill by watching his father teach Dr. Kennedy of Mabou.

In the 1920's, Ronald took first place in a number of fiddling competitions. One particular contest in Inverness, in 1925, involved many of the noted players of that era.

Facially, Ronald bore a slight resemblance to Scottish composer James Scott Skinner. A hard-working farmer most of his life, he was a strapping man, all of forty-four inches across the chest; however, while sowing the land by hand at eighty-eight years of age he finally collapsed.

Of his children, Danny, Archie, Joe and Mary have demonstrated talent on the violin.

Paddy LeBlanc

Dates: 1923-1974, a native of East Margaree
Parents: Jim LeBlanc and Margaret Poirier

Paddy, the son of dance-fiddler Jim LeBlanc, took stepdancing lessons as a youth and became very proficient at this art. He was also privileged to study the violin under Professor James MacDonald of North Sydney, which tutelage enabled him to read music well, and soon he was playing for dances all over the Island. Besides being active as a fiddler, Paddy also specialized in Highland drumming, having spent twelve years with the Cape Breton Highlanders Regiment. Later, he became a barber in the Sydney area, but always maintained a busy fiddling schedule as he performed weekly on CJCB-TV with singer Charlie MacKinnon and a group called "The Lumberjacks". In addition, Paddy worked with Winston "Scotty" Fitzgerald on the television show "Cape Breton Ceilidh", originating from Sydney.

Celtic Records recorded Paddy following a glowing recommendation from fiddler, Dan R. MacDonald. George Taylor, employed by that record company, made these comments regarding Paddy's violin playing and his French background: "After listening to Mr. LeBlanc play, I was prepared to stake my reputation that none could play the fiddle with such feeling unless deep down beat the heart of a Scot!" With Celtic, Paddy released two albums under the name "Scotty" LeBlanc, and these records are numbered CX 29 and CX 41.

Music earned Paddy the opportunity to travel to such diverse places as Sudbury, Ontario and Ayr, Scotland; his overseas performances were broadcast over the BBC network.

In February, 1974, the untimely death of Paddy LeBlanc left all Cape Breton Scots saddened.

Dan R. MacDonald

Dates: 1911-1976, a native of Judique, Cape Breton
Parents: John R. MacDonald (Iain MacGhilleasbuig Iain 'ic Ruairidh) and Jessie O'Handley

The legend that is Dan R. had its beginnings in the home of his father, John R. MacDonald of Judique. John R. was a good "ear player", but his small son paid little attention to music until the fateful day described here by Dan Rory himself (transcribed from a taped interview by Ron MacInnis of Halifax):

"My father took me up to Hugh A. O'Handley's in Judique South in 1921. Angus A. MacDougall and Allan MacDougall were playing the fiddle, and I took an interest in the violin. So, Hugh O'Handley got a violin that his brother had - that is my grandfather, Allan O'Handley up in Hastings - and there was no strings on it. I took the violin down to Alexander MacDonnell and he rigged it up for me, and I started from there."

Coached somewhat by Mr. MacDonnell, Dan R., while still in his teens, progressed by ear to a point where he could play for dances near his home. This, however, did not satisfy him. "I didn't get anywheres in playing the violin there - nobody read any music around Judique; Alexander didn't read music - till I went over to Glendale in 1930. I learned to read from John Willie MacEachern. He had a little book there, an instruction book with 'The Irish Washerwoman' in it and figures on it, and he showed me how it was done. I studied it under lamplight up in bed till 2 o'clock in the morning, and, next day when I got up, I took up the fiddle and could read a tune out of the book!"

Dan R. adeptly solved the puzzle of understanding the notes and became an avid collector of music. As for the suggested bowing patterns with each piece, however, he had a different approach: "I don't go by that - I use my **own** bowing. If you're gonna be going by signs and by the way everything is written in the book, you're gonna be mechanical, and I don't want to be a mechanical player!" Instead, he applied the traditional bowing techniques as practiced by the elders of Inverness County.

In time, Dan Rory developed a flair for Scottish composition which bordered on genius. It has been suggested that if Scott Skinner was "The Strathspey King", then surely Dan R. must have been king of the reels! During the forty years in which he created original music, it is estimated that he "made" over two thousand tunes, many of which sparkle with his special brilliance for melody. "The very first tune I composed - it's in Gordon MacQuarrie's book - was 'The Red Shoes'," said Dan Rory. That particular piece was named for some homemade footgear crafted by Angus D. MacEachern of Glendale. The adventurous shoemaker had stained the shoes a bright crimson with Sherwin-Williams Paint, and the incident was the inspiration for Dan R.'s reel.

THE RED SHOES

Reel   By Dan R. MacDonald

Today, literally every Cape Breton fiddler plays his compositions, tunes like "Trip to Windsor", "Devil's Delight", "Glencoe March", "Strathlorne March", "Mrs. Norman MacKeigan" and "The River Bend Jig".

1941 found Dan R. in Scotland with the Canadian Army. It was there that he befriended composer J. Murdoch Henderson, who made him aware of the valuable music collections available in Britain. Dan R. quickly made it possible for his fiddling companions back home to obtain these important books. While overseas, he played over the BBC network, and he penned one of his most performed tunes, "Heather Hill" (or "Heather on the Hill"), which he claimed to have originally jotted down on a tree stump while working in the woods.

After military service, Dan Rory returned to Canada and spent the next twelve years in Windsor, Ontario. In 1957, he recorded his first album with The Five MacDonald Fiddlers, a popular group of ex-Cape Bretoners. A victim of failing eyesight, he decided to settle on his native island in 1959. In the years that followed, this huge man, his eyeglasses held together with Band-aids and tape, became a familiar figure at fiddling festivals and parties all through Nova Scotia. He performed regularly on CBC TV's "Ceilidh" in the early 1970's, and was featured in Ron MacInnis' historic film, "The Vanishing Cape Breton Fiddler".

Dan R's reputation as a bona fide "character" became far reaching. Married only to his violin, he travelled extensively, spending a week here and a week there among his friends and relatives, invariably leaving behind a trail of wonderful anecdotes and precious music. He continued to astound his associates with his photographic mind and the ability to recite the most difficult verses of Dante and John Milton at will. Regarding his memory, he used to say, while gesturing towards his head, "I read a lot. It sinks right in here and it stays in here!"

Filled with a love for God and nature, Dan Rory was a man of strong convictions: "Look - there was a priest told me one time,
> 'Only for God, you wouldn't be able to put rosin on your bow; you wouldn't be able to compose music or nothing - only for God!' Well, I believe that. So, everyday I get up I say, 'God Almighty, give me the strength to compose a tune', and it comes to me right like that! Never failed yet." Dan R. MacDonald created jigs and reels right up until the last hours of his life.

On September 20, 1976, Cape Breton lost one of her most colorful and talented sons when Dan. R. passed away in Inverness at age sixty-five. A few days later, mourners and admirers filled St. Mary's Church in Mabou, while a symphony of musical friends played his most beloved marches. Today, his manuscripts are treasured by the countless fans who realize that his contribution to Scottish music will never be forgotten.

"The Devil won't do nothing to me because I played music all my life, and I was enjoying people. He can't do nothing to me - God will see to that. God is supreme in this world; He's not gonna let the Devil get a hold of me!"

- Dan R. MacDonald

Some of his recordings:

"Dan R. MacDonald" Celtic CX 28
"The Five MacDonald Fiddlers" Celtic CX 20
"The Five MacDonalds" RLP 27
"Five MacDonald Fiddlers" Celtic CX 30

Hughie A. MacDonald

Dates: 1889-1976, a native of Lanark, Antigonish County
Parents: Angus MacDonald and Mary MacInnis

Hughie was born on the old homestead at Lanark. "Lot Eleven" was the land number given to his ancestors, early settlers of the Antigonish area, and was the source of one of his nicknames - "Hughie Eleven". He was also occasionally referred to as "Hughie the Fiddler" and "The Polka King".

Hughie A.'s father could read and write music, while his mother was both a violinist and a pianist. The six children - Jim, John Duncan, Hughie A., Mary, Janie and Kate - all could produce music on the violin. Jim, in fact, once constructed a special fiddle using wood from the old family home; the top was made from spruce taken from the stairs, while the back section was built from a table top.

Hughie was a Scottish fiddler from the age of nine, having been influenced by uncles Dan MacInnis and John MacDonald, as well as neighbour Dan "the Ridge" MacDonald who had strong Mabou roots. The possessor of an amazing ear, Hughie "the Fiddler" was able to master very difficult tunes without the aid of notation, though in later life he had a fair grasp of music theory. While he was comfortable with many types of pieces, his specialty was the polka, many of which he obtained from his cousin, John Willie MacDougall of Westville. He also had a preference for "the flats" - "He loved to play in the key of 'F'," says his wife, Winnie.

Near his home, Hughie's name and music were closely associated with the barn-raising and plowing frolics. After a vigorous day's labour was completed at such an event, the music would begin in earnest and continue all through the night.

Spurred on by the encouragement of Bernie MacIsaac of Antigonish, Hughie A. went to Montreal in the mid-thirties and recorded his first 78 rpm's for the Celtic label, accompanied by Bess Siddall MacDonald on the piano and Jim Dale on string bass. Among the tunes released were "The Honeymoon Polka", "The Crooked Stove Pipe" and "The Starlight Waltz" (Celtic 018). "He sold an awful lot of records for those days," says Winnie. "Everyone bought them!"

It was also in the thirties that Hughie performed with the Antigonish Orchestra, besides winning first prize in a fiddling contest. Eventually, he became a regular contributor to the Highland Ball, at the Highland Games and on CJFX Radio.

In 1967, Hughie A. was paid a great tribute when his recording of "MacDonald's March" was featured in the Canadian Pavillion at Expo. Nine years later, "The Polka King" passed away. A fiddle now decorates his headstone.

"Little" Jack MacDonald

Dates: 1887-1969, a native of Creignish, Cape Breton
Parents: Donald Rory MacDonald and Flora MacDonnell
(Floiri Eoghainn 'ic Alain Bhàin)

Following the premature death of his parents, "Little" Jack was raised in Judique by Annie MacMaster MacDonnell, the wife of his mother's brother, Allan "Tal". In the home of another uncle, Angus "Hughie" MacDonnell who lived on the River Denys Road, Jack was introduced to Cape Breton fiddling and dancing in great abundance. In fact, it has been said that as you approached Angus "Hughie's" house, you were always likely to hear the music resounding through the walls; if you entered, you would probably see one of the boys (ie. Allan, Archie, Hughie or Alexander) playing the violin in the corner while the whole family was up stepdancing. Angus "Hughie" himself taught stepdancing and could play the pipes, and a Gaelic-speaking youngster named "Little" Jack MacDonald took it all in.

Once, as a lad, Jack attempted to construct a fiddle from a wooden cigar-box. This apparent interest in the music caused the boy's foster father to build a half-size instrument for him, and so Jack's playing career began. Mr. Bernie MacNeil of Michigan, an expert on "Little" Jack's life, contributes the following information: " 'Big' Dan Beaton of Mabou, one of Cape Breton's great players, was definitely responsible for showering his talent on this young student. Each year, he would spend several days at Jack's home, and each year Jack's repertoire of tunes would increase."

"Little" Roddy, Jack's brother, was also musical, being both a fiddler and a good stepdancer. In addition, the Judique area had spawned a fine array of violinists and many of these became acquaintances of Jack's: Danny Angus MacDonnell, Angus "Donald Duncan" MacMaster, D.A. MacPherson, Robert Hughie (Rob Eoghainn) MacInnis, Sandy O'Handley, Angus T. Campbell, and so on.

"At the early age of sixteen," says Bernie MacNeil, "he left Judique and joined up with a travelling 'Home Products and Medicine Man', playing the violin and doing various chores. They travelled throughout Cape Breton and then worked their way westward to Montreal." In the latter city, Jack improved his education and applied himself to rudimentary music reading. At this point, he passed up an opportunity to attend a conservatory, a decision he regretted the rest of his life. In the next few years, Jack spent time in New England and Northern Ontario. After meeting Jeanette MacDonald in Timmons, he married her in 1918, and the first three of their five children were born in North Cobalt.

In 1923, Jack, who by now was trained as a hoisting operator and a steam boiler repairman, moved his family to Detroit, Michigan. During the Depression, he turned to his music for survival. Bernie says, "Accompanied by a guitar player, he barnstormed the clubs and pubs around Detroit." Later, as an established entertainer in the Detroit-Windsor area, Jack performed for the Lewis Scottish Society, the St. Andrew's Society, the Nova Scotia Club of Detroit, the Maritime Club in Windsor, radio station WMBC, as well as at scores of parties, weddings and "ceilidhs". His regular accompanist during this era was Mrs. Bernie MacNeil.

Bernie continues, "His first and greatest love was Highland music, and it was in this traditional art his playing showed brilliance and control. He also had a singular gift of expression that was quickly recognized and admired by other players. His motto, which he often repeated, was that 'music must have soul to make it worthwhile.' Days of diligent practice were a necessity with him for the more difficult compositions, and he looked with disfavour on the custom of absorbing an unlimited number of tunes as a sign of distinction. He would listen for hours to Fritz Kreisler's old seventy-eight recordings, and on several occasions attended both Kreisler and Heifetz recitals at the Masonic Temple in Detroit. Inspired by these classical artists, he would take on the task of trying to develop our Highland music on the violin the way the great Scottish composers wanted it played.

"Jack," says Bernie, "was unable to return to his homeland, since leaving there in 1904, until about the early fifties. When visiting the old home in Judique and reminiscing with the folks there, he recalled keeping the fiddle in a wall recess, and, to everyone's amazement, he reached into the opening and discovered that the old home-made 'fiddle' was still there. This incident brought a flashback of memories while he tried to piece together the effect this old instrument had had on his life."

Bernie recalls, "It was in 1939 that the Celtic Music Co. in Antigonish, Nova Scotia urged him to record some of his music and, in the next six years, he produced five '78' discs (Celtic 022, 024, 026, 031 and 034); much later he taped an album while living in Glengarry, Ontario."

Though remembered as a man with a sense of humour, when it came to fiddling it was a different matter. Angus A. MacDonnell of Judique recalls, "He'd have to be in the right cheer to play good music!" Even then, if his audience was less than perfectly attentive, "Little" Jack would sometimes end his playing with an abrupt motion and a cold stare. However, when all conditions were to his liking, the music was stirring and distinctive, abounding with "cuts" deftly, if not ingeniously, delivered. His recording of the tune "Devil in the Kitchen" demonstrates a special right-hand technique termed "double cutting", an effortless exercise for such a master. That bowing, touted by noted players such as Sandy MacLean, helped to make "Little" Jack a legend in his time, and earned him the title "The Bard of Scottish Fiddling". Particularly outstanding and progressive was his treatment of pastoral airs like "Highland Queen". With bold portamentos and precise position work, he introduced new life to a type of tune seldom attempted or sweetly executed by traditional-style players of that time. Today, Bobby MacNeil of Dearborn, Michigan, a friend and student of "Little" Jack's, possesses much of the master's flair for this style of music.

"During the late forties," Bernie MacNeil says, "Jack moved from Windsor, Ontario and lived for some years with Clifford (his son) in Toronto, after which he moved to Dalhousie, Quebec, playing at a night club there for several years." He also performed at the Maxville Highland Games and at Scottish concerts in Alexandria, Ontario. During this period, his piano player was Viola MacCuaig of Dalhousie.

Jack's last years were spent in Moore Township. On August 8, 1969, one of Cape Breton's best travelled and most widely respected musicians, "Little" Jack MacDonald, passed away. He lies buried in Sarnia.

"Little" Jack MacDonald, Lauchie Meagher and Dan MacEachern (Hillsdale)

John Alex "The Big Fiddler" MacDonald

Dates: 1877-1958, a native of West Mabou
Parents: Ronald MacDonald (Raonull Eoin) and Mary "Meshag" MacDonald

When John Alex MacDonald was about twelve years of age, he yearned to play the bagpipes, but his mother prevailed upon him to be a fiddler and obtained an instrument for him. Mary "Meshag" had a good knowledge of the repertoire for Scottish violin, and so did her husband, Ronald, who was a stepdance teacher. John Alex would slip away to the woods to practice and when he would return he would play for his mother. Sometimes she would exclaim in Gaelic, "Put it away - you're killing the tune!" Persistence on his part, however, paid off, and by age fourteen he was already supplying music at dances. A child of low-income parents, John Alex used to walk barefooted from West Mabou to Harbourview to perform, yet his pay would only amount to three dollars!

John Alex, who was lean of build and stood 6'4'' high, became known as "The Big Fiddler". A lively player with excellent timing, his dances in Mabou, Port Hood and Glencoe attracted enthusiasts from miles in every direction. Judique musician Buddy MacMaster has said, "If John Alex was playing, it was sure to be a great dance!" Even in 1937, at the age of sixty, he was still making frequent appearances at halls such as St. Peter's and Earl's.

In competition at the Judique picnics, he earned three medals - two gold and one silver. Of the many tunes he could deliver with flourish and gusto, two were "Flora MacDonald" and "Cuir 's a' Chiste Mhóir Mi".

In 1920, some years after his marriage to Margaret MacLellan, he moved his family to Port Hood where he took employment in the mines, all the while maintaining his busy dance schedule. Of this period, his daughter Esther recalls, "We ate music - morning, noon and night! On Sunday afternoons, especially,

you'd find seven or eight fiddlers at the house - men like Peter MacPhee, Ambrose Gillis, Dan R. MacDonald, Jim and Alex "Lewis" MacDonald and Alex Michael MacDonald. Alex Michael (who used to charge a 25¢ admission for dances held in his house) was a good friend and neighbour, and he and Papa often played together in the later years."

At one point, John Alex owned a violin which he nicknamed "the big, white fiddle". Its original owner had done a rough job refinishing it, thus spoiling the tone. John Alex purchased the instrument for fifteen dollars and stripped it down to the natural wood, which gave it a light-coloured appearance. Donald Angus Beaton strung it up and it was found to have regained its beautiful sound. From then on, that white violin became "The Big Fiddler's" trademark.

When it came to learning a tune, John Alex always preferred the "ear method" to the note method. He did, however, pick up the skill of reading music while in his late sixties. By then, he had become a famous Cape Breton fiddler, but, curiously enough, he would sometimes take a chanter and play a few selections, calling up memories of his childhood when he had longed to be a piper.

A few years ago in Detroit, an anniversary party was held at 2576 Honorah Avenue, and a group of former Cape Bretoners were listening to wire recordings of "The Big Fiddler". One of the company spoke the following words: "Well, folks, it makes me lonesome to hear that music when I think back of the many times I had listened to that man playing the violin. In his heyday, the best of them would have to swing a mean bow to beat him, but I'm very happy to hear him play again, even if it is a recording, and I meant to add if the recordings are as willing to play for you as Big John Alex always was, you would hardly need a switch!"

In 1957, while staying with his son in Halifax, John Alex took a serious fall and subsequently died of his injuries the following January. In Port Hood, a stone marking his resting place bears a name once spoken in all corners of this Island - "THE BIG FIDDLER".

Johnny "MacVarish" MacDonald

Dates: 1852?-1934, a native of Broad Cove Marsh
Parents: Mr. and Mrs. Angus Hugh "MacVarish" MacDonald

The name "MacVarish" can be traced to the Gaelic words for "son of the sea" - "MacMhariche". For some unexplained reason, certain members of Johnny's family were known by this name instead of "MacDonald".

Johnny was identified in the local tongue as "Iain Aonghais 'ic Eoghainn", or was sometimes referred to by the title "Johnny from the Marsh" to distinguish him from all the other John MacDonalds of Inverness County. Though his father was a fiddler, his most important instruction came from Angus "The Tailor" MacPherson, a dance player from Antigonish who was one of the best violinists in Nova Scotia at that time. Even when Johnny was in his prime, he received tutoring from MacPherson who later admitted that his student was at least his equal. These two musicians used to meet regularly at Ronald Kennedy's home in Broad Cove.

Johnny became an avid note-reader, which was somewhat of a rarity at that time. A neighbour, Dave Beaton, recalls, "He was very correct - he wouldn't play tunes with mistakes in them!" Gradually, this accomplished musician collected a fine array of fiddle-tune books. His style was once described by writer Joe MacInnis in the following manner: "Mr. MacDonald is said by those capable to judge, as having been a profoundly neat, clean violin player. What he lacked in volume was made up in ornament and finish. Mr. V. A. MacLellan, speaking in Gaelic of Mr. MacDonald, remarked: 'Fidhlear sàr-mhath. Fidhlear grinn, glan' ('An excellent fiddler. A neat, clean fiddler.')."[19]

Not only could Johnny MacDonald play exquisite versions of tunes like "Sir Alexander Don Strathspey" (in G minor), but he could also turn his hand to novelty pieces; for example, he would run some of the bow hair under the violin strings to create a bagpipe effect behind the actual melody. Sandy MacLean of Foot Cape clearly remembers Johnny and says, "He could play lots of the tunes in three or four keys, and he could turn his left hand around on the neck (ie. finger the strings from above instead of below) and play just as well like that!" Often Johnny would shock his fiddling companions by producing "secret tunes" that no one else had ever heard. Another habit he had was that of relating the history behind a piece of music so as to better prepare his listeners.

A man of many talents, Johnny was equally at home composing music, stepdancing and, when necessary, repairing violins. To make his living, however, he relied on his small watch repair business, as well as some mackerel fishing with his brothers out of the then-thriving fishing community of Broad Cove Marsh. Though a fluent Gaelic speaker, he was well educated in English and possessed a collection of books dealing with Scottish history.

Johnny is fondly remembered as a true gentleman and a regular church goer. He used to spend some of his winters at Archie MacDonnell's in Inverness. On holidays, or immediately after Sunday Mass, his musical comrads would join him at the house and the fiddling would continue until daylight without a break. Sometimes his grandniece, Christy MacDonnell Gillis would press down the organ keys to provide a drone accompaniment to Johnny's long, driving medleys. Among the friends who participated at these gatherings were Ronald Smith (a relative), Sandy MacLean, Ronald Kennedy, "Little" Murdoch MacLean and "Big" Ronald MacLellan. Besides these sessions, Johnny made frequent appearances at the house parties and "frolics" which were the main source of entertainment during that period.

Johnny never married, but lived alone near Deepdale. His last few years, however, were spent at the home of Roddy MacEachern. At eighty-one years of age, he died of heart trouble on May 18, 1934, and, in accordance with his wishes, received the last Sacraments of his Church.

DAN RORY MacDOUGALL

March

as played by Mike MacDougall

Mike MacDougall

Dates: 1928-1981, a native of Ingonish Beach
Parents: Dan Rory MacDougall and Mary Anne Whitty

The MacDougalls of northern Cape Breton have long been acclaimed for their fine musicianship. Mike's father, Dan Rory, and his grandfather, Rory, were accomplished on both pipes and violin. It was, therefore, quite in line with family tradition when Mike and his brothers became captivated with the fiddle as small boys. "When I learned to play at the age of eight, I put every moment I had free on the violin. There was usually an argument among the four brothers as to whose turn was next; the fiddle didn't get a chance to cool off!" said Mike. "We never had anyone come to us and say, 'Here's how to start a tune' - we figured it out for ourselves. If there was anything we didn't play right, well, our father would set us straight. We each practiced in the bedroom with the door closed. Our father would knock on the wall whenever he heard us play a bad note." By age sixteen, Mike was entertaining at dances and concerts in Cape North, Dingwall and Ingonish. "Tim, my brother, and I eventually played a lot together at the old St. Peter's Parish Hall here - in the forties, I believe; we'd get $2.50 each. We did it more or less as a favour," he said.

Growing up, Mike experienced the music of the many talented players in his area, including "Little" Charlie Williams and Murray Hawley of Ingonish Ferry, Joey Doyle of Ingonish Center and Simon Morris of Ingonish North.

Mike developed an interesting way of holding the violin, keeping the instrument tucked in close to him. This style was derived from his early involvement at "kitchen rackets". At such affairs, there wasn't much space for fiddlers once the dancers got going, so the musicians would huddle close together, often having to defend themselves with solid shoves when flying bodies came dangerously near. Whatever the conditions, Mike's music, pipe-flavoured and foot-tapping, remained consistently good and thankfully abundant.

In the mid 1970's, Mike took his Cape Breton style of playing to the British Isles and, in Ireland, thrilled traditional music-lovers time and time again. He performed on five Irish radio shows, entertained at the famous Embankment and, in County Meath, met and dueted with world-famous fiddler Sean McGuire. "I got excellent treatment by all the folks in Ireland," Mike recalled, "and I was impressed with the Irish - both as people and musicians." In April, 1975, Gerald O'Grady of the Irish Free Press wrote, "We hope Mike will return many times to Ireland with his delightful personality and his excellent music. His contribution to world fellowship will long be remembered by those who were fortunate enough to see, hear or meet Mike MacDougall."

Mike befriended and performed with many British Isles entertainers, notably Ryan's Fancy and Barley Bree. With the former group, he was involved in an RCA Victor recording, and often appeared on television and in concert.

Generous in his praise of all the accompanists he worked with through the years, Mike was especially fond of the guitarists, some of whom were Tim Donovan, Buddy MacDonald, Kevin Donovan, Donnie Campbell and Ralph Williams.

A composer for the violin since 1965, Mike created several beautiful melodies, including "Peggy's Jig", "Memories of Fr. Angus MacDonnell" and "Fr. Eugene's Welcome to Cape North". Of the latter piece he said, "Fr. Eugene was, and is, a great friend of mine through music. He has always impressed me as a fellow who loves the fiddling. When I found out that he was to be transferred to St. Joseph's Parish in Dingwall around 1976, I was so delighted that I composed a march in his honour. After he heard it, he complimented me on it, and then I told him it was named for him." Mike's unique repertoire of tunes also featured an inspired march attributed to the pen of his father, Dan Rory MacDougall.

"Music," Mike admitted, "made a happy home where I was brought up - crowds coming to hear my father and my brothers and me play - and to hear my mother sing. There was always a feeling of joy! All down through my life, the most important thing to me has been music. If it wasn't for the fiddling, I wouldn't have met all those wonderful people."

"Fiddler's Dream", the boat he loved, stands captainless now, but the cherished memory of Mike MacDougall will ever glow as a warm ember in the hearts of his family and friends.

Mick MacInnis

Birth: 1870-1946, a native of Terra Nova (Glengarry), Cape Breton County
Parents: Rory MacInnis and Mary MacPherson

Mick was one of eight children. His brothers Jonathan (1863-1946), Martin (1865-1928) and Jim (1879-1954), all Gaelic speakers, were also fiddlers, with Jim being a particularly gifted player. This latter brother, a noted classical violinist and title-holding boxer, was the man responsible for teaching Angus Chisholm how to read music.

Though trained in Glengarry as a carpenter by Hector MacKinnon of Loch Lomond, Mick's true calling was that of a musician. Regarding the fact that he never experienced a single lesson and played completely by ear, he once commented, "All I have to do is to hear a piece once or twice and I can sit down and play it!"

In an interview printed in the Cape Breton Post in the 1940's, Mick, as an elderly man, once reflected on a long and distinguished fiddling career: "I was practically born with a violin in my hands seventy years ago at Terra Nova, C.B. At that time, the community was called Glengarry. While other youngsters in the community in which I lived enjoyed boyhood games, I often would be found back of the barn picking out the notes on a violin which I had made myself. It seemed to come natural to me and within a short time I was able to play the easy reels, jigs, strathspeys and clog dances that I had heard the older people play.

"Later I left my home community and went to work at No. 3 Coal Mine, Sydney Mines. However, my evenings and spare time were spent in practicing on my violin. My big chance came at North Sydney in 1926. A competition was held to send the best Cape Breton fiddler to Boston to engage in competition with fiddlers from the mainland of Nova Scotia, Prince Edward Island, New Brunswick and the New England States. Following stiff competition, I was adjudged the winner.

"The Boston competition lasted for one week and I finally won out from over a hundred fiddlers. The Intercolonial Club of Boston presented me with a trophy on which was enscribed 'Michael MacInnis, best old fashioned fiddler, 1926, Intercolonial Club, Boston.' The fiddling competition idea caught on. Competitions were held at Saint John, N.B., Charlottetown and New Glasgow. I participated in them all and won first place. At New Glasgow I was presented with a trophy enscribed as follows: 'Eastern Nova Scotia Fiddler Championship, 1926'." In the late 1920's, for his efforts in a contest held in Charlottetown, P.E.I., Mick was awarded a pin in the shape of a violin.

Upon moving into the industrial area, Mick took employment as a miner. He spent time in New Waterford, Bras d'Or, Sydney and the State of Maine, but no matter in which locality he found himself, he managed to pass countless hours visiting acquaintances and providing Scottish music. Occasionally, especially in later years, he served as judge in local fiddling competitions.

Mrs. Margaret MacKinnon, a niece of Mick's, maintains a vivid memory of him, and she says, "They used to have picnics at Big Pond, and he played. I remember seeing him there, fiddling unaccompanied for a square set - it was around 1930. There was a demand for him all summer and fall. In October, he'd come to our place to stay - I suppose he'd be in his sixties then. He'd entertain at kitchen parties in the winter. He was gentle and kind, and never said a cross word to us children. He'd play the fiddle in the evenings in the old country kitchen, and we'd all try to stepdance. Sometimes my mother would say to us, 'Be quiet so we can hear the music!' "

After over six decades of playing the violin, Mick once made the estimate that he had worn out about one-half mile of gut and steel strings; however, even while in his seventies, his fingers were reported to be as nimble as they had been when he was a youth.

In February of 1946, the following article appeared in a local paper: "Cape Breton's champion fiddler for many years, Michael MacInnis, died Sunday night in Saint Anthony's Home where he had been a patient for some time. . . . The late Mr. MacInnis carried off awards in fiddling competitions held in Boston and in the Maritimes and his services were in great demand for years."

Dougald MacIntyre

Dates: 1878?-1934, a native of Cape Mabou
Parents: John Dan MacIntyre (Iain MacGhilleasbuig 'ic An T-Saoir)
and Mary MacIsaac (Nighean Illeasbuig Oig)

John Dan MacIntyre, a violinist as well as an authority on Scottish fiddle tunes, was a perfectionist regarding the interpretation of the old-time melodies; Dougald (Dùghall Iain Ghilleasbuig) and his four musical brothers were constantly warned against modern variations in accepted traditional arrangements. Dougald's mother, meanwhile, was one of the "dancing" MacIsaacs.

Being basically a self-taught player whose repertoire was acquired entirely by ear, Dougald was ever noted for his bowing, strict timing and precise position work. After taking employment as a miner in Inverness in 1900, he and his friend, Joe Smith, were invited to entertain at the picnic celebrating the town's incorporation in 1904; this event was recorded in a photograph.

Following the death of his wife, Sarah, in 1922, Dougald moved to the mining town of New Waterford, where he was to remain. On April 1, 1926, he took first place in the finals of a fiddling contest staged at the Strand Theatre in Sydney. One of the judges, Joseph Pickup, told the Post-Record that Dougald displayed the finest bow hand he had ever seen and raved about the winner's "superb" interpretations. As "South" Cape Breton's representative in a further competition held later that month in Boston and adjudicated by the famous J. Scott Skinner of Scotland, Dougald once again reached the final round and was awarded a handsome silver trophy. A friend who had witnessed his performance in the States commented, "When Judique took the floor, the judges knew they were listening to a fiddler from the land where they grow them!" Margaret MacPhee, Dougald's daughter, remembers her father's playing well and has said, "He was a marvellous fiddler and took a lot of pride in his music. Everyday, after work, he'd take out the violin - no matter how tired he was! He was also a good stepdancer."

Dougald passed away in 1934, and a local paper offered the following: ". . . His fame as a violinist, particularly of old-time melodies, was known throughout the Island of Cape Breton and far beyond its boundaries. He was in great demand at entertainments and wherever lovers of music gathered, and, as an admirer of his said, 'He brought pleasure and enjoyment into the lives of many people.' He will therefore be greatly missed and his place will be hard to fill."

Of his children, Florence became a noted stepdancer, and Margaret, a pianist. A grandson, Doug MacPhee, is both a recording artist (piano) and an authority on Cape Breton music.

Johnny MacIsaac

Dates: 1867?-1941, a native of Blackstone, Inverness County
Parents: Alexander MacIsaac (Alasdair Mhurchaidh) and Anne MacIsaac

Johnny, a very accomplished "old time" fiddler, was the grandson of Murdoch MacIsaac, a pioneer settler at Broad Cove Interval. "Alasdair Mhurchaidh", Johnny's father, moved from Strathlorne to Blackstone in 1865. There, a family of twelve was raised which boasted three good fiddlers: Alexander (Sandy), Donald (Danny) and of course, John (Jr.).

Having started as a youngster, Johnny's violin playing progressed at a tremendous rate. His maternal grandmother, Sara Beaton, was a noted stepdancer and he often supplied music for her nimble feet; partly through her influence, he too became an able dancer.

Johnny was not a note reader, but his great ear and extensive exposure to good music stood him in good stead. He had a version of "The Tullochgorum" which has been described as "wickedly good!" On some old tunes, such as "Lord MacDonald's Reel", he displayed a flavour reminiscent of Mabou Coal Mines playing. Among his friends in the fiddling circles were Ronald Kennedy, John MacQuarrie of Black River and Dan J. Campbell.

Agnes (Beaton) Walker, another Cape Breton violinist, knew Johnny when she was a young girl, and chorded for him on the organ. She remembers, "He was a shy, nice man and was sometimes reluctant to play, but he was generous regarding the teaching of any tunes he knew. About the year 1915, he was a well-known violin player in the surrounding area; he was certainly a favourite for stepdancers. Many a night after going to bed, a neighbour would go to his house and ask him to come and play at a house party. In those years, the younger generation would drive for miles with horse and buggy (or sleigh if it was wintertime) and go somewhere for a surprise party, where a few of the neighbours would gather and dance for three or four hours."

Johnny was known to put a very lively beat to his jigs, as well as for lending his own distinctive flavour to the old-time strathspeys and reels of which he was a master.

In 1897, Johnny was selected as one of the "official" violinists at the first Mabou parish picnic during the pastorate of the late Rev. Dr. J.F. MacMaster. Others on the program included the following: Angus Archibald MacDonald, piper and violinist of Mount Young; Alex Archie MacDonald, Jr. of Mount Young; Malcolm H. Gillis, bard and violinist from S.W. Margaree; Johnny Ranald Beaton, Mabou Coal Mines; Angus Ranald Beaton, Mabou Coal Mines; John "Sandy" Beaton, Mabou Coal Mines; Donald John "The Tailor" Beaton of North East Mabou; John Alex "The Big Fiddler" MacDonald of West Mabou; John MacQuarrie of Black River; Donald Allan "Red John" MacLellan of Glenville; Johnny "MacVarish" MacDonald of Broad Cove Marsh; John Campbell (Aonghas Iain) of Glenora Falls; and Archibald Beaton, the famous Mabou Coal Mines piper.[20] Surely this must have been one of the greatest Celtic gatherings of all time!

One day, Johnny's brother Sandy took a stroke while working at the forge and soon died. In grief, the family violin, which hung on the kitchen wall, was not touched by anyone for seven years because that fiddle still had Sandy's tuning on it from the very last time he had played. Eventually, Dan Angus Beaton's father, Finlay J., ended the fast by deliberately playing that violin one day when he was visiting the MacIsaacs. Following this latter incident, Johnny resumed his fiddling.

Johnny never married, his constant companion being the violin. In the fall of 1941, he passed away, but his reputation as one of Cape Breton's finest traditional-style players will long be sustained.

CHRISTY CAMPBELL

a Cape Breton setting of the traditional strathspey; tuning: A/E/A/E (transcription by Roddie MacDonald of Inverness Town)

Archibald J. MacKenzie

Dates: 1861-1939, a native of Rear Christmas Island
Parents: James MacKenzie (Seumas Dhomhnuill 'ic Eachainn) and
Catherine MacDougall (Catriona Eachainn Ruaidh)

Archibald J., or "Eairdsidh Sheumais" as he was called in Gaelic, was the youngest child in the family of James MacKenzie who arrived from Barra, Scotland on the ship "Harmony" in 1821. His mother, the former Catherine MacDougall, was an exceptional Gaelic poet, and her people were renowned for their dancing and piping.

Near the MacKenzie home, a large pine stump stood alone in a field, and, at age twelve, Archibald cut a block from it. He gouged out the centre, covered its top with a shingle, added a neck, and thus manufactured his own violin. Years later, he would point out the old stump to his children and say, "The fiddle I learned to play on came from there!" At age eighteen, he began to teach school, and with his first pay bought a new violin in Baddeck, passing on his homemade one to his friend, Dan C. MacNeil, who used it often.

There were two strong musical influences in Mr. MacKenzie's life, one was the famous piper, Stephen B. MacNeil who was a friend and fellow teacher. The second was Michael MacKinnon, "The Little Fiddler", from the Castlebay area. Michael, who was Archibald's brother-in-law, was an exceptional player, and he could always recite the Gaelic words and history associated with each tune he played.

Archibald, who specialized in unaccompanied traditional music, held the fiddle into his shoulder like many players of that time, He had an extraordinary bow hand and could "cut" going up and down. Among his favourite pieces were "The Yowe with the Crooked Horn" and "Cairistiona Chaimbeul"; he excelled at this type of tune, and he seldom performed without utilizing "high bass" tuning. While he was in his prime, he played at dances and weddings all over Christmas Island parish.

Archibald's son, Archie Alex, relates this tale about his father: "He was the president of The League of the Cross. Once, the organization made an excursion by boat on the Bras d'Or Lakes, and he prepared for the occasion by thoroughly cleaning his violin with egg whites. On board, **he** provided the music while the others in the party danced on the deck. It was a temperance gathering, but they made it as lively as possible!"

Archibald's home became the center for Scottish culture in the area. The ceilidhs attracted people of all age groups who came to share in the pioneer stories, the Gaelic songs and music from Mr. MacKenzie's violin.

A teacher for over thirty years, Archibald was a master of both Gaelic and English. In the former language, he wrote beautiful poetry, songs and fairy tales. Some of his most celebrated poems are those entitled "Failt'a Bhonnaich Choirc", "An Tulach Bhoidheach" and "Oran na h-aois". In

English, he published "The History of Christmas Island and Parish", an important and fascinating genealogical work.

Just a few months before Archibald passed away, his grandchild took the old man's fiddle from its case and handed it to him. One last time, he movingly played the music of his heart.

Of his children, sons Hugh F. (d. 1971) and Archie Alex continued the fiddling tradition.

Dan MacKinnon

Dates: 1864?-1949, a native of Washabuck, Iona Parish
Parents: Murdoch MacKinnon and Catherine Anne MacKenzie

Dan MacKinnon was an important contributor to the musical history of his section of Cape Breton. His fiddling career began in rough fashion on an old shingle strung with horse hair; he would "jig" tunes out behind the barn while pretending to play. Later on, his older brother, Neil, brought the first real violin into the home, and Dan, the youngest boy, immediately took an interest in the instrument. When Neil left for California, he gave the fiddle to Dan, who by this time was making good progress. This very violin, made with a fir top and a beech back, is still in the family's possession.

Of his various violins, Dan grew to love his 3rd one, obtained from John Neil MacKenzie, a native of Washabuck, who spent time in Boston. "My father was crazy about that fiddle," says Dan's son, Jimmy.

When Dan MacKinnon first started to play, he was the only fiddler in the area. The source of some of his tunes is still a mystery, but the quality of his music was well known. His son Hector recalls, "He was an ear player. Good violinists have told me that his music was wonderful and very good for stepdancing. He was great on tunes like 'Caber Féidh', 'Braes of Mar', 'Lord MacDonald's Reel' and 'Calum Crùbach'. He used that last tune quite a bit when playing for stepdancing. He often used the 'high bass'. When he played around home, there'd be crowds out there to hear him. Sometimes on Saturday nights or Sunday afternoons, Vincent MacLean and his sons would arrive with something to sip on and the party would be on!" Vincent was a "neat" stepdancer and loved to dance to Dan's lively selections. Besides the MacLeans, the Brown family, known far and wide for their antics and their love of music, sought Dan's fiddling to accompany their dancing.

Pianos and guitars being a rarity then, Dan usually performed on his own. Sometimes before or after a medley, he would sing out the Gaelic or English words associated with each violin tune; these words were generally of the comical variety.

Cape Breton dance music was provided at weddings, milling frolics, picnics and "pie sales", but among the most popular gatherings were those held at the many one-room schoolhouses in the district.

Dan would earn only $3.00 per night at these events, but he was always a willing participant. At the Orangemen's Picnic at Little Narrows, his earnings could run as high as $10.00.

Dan MacKinnon influenced and encouraged the development of Scottish music in the Iona area of Cape Breton. Nine sons and a daughter enthusiastically carried on the fiddling tradition, and they were by name: Philip, Johnnie, Dan Joe, Jimmy, Roddy, Hector, Columba, Murdoch, Neilly and Sally. Jimmy remembers, "My father, like my brother Hector, was a very good stepdancer. We'd all take turns playing for him when he danced at home. At one point, there were seven violins in the family - all tuned up. Once, 'Big' Ronald MacLellan came to our house and stayed up until 3 o'clock in the morning, trying all the violins." Dan, himself, could fiddle for long hours without interruption, but, when the dancers tested his endurance, he would secretly use his fingernails to cut through the gut strings of his violin; this "unfortunate accident" would then earn him a few minutes break while a replacement string was located.

Besides being a good fiddler, dancer and Gaelic speaker, Dan MacKinnon was a talented carpenter. In this regard as well, his sons have followed in their father's footsteps.

A staunch supporter of Cape Breton music, Dan never lost his vitality. "He took a crack at the fiddle every evening before bed, and he played up until the last days of his life," remembers Jimmy. The following was taken from the old family Bible, now at Jimmy's home at MacKinnon's Harbour: "Daniel MacKinnon departed this life at Cain's Mountain on Monday afternoon, 1:30 o'clock, August 8th, 1949, aged 85 years. Burial took place on Wednesday morning from Holy Rosary Church, Washabuck Center, Rev. Fr. D.J. Rankin officiating. R.I.P."

Dan MacKinnon's name, along with those of Gillis Point favourites "Big" Ann Morrison and John Alex "the Fiddler" MacNeil, is still spoken with fondness whenever discussions concerning Scottish music take place in modern-day Iona.

"Red" John MacKinnon

Dates: 1870-1940, a native of Meat Cove
Parents: Sandy MacKinnon and Catherine MacDonald

"Red" John - fiddler, piper and stepdancer - was one of seven children by his father's first marriage. In the family, only he and his brother, Angus "Mossy", played the violin. John's daughter, Mrs. Alice Aucoin, tells her father's story: "He started playing at ten or twelve years of age. He and Angus used to go over to their uncle's, Hughie MacDonald of Meat Cove to learn. Hughie's sons Jimmy, Hector and Angus played, and they stepdanced too." Both the MacKinnon and the MacDonald boys worked in the lumber camps in St. Ann's, Cape Breton and in Maine; they always took their music with them wherever they went.

Though he had little formal education, "Red" John was a gifted musician. "He was an ear player," Alice continues. "He learned the fiddle and the pipes from the older players down north. In those days, there were rough fiddles being made in Meat Cove, and there was all kinds of music there. My father built a set of pipes once, and he mounted them with silver that had washed ashore where the ships used to pass by. And, he bought an old French fiddle - a LePage - for twenty-five dollars. It was very old, and he had a MacKinnon-tartan ribbon hanging from it. Down north, he played at dances; he would change back and forth from the violin to the pipes. He was a terrific piper - he played the pibroch, and he could play for sets.

"In 1897, he married my mother, Elizabeth MacLellan of Broad Cove," Alice says. "When he was still in his twenties, they moved to Sydney, where he worked 'on the city' and played at dances for five dollars per night. At home, he'd often take out the violin first thing in the morning, before his first cup of tea! Then, we'd have a ceilidh on many a night and the kids would stepdance - Jimmy Angus, Florence, Jessie, 'Kit' and me. I remember two of my father's favourite tunes were 'Down in the Meadow Where the Farmer Lost His Ox' and 'Tullochgorum'."

The MacKinnons lived on Hardwood Hill in Sydney for over ten years, and Alice relates this tale about her father, which took place during that period: "Allan Donahue of New Victoria was getting married, and my father was invited to play at the wedding. When the big day came, he got up at 5:00 a.m., had his breakfast, and then walked all the way from Hardwood Hill to Brown's Road, New Victoria and played the whole night! They had quite a time. He left at eight or nine the next morning after breakfast, and he walked back home. There's living, what! He had the nicest shape a man could have - 48'' across the chest and 31'' around the waist, and he was all muscle! But, he was gentle and very good natured, and he'd never show off with his fiddling.''

Occasionally, "Red" John and his family spent a few months in Meat Cove. He would take part in the spring's fishing and in the lively "wood frolics" in the fall. But Sydney being his new home, it was there that most of his Scottish-music associates lived, men such as J.J. MacInnis, a close friend; Mick MacInnis; Joe MacKinnon, the magistrate; Jim MacDonald, formerly of East Bay; Martin Campbell; Hector MacDougall, who'd be home from Boston; and "Little" Simon Fraser, a relative from Meat Cove. The accompanists he employed included Bessie MacKinnon, Mary MacLean Gillis, Mary MacInnis and his son-in-law, Johnny Aucoin, who played the guitar.

"Red" John's brother, Angus "Mossy" MacKinnon, a famous stepdancer, was also a good violinist, even though the index finger on his left hand had been permanently injured in an accident. Alice says, "When my uncle Angus played, even if you couldn't dance, you'd still feel like trying. He was a rougher player than my father, though. My father's playing was sweet. He (ie. John) had about seventeen medals for fiddling and dancing. In 1925, he won a fiddling contest at the Lyceum. The judges were from away, and one of them asked my father where he got his music. He answered, 'I learned it from the singing of the birds in Cape North!''' A collection of medals, still in the family's possession, stands as proof of "Red" John's success.

On September 17, 1935, a plaque was presented to Mr. & Mrs. John MacKinnon on the occasion of their fortieth anniversary. The following is an excerpt from the inscription: "John is well known to every Scottish and Gaelic audience of the whole Island, to whom he has given the choicest entertainment in violin and bagpipe music and stepdance in every Cape Breton theatre. . .''

In 1940, at seventy years of age, "Red" John was invited to play his pipes in Scotland. Alice remembers, "He had just got a new suit and his suitcase was packed for his first trip to the home of his ancestors - he died before he could go. He took a stroke from high blood pressure; he had never been sick a day in his life up till then. He played the fiddle until he died - as good as when he was twenty!''

Today, "Red" John would certainly be proud of the manner in which his grandchildren have continued his work of bringing joy to the world through music.

Ned MacKinnon

Dates: 1876-1926, a native of Cooper's Pond, Christmas Island parish
Parents: Angus "Neil" MacKinnon and Mary Curry

Edward A. "Ned" MacKinnon was the great-grandson of Donald MacKinnon ("Domhnall Bàn MacChaluim"), who settled in the quaint village of Cooper's Pond in the first decade of the 1800's. All of Angus Neil's children could provide fiddle music; notably, Joseph A., Rod (1872-1969) and Ned, of course, who was considered one of Cape Breton's most proficient performers.

Rod MacKinnon, who had begun to play at age twelve, had much to share with his younger brother, Ned, by the time the latter was old enough to hold the violin. Developing into a note reader, Ned eventually possessed a collection of fiddle-tune books, some of which contained arrangements and compositions by J. Scott Skinner. Ned was apparently among the first Cape Breton fiddlers to specialize in Skinner's music, tunes such as "The Bonny Lass of Bon-Accord". On the other hand, he had an obsession with the traditional melodies which had been handed down through successive generations to Christmas Island residents. A.J. MacNeil, the son of Joe "the Blacksmith" of Cooper's Pond, relates this story: "Ned used to walk from his home up along the old Grand Narrows Highway. If a tune came into his head, he'd run into my father's house and grab the old four-dollar fiddle. He'd make that cheap violin sound like a very good instrument. He'd play three or four versions of that tune he'd been thinking about, but he'd always know which version was the oldest!" A.J. continues, "Ned was a good woodsman - good with an axe. But if he was working and an old tune came to mind - some tune he had once heard the old folks play - he'd stop cutting and start whistling. Then, right after work, he'd race home to get his violin and try out that piece."
Though Ned took employment from time to time, his niece, Peggy MacLean, states, "He had no real trade - he was a travelling musician. Ned was in love with his violin; he never married."

In honour of his wonderful ability, Ned was once given a beautiful violin by a member of his community. It was one of three or four fine, old instruments which had been brought to the area by some of the early Scottish settlers. He played this violin with the pride and exactness of a worthy owner.

For scores of miles in every direction, Ned MacKinnon came to be spoken of as a great violinist. Occasionally he would play at dances, but it was always understood that his services were slightly more expensive than the average fiddler's.

Having friends over in Inverness County, Ned made a number of trips there. During one such excursion, his music was heard by a very young lad named Dan R. MacDonald. Many years later, Dan R. still spoke of Ned's playing as impressive. Sandy MacLean of Foot Cape recalls, "Ned MacKinnon worked in the mine in Inverness, and he boarded at Alex MacInnis' - he was a very nice player!" Once, while on the Island's west coast, Ned met Jessie Maggie MacLellan, a famous piano player who had studied music. As she accompanied him, Jessie Maggie was amazed at Ned's ability to sight-read music from books he had never seen before.

In the winter, and closer to home, Ned and his brothers often travelled by horse and sleigh on Sunday afternoons to the home of Archibald J. MacKenzie, a violin player from Christmas Island. Archibald's son, Archie Alex, describes Ned's music as follows - "It was sweet - he was a very pleasing player to listen to!"

Ned and his brother, Joseph A., who was also a talented fiddler, spent an extended time in America. It was there that Ned took seriously ill and was forced to return home. He died in 1926 at just 50 years of age, leaving only memories to attest to his musical wizardy; but, the elder folk of Christmas Island Parish still refer to him as "one of the best".

PUT ME IN THE BIG CHEST [CUIR 'S A' CHISTE MHÓIR MI]

Reel transcription by Roddie MacDonald of Inverness Town

Dan Allan MacLellan

Dates: 1870-1946, a native of Glenville (Gleann Dubh), Inverness County
Parents: "Red" Allan MacLellan (1832-1907) and Catherine MacLellan

Dan Allan, also known as Donald Allan, was the grandson of "Red" John MacLellan of Morar, Scotland who was the third man to settle in "Gleann Dubh". A former good friend and neighbour, Monsignor M.A. MacLellan, offers this first-hand information on the noted violinist: "Donald had two brothers, Malcolm (1876-1959) and Johnnie (1859-1951), both of whom played the fiddle quite well, but were over-shadowed by Donald's preeminence. Donald Allan was our music master in the Glen. He played completely by ear and, in his day, was recognized as one of Cape Breton's leading fiddlers. He was both a farmer and a carpenter, but he clearly was not born for farming and was far more suited to have been a musician or a cabinet maker. His outstanding ability as a fiddler provided many a lively hour of entertainment and enjoyment to the Glen folk. With all his brilliant skill, he was a very modest person, always protesting his own deficiencies and what he would describe as 'scratchings'."

Dan Allan's nephew, Allan Albert Kennedy, has the following recollections of his uncle: "He had a terrific ear, and he was a master on the back strings. His music was so lively for dancing! He was one of the experts on Scotch-four playing - he'd put a wooden man to dance! He and his brother Malcolm were great stepdancers too, and Dan Allan also composed a good many strathspeys and reels.

"When he was a young fellow in stove-pipe pants," Allan Albert continues, "he was invited up to Judique to play for a wedding. Sometime during the course of the day, Dan Allan was relieved by another fiddler, and so got up to dance in the same set as 'Wild' Archie MacLellan, a local character. With 'Wild' Archie to back him up, Dan Allan called out, 'MacLellans on the floor - who'll dare put them off?' The Judiquers got quite a charge out of this challenge.

"Dan Allan had a great love of music and company," Allan Albert recalls. "He was a great extrovert. Once a group of neighbours and friends in Glenville chipped in and bought him a good violin and presented it to him. It was an original 'Simon Leroux' of Montreal. The people of the area nicknamed it 'The Big Fiddle' on account of its volume and clarity.

"The old home was on a hill," he adds, "in the center of the Glen. Dan Allan would go out on the portico after the chores were done and play. They'd hear him all through the Glen because of the location of his house."

A bachelor farmer who hardly ever left home, Dan Allan lived on the old homestead with his brother, Malcolm. Utilizing a technique which is referred to on the Island as "the long bow", Dan enhanced the Gaelic flavour of each tune with the beautiful "cuts" always associated with great Cape Breton fiddling. The Monsignor continues, "Regarding the style of Dan Allan's music, it was largely traditional - jigs, reels, strathspeys, lively and sweet, clear and distinct. There is no doubt that he was a gifted fiddler! Sometimes a drink of good Scotch would be available and then one could sense that, whatever the evils associated with alcohol, certainly it had enormous potential for maximizing the fiddler's dexterity, enhancing his rhythm and thereby raising the level of harmony and joy to the highest pitch. In his own way, Donald Allan was an artist, sensitive and impatient with the coarse, the vulgar and the mean. He gave most generously to the happiness of the neighbourhood and he was never forgotten by all who were honoured to have known and listened to him.''

In 1897, Dan Allan participated in the musical extravaganza which marked the beginning of the Mabou parish picnics. In later years, his thrilling music was enjoyed by two other noted fiddlers,

Donald Angus Beaton of Mabou and Dan J. Campbell of Glenora Falls. Recently Donald Angus said, "He could play all night on the high bass and tenor - hundreds of tunes; that was unusual!"

Dan Allan's brother, Malcolm, was known as a sweeter player, but was shyer and more retiring; and, these MacLellans had a cousin called Allan Donald who occasionally made a small contribution to the musical gatherings in the community.

In 1946, the highly-sociable and multi-talented individual known as Donald Allan "Red John" MacLellan went to his final reward. He lies buried with his family in the Inverness Cemetery.

"Baby" Joe MacLellan

Dates: June 15, 1915 – March, 1935, a native of Riverside, Cape Breton
Parents: "Big" Ronald MacLellan and Mary Ann MacDonald

"Baby" Joe, the son of fiddler "Big" Ronald MacLellan, received his nickname because of the fact that he was always slight, frail and youthful-looking. His rapid development into a mature violinist left both family and friends stupefied. At only twelve years of age, "Baby" Joe was supplying music for schoolhouse dances, using a three-dollar fiddle he had earned by selling garden seeds from door to door. He would often play from dusk until dawn for little or no pay.

Joe's younger sister, famed fiddler Theresa MacLellan, has always heard wonderful accounts of her brother's playing. She has been led to believe that "he had an awful pretty tone - his music was like a little bird singing."

"Baby" Joe's musical services were often sought for the house parties and "kitchen rackets" held in such places as Port Hawkesbury and West Bay Road. Sometimes a twenty-five cent admission would be charged at these functions, with part of the money going to the fiddler and part to the organizer.

Two of the boy's biggest supporters were his parents. On one occasion when Joe was only about fourteen, his mother requested that he play a few selections for her in the sitting room. As he proceeded to produce beautiful melodies unaccompanied, Mary Ann turned to the children at her side and whispered, "What music can there be in Heaven when we have **this** here on earth!"

Coached well by "Big" Ronald, Joe began to take a prize in every contest in which he participated. In 1928, at only thirteen years of age, he earned a second-place medal at the Lyceum Theatre in Sydney; on October 30, 1929, at fourteen, he won a fountain pen in a North Sydney competition; and in 1930, at fifteen, he took the first-place medal at the Judique Highland Games.

In 1932, "Baby" Joe decided to enter the old-time fiddling contest in Sydney. Theresa picks up the story: "He went down on the train alone; Hughie R. MacDonald of South Bentinck Street looked after him. He was very shy coming out on the stage - he sort of eased out sideways. The audience didn't expect him to be in the running with all the older players in the contest." But, on October 5, 1932, the following article appeared in the Sydney Post-Record: "Joseph MacLellan, seventeen year old violinist from Cleveland, C.B., carried off first prize honors in the Cape Breton fiddling contest last night at the Capitol Theatre. A son of Mr. & Mrs. Ronald MacLellan, well known residents of Cleveland, he is a familiar figure in Cape Breton competitions, having . . . played his way to major awards at other events staged in various centres on the Island in recent years." "Joe took the twenty-dollar first prize," continues Theresa. "He bought me a pair of gumboots from the money he won - he had them coming home with him." While in Sydney, "Baby" Joe took the opportunity to play over CJCB Radio, but unfortunately the MacLellans back in Riverside were unable to pick up the program, as Theresa explains: "We had no radio at that time, but everyone in Sydney who heard the broadcast said it was fantastic!" Fr. John Angus Rankin claims that, after hearing "Baby" Joe perform in Sydney, Sandy

MacLean of Foot Cape announced, "If that young fellow continues the way he's going, then in a few years the rest of us can all to out and break our violins!"

Of Joe's victory at the 1930 Judique Highland Games, Theresa says, "He was a very religious-type boy. Since he didn't have any money to get into the picnic, he went into the Judique church to pray. When he came out, he found an entrance ticket on the ground! That day, he won the first-prize medal; I think one of the judges was Gordon Mac Quarrie."

In the early 30's, "Baby" Joe sometimes accompanied his parents on the train to Port Hawkesbury, where the three would entertain at the two-day picnic at Saint Theresa's Convent. "Big" Ronald and "Baby" Joe supplied the violin music, and Mary Ann provided piano or organ accompaniment when possible. The music continued in a steady stream from 9:00 a.m. until 1:00 a.m.

But fate dealt Joseph MacLellan a cruel blow. "Up until about age sixteen, 'Baby' Joe was healthy," Theresa says. "What got him was playing for dances - you'd eat the dust in the corners at the schoolhouse! He was out making money for the family, and he always brought it all home (i.e. the $3.00 - $5.00 wage). When he got weak, it was discovered that he had TB. He was sent away to Antigonish for two years, and he took his fiddle - it was there he died. He played the fiddle right to the end. He had orders from the doctor not to play, but he took the fiddle out when some boys came to visit him in his room - I guess that's what killed him."

Ronald MacLellan always intended that his son, Joe, should be his equal or better on the violin, but it was not to be. After extended medical confinement, "Baby" Joe died at the age of nineteen - Cape Breton's most astounding prodigy was gone.

Fiddlers in his family tree:
grandfather, Rory Malcolm MacDonald; uncle, Dan MacLellan; father, Ronald; sister, Theresa; and brother, Donald. A second sister, Marie MacLellan, is a famous Cape Breton pianist.

"Big" Ronald MacLellan

Dates: 1880-1935, a native of Broad Cove, Inverness County
Parents: John MacLellan (Iain MacIain 'ic Aonghuis) and
Peggy MacEachern

The son of fisherman-poet John MacLellan, "Big" Ronald (called "Raonul Mór") began playing the violin while living in Glendale with his uncle, Archie MacEachern. Some people believed that Ronald was predestined to be a fiddler, and the following tale is still told by members of his family: Musical individuals were often said to have been visited by fairies or "little men". One day, Ronald's aunt discovered a bow-shaped arrow projecting from a mound in a field near her house. Knowing its significance, she took it home and hid it in a basket over the doorway. She believed that this "fairy bow" would one day enhance the abilities of some great fiddler who would know in his heart that it was meant for him. When Ronald's musical talents began to manifest themselves, he took the mysterious bow out to the barn and strung it up with the white tail-hair of a horse. From then on, he was able to produce violin music which was magical in its strength and expression.

Ronald grew to a height of about 6'5" and weighed in the vicinity of 270 pounds. His huge, powerful blacksmith's hands were deceptive, for they could lure beautiful strains from the violin. In the words of one of his biggest fans, Dan R. MacDonald, "He'd make the hair on your head stand; he'd charm the snakes out of the woods!"

Ronald's son, Donald, is of the opinion that his father mastered note reading with the assistance of prominent Cape Breton musician, Vincent A. MacLellan. Be that as it may, Raonul Mór was probably better known for his driving renditions of the "big tunes", meaning the Gaelic-flavoured traditional beauties often associated with Inverness County; for additional dynamic dimensions, he frequently employed the high bass and tenor tuning. It was universally agreed that Ronald excelled at marches, one of his personal favourites being "Lord Alexander Kennedy". His own compositions for the Scottish violin were highly acclaimed as well, and six of these are included in the book which was published in 1940 by his close friend and fellow player, Gordon MacQuarrie; both "Miss Christy Nicholson's Strathspey" and "Port Hawkesbury Reel" receive periodic treatment by Cape Breton fiddlers.

As a blacksmith, "Big" Ronald travelled all over the Island, occasionally demonstrating fantastic feats of strength. A horseshoe, bent by Ronald into the shape of a figure-eight, used to hang in the River

Denys railway station, stark evidence of his incredible power. Even after working a 2½-day shift shoeing horses in the Inverness mine, his endurance was such that he was still able to seize the violin and produce enchanting music from dusk until dawn without the benefit of sleep.

In the words of Donald MacLellan, "Angus MacIsaac used to say that my dad often played in his kitchen in Port Hawkesbury, leaning back on a chair with his head against the wall - the music would bring Angus to tears. When the painters came to remodel Angus' house some years later, he wouldn't let them touch up the spot where my dad's head used to touch the wall!"

On Christmas Day, 1935, "Big" Ronald MacLellan passed away at the home of Ronald Allan "the Baron" MacDonald of Mull River. The body was transported by truck to his home, and he was laid to rest at the Princeville Cemetery. Of his surviving children, three are noted musicians: Donald, Theresa (violinists) and Marie (pianist). Another son, Joseph (1915-1935), was a fiddling prodigy.

A man from Mabou is reputed to have been responsible for the following tribute to our musical giant: " 'Big' Ronald could play just fair, he could play middlin' and he could play good - but when he played good, the Devil couldn't beat him!"

> "Those Scottish tunes he'd play so sweet
>   You'd think 'twas Orpheus come again;
> And he could make us smile and greet,
>   So gay or sad the lilting strain.
> His melodies would bring to mind
>   Far distant glens and rippling streams.
> Though gone himself, he left behind
>   His strains - we hear them in our dreams.
> He's gone to join that noble throng,
>   Cape Breton's talent gone before
> Who lift their music and their song,
>   Though they themselves are seen no more.
> Though gone, he still with us will stray;
>   Although he in his grave does lie,
> The melodies he used to play
>   And left behind will never die."
>
> — "Red" Gordon MacQuarrie

Vincent A. MacLellan

Dates: 1856-1935, a native of Broad Cove Intervale, Inverness County
Parents: Donald MacLellan (Domhnull Gobha) and Mary MacIsaac (Mairi Iain 'ic Ailean)

Vincent (called Bhinsent Dhomhnuill Ghobha) was the son of Donald MacLellan, a blacksmith and bard who was able to compose songs on the spur of the moment. The obvious inheritor of his father's creativity, Vincent was highly touted in the 1943-44 edition of Eilean Cheap Breatann: ". . . He applied himself to music at a very early age, taught himself to play the violin and to write down his compositions, thus showing he possessed a wonderful amount of natural ability."[21]

Though born in Inverness County, in 1868, with his parents, Vincent moved to a farm once owned by Alex Gillis in Grand Mira North. In the words of Mrs. Elizabeth MacLellan, the wife of Vincent's nephew, "There were an awful lot of violin players in the Mira area. For instance, there were the two Duncan MacDougalls - one from Broad Cove Chapel and one from Grand Mira - living across the road from each other; they were friends of Vincent's. One Duncan was a sweet player; the other was a powerful dance fiddler who played at weddings. Then there was Steve and Dan MacEachern, and Jim and Archie Gillis - all from Victoria Bridge. And, John Gillis (Iain Sheumais), John R. MacDougall, plus several on the French Road. Vincent knew them all, though some were younger and had less ability on the violin.

"Vincent was often called to weddings to play for dancing," Mrs. MacLellan continues. "He was a powerful player, but you had to pay attention to him. 'If you don't want to listen, there's no use playing!' he used to say if his audience wasn't attentive. He was a big, heavy man with broad shoulders and was a good stepdancer, though his brother Frank was the outstanding dancer in the family. All the MacLellans were full of music, and they were witty."

Vincent's older brother, Angus (called Aonghas "Pushie"), was also a fine fiddler. He married and set up a successful carriage-making business in Sydney, but, being burned out in a fire around 1880, settled in California in 1883. Vincent, John, and Frank, following their brother's lead, also decided to head for "the Golden West". Since they were all competent musicians, the MacLellan boys were popular citizens no matter where they made their homes. In addition to being a very good fiddler, Vincent was a fine carpenter and built violins. "Before he left for the west coast," Mrs. MacLellan says, "he was in an old, abandoned house and spotted some wood that he thought would be good for making violins, especially because it was so dry. After moving to America, he wrote and asked a friend to go to that house and gather all the old wood the length of a violin and ship it out to him."

In 1890, Vincent came back home to Canada. A creative writer both in Gaelic and in English, in 1892, he published a book of songs entitled "Failte Cheap Breatuinn", which Joseph MacKinnon once called "that literary and bardic landmark of our Island's Gaelic." In 1905, also in Erse, he composed a few lines which were used on a poster advertising a picnic to raise money for the Stella Maris Church in Inverness Town. Roughly translated, the words read, "Get up and come along to the picnic of the big church. We'll see many friends and relatives there from near and far away. There'll be food and drink and tasty treats and music that will bring cheer to your feet. So, dip your oar and come along!"

Unmarried though popular with the ladies, Vincent continued his wanderings, being a veritable itinerant musician. For a while, he worked in Inverness Town with the telegraph service, and then was employed in the drugstore. Around 1912, he went to work with his nephew, W. J. MacDonald, in New Waterford. W. J., too, was a good fiddler, and they occasionally performed together at dances in the old St. Agnes Parish Hall.

Always putting stress on the art of reading music, Vincent became an influential member of Cape Breton's fiddling community. He assisted fellow players such as Gordon MacQuarrie and J. J. MacInnis in their study of music theory, and he judged fiddle contests and taught music in the metropolitan area.

After retiring, Vincent stayed with his sister. One day, he received a friendly note from his brother, Frank (d. 1929), who had remained in California. It cheered him up so much, that he sat down and composed his most famous tune, "My Brother's Letter", a rousing reel which was published in "The Cape Breton Collection" in 1940.

A glowing tribute was paid to Vincent in 1933 by his friend, the aforementioned Joseph MacKinnon of Sydney: "Bhinsent Dhomhnuill Ghobha is physically a magnificent specimen - big size, good proportions, easy bearing, noble carriage. His manner is confident and gracious; his presence, impressive but not obtrusive. He is both practical and adaptable - not aloof. His conversation is ready and intelligent; his wit unexcelled. He is a dancing master, a composer of songs, a good singer, with good taste for the songs of others. He is clever in vocal music (having directed choirs and orchestras) and the theory and rendition of instrumental music, performing with skill on the piano, violin, bagpipes and some brass instruments. Vincent is well versed in dramatic art, having acted in casts, and directed and composed local plays of merit. As an entertainer, he is without peer, Charlie Chaplin and Harry Lauder being not in his class. Vincent MacLellan is perhaps, above all else, a Scot who will be forever one of our Cape Breton landmarks in matters dear to the Highland heart."

In the fall in 1935, Vincent MacLellan passed away in St. Anthony's Home in Sydney. "He was considered one of the best violinists of his day, was a real musician and a great Highlander!"[22]

-J. J. MacInnis

Peter MacNeil

Home: Castle Bay, Christmas Island parish
Parents: John MacNeil (Iain MacRuairidh) and Ann MacDougall

Peter was the son of John MacNeil, who, along with his three brothers and a sister, was among the first immigrants to come from Barra, Scotland to "the Gulf"; John eventually sailed for Cape Breton and settled at Castle Bay.

Peter's brother, John "Og" MacNeil, was also a fine violinist, having been taught by the famous Donald Campbell (d. 1878) of St. Peters who, in turn, was supposed to have received his knowledge of the violin from the fairies in a "sithean" or fairy hill.

The following tale is taken from "The History of Christmas Island and Parish" by A.J. MacKenzie: "Peter MacNeil (Iain MacRuairidh) was a noted violinist, and his service was in great demand at match-makings and weddings. As a player of Scottish music, it is the general opinion that he never had an equal in this district except his brother, John Og. The latter had a sweeter finger and a neater bow; but for the loud, lively music for 'break-downs', Peter had no equal. He was playing at a wedding one time and a piper happened to be playing there too. They played 'spell about' during the night; but at dawn when the morning wedding reel was going on the floor, the groom told the piper to set up his pipes and play the 'morning reel'. Now, in those days this was as much as to say that the piper was the better musician. Peter felt offended, but he made way for the piper. When the reel commenced, Peter went and stood at the door with the violin under his arm. His temper was up, and he said to a friend in Gaelic: 'Cuiridh mi suas i' ('I'll show the pipes up'). 'No,' said his friend, 'don't do that.' 'E bhi damainte; cuiridh mi suas i' ('He be damned; I'll show the pipes up'), said Peter; and he began to play the violin so loud that he drowned the music of the bagpipes. The piper had to give up the contest; and Peter played the reel to the end."[23]

Peter married Jessie MacKinnon and settled at the rear of Castle Bay. They were blessed with ten children.

Duncan MacQuarrie

Dates: 1884-1979, a native of Glenora Falls, Inverness County
Parents: John MacQuarrie and Maggie Boyle

John MacQuarrie, a fiddler, had eight children, and they all tried their hand at the violin, though only Duncan and his younger brother John Alex persisted. Mrs. Belle Kennedy, Duncan's sister, relates this story: "Our father played at parties, dances and picnics. He was very fussy about the music **and** his violin. When Duncan got that he could hold that fiddle (around age twelve), he'd steal it out. He'd get away from the house and go to the barn to practice; at first, our father didn't know anything about it! Later, when Duncan started stepping out and playing at parties, he had to have his own violin."

By surrounding himself with good music all the time, Duncan compiled an impressive store of traditional tunes. Dan J. and Angus, the Campbell brothers from Glenora Falls, were neighbours and friends of his, and many were the hours they spent together fiddling.

"Duncan played at many dances," Belle remembers. "Think of how hard it was for the fiddler - no piano! After a while though, my sister, Mary, bought an organ for home. When we were young, everyone would be dead without the music! You wouldn't think of having a night's entertainment without the fiddler!

"Duncan worked at the Port Hood and Inverness mines," Belle continues. "He'd board in the areas where he was working, and he'd always take his violin with him."

In 1919, Duncan moved to New Waterford, where he began his long friendship with Margaret MacPhee and her son, Dougie. The latter still speaks admiringly of Duncan's bow arm, good timing, sweetness of tone, "lift", repertoire and effortless delivery, stressing that he always played with the perfect blend of grace and authority. "And, Duncan was the wittiest man on the face of the earth!" Dougie says.

Having performed for over eighty years, Duncan knew and was appreciated by all the local Scottish musicians. One special friend was the late Johnny Archie MacIsaac - their duets were unforgettable.

Duncan never married, and, when asked why, he used to say in jest, "Nobody ever asked me!" However, he was deeply loved by the community at large. "I don't think there was anyone as fond of music and company as Duncan was," says Belle. "And, he never had any enemies - he got along well with everyone."

Gordon F. MacQuarrie

Dates: 1897-1965, a native of Dunakin, Inverness County
Parents: Angus Forbes MacQuarrie and Margaret MacLean

Following the sudden death of his mother when he was just an infant, Gordon was raised by Neil MacLennan of Melford. Having received a good education at the Melford school, he developed a consuming love of music and the written word. Literate in both Gaelic and English, he became familiar with the Classics and embarked on a career of poetry writing. As a musician, Gordon grew fond of both the bagpipes and the violin; however, in 1935, in a letter to Joseph MacInnis of Sydney, he once said, "Although I own both instruments, I very seldom now blow up the pipes, not because I don't like them as music, but because I feel I can do the violin more justice and no one can be at both very much."

It is believed that Gordon became a note reader quite early in life due to a correspondence course he received on the subject. In addition, however, he benefited from the assistance and encouragement offered by both John Alex Gillis of Alba (a violin builder) and Vincent A. MacLellan, a prominent Cape Breton violinist. His list of musical friends came to include Dan R. MacDonald and "Big" Ronald MacLellan. Then, in the mid-twenties, Gordon played with Ronald's son, "Baby" Joe, at a picnic celebrating the opening of the Creignish Hall.

"Red" Gordon, called so on account of the color of his hair, was considered extremely creative and wildly eccentric. A travelling musician, he became famous for his escapades, his inspired playing and his countless abodes. One of his temporary homes was that of Rannie MacIsaac of Creignish. Rannie's son Norman recalls, "He'd come by bus with his pipes and fiddle under his arm - if you heard him whistling, you knew he was in good trim for playing. One Saturday afternoon, on our front veranda, he played the pipes and fiddle, spell about, for a couple of hours. You could hear the music a long ways off. He had the American cars all lined up on the road for quite a distance - they were just parked there listening! Sometimes John H. and Alex Joe MacDonald would hear the music and walk over, but you couldn't make a sound; if you interrupted him, he'd just stop and put the pipes and fiddle in their cases."

In 1935, following the death of "Big" Ronald MacLellan, Gordon grieved at the loss of his friend and fellow musician, and, in tribute, wrote a moving sixteen-line poem beginning: "Those Scottish tunes he'd play so sweet/ You'd think 'twas Orpheus come again . . ." In 1939, largely due to the efforts of Johnny Archie MacDonald, he performed at a concert in Detroit along with fellow violinist Mary "Hughie" MacDonald.

In 1940, with the very able assistance of Joe Beaton, Gordon compiled "The Cape Breton Collection of Scottish Melodies". This book, a pioneer effort in the field of Cape Breton music publication, contains not only Gordon's original tunes, but those of Dan R. MacDonald, Ronald MacLellan, Vincent MacLellan, Dan Hughie MacEachern, Peter MacPhee, Sandy MacLean, J.D. Kennedy and others. Of Gordon's own works, the piece which enjoys the most popularity is "The Bonnie Lass of Headlake", an air composed for Hattie MacDonald of Lake Ainslie.

As a member of the Cape Breton Highlanders, Gordon served in the British Isles during World War II. He often played the reveille on his bagpipes to rouse his slumbering comrades. While in Scotland he capitalized on the chance to obtain music collections unavailable back home. Among his favourite tunes for the violin were "Niel Gow's Lament", "The Duke of Gordon's Birthday" and "King Robert the Bruce". Many remember his stirring version of the latter piece, complete with all the suggested musical slurs.

For the families who experienced visits by Gordon through the years, the highlights include long evenings of music, recitations and the writing of clever and impromptu verse. His unbridled vitality has certainly left its mark on all those whom he encountered.

On October 31, 1965, Gordon MacQuarrie met a tragic end in a car-pedestrian accident near Inverness. He was laid to rest at the Stewartdale Cemetery.

Lauchie Meagher

Dates: 1881-1942, a native of Brook Village, Cape Breton
Parents: James Meagher (d. 1894) and Mary Jamieson

Lauchie's grandfather, Daniel Meagher (1794?-1865), was born in Ireland but immigrated to Canada around 1820, settling in beautiful Brook Village between the years 1823-24. Lauchie's father, Jim, was a violinist and an ardent defender of Cape Breton music, having refused to surrender his fiddle to the infamous Fr. Kenneth MacDonald, parish priest in Mabou from 1865-94.

Lauchie, a miner for forty years, had the reputation of being a very good traditional-flavoured fiddler. He had learned the intricate nuances of the old style by observing and absorbing, not by depending on the written notes. When he had attained the level of an accomplished player, he was called upon to supply dance music in most parts of Inverness County. Lauchie, renowned for his strict time when providing the tunes for "Scotch Fours", was himself a talented stepdancer. On certain occasions, he joined forces with other Scottish violinists; such as Ronald Kennedy, Ronald Smith, Ranald "the Baron" MacDonald, "Little" Jack MacDonald and Dan MacEachern, the latter from Hillsdale. Lauchie and his wife raised ten musical children, including six boys who specialized in violin music; namely Jim, Donald, Allan, John Nicholas, John A. and "J.D.".

Lauchie Meagher passed away on December 31, 1942 and lies at rest near his birthplace in Brook Village.

Ronald Smith

Dates: 1876-1979, a native of Broad Cove, Inverness County
Parents: Alexander Smith and Catherine "MacVarish" MacDonald

Ronald's great-grandfather, Angus Smith (Aonghas Bàn Gobha, born 1766), is believed to have been the second man to settle at Broad Cove, landing around 1804 and bringing with him his Gaelic language and music. The legacy of rich folk-culture was eventually passed down to Ronald, who nurtured and exhibited it with pride. On the maternal side of his family tree were the "MacVarish" MacDonalds, who were famous for their fiddling; one excellent example being Ronald's uncle, Johnny (1852?-1934).

Ronald started playing by ear in 1884, sharing with his brothers - especially Jim and Joe - the Smiths' only violin. His music was basted with threads from Highland Scotland, threads which he had picked up in his youth via a keen ear, threads which connected his playing to a time long past. As a mature fiddler, he would possess tunes which no one else had, being able to satisfy the most discriminating listener with rare musical gems, night after night.

By the turn of the century, the Smith brothers were in great demand at weddings, house parties, "garden parties" and picnics. At age twenty-one, Ronald married Catherine Gillis and, in time, they were blessed with eleven children, of which family John Alex and John Francis continue to play the violin. As for his occupation, Ronald was versatile; for example, he was a trapper, a miner (at seventy-five cents a day), a fisherman, a violin builder and an early construction worker, the latter being in connection with the Port Hawkesbury-Inverness Railway. Always, however, he and his brothers sustained their busy playing schedules.[24]

Besides the lively tunes which are universally associated with Cape Breton fiddling, Ronald loved the more contemplative pieces such as "Hector the Hero", "Highland Queen" (as played by "Little" Jack MacDonald) and "Lord Lovat's Lament". Ronald's version of "Lord Lovat" featured a high-bass tuning which served to harmonically adorn the moving melody. He could entertain without a violin too; Father John Angus Rankin called him "a great raconteur", because Ronald could keep an audience spellbound by building a captivating story from a small seed of information.

On the occasion of Ronald's one hundredth birthday, a large celebration was staged, and in attendance were fiddlers Greg Smith (his grandson), Buddy MacMaster and Francis MacDonald. The oldest living Cape Breton violinist at that time, Ronald continued to thrive on music and all other aspects of Highland culture.

Back row: Peter MacIntyre of Benacadie, Joe Walker of Lake Ainslie, Alex MacIntyre of Benacadie.
Front row: Bernie Gillis of S.W. Margaree, Mike MacLean of Iona, Jack Gillis of S.W. Margaree, Alex Gillis of S.W. Margaree. Photo taken in New Bedford Mass., 1922-23

JIMMY "MALCOLM" GILLIS,
South West Margaree

JACK "MALCOLM" GILLIS,
South West Margaree

CASSIE MacISAAC MacINTYRE,
Inverness Town

JOHN ALEX "THE FIDDLER" MacNEIL,
Gillis Point, Iona

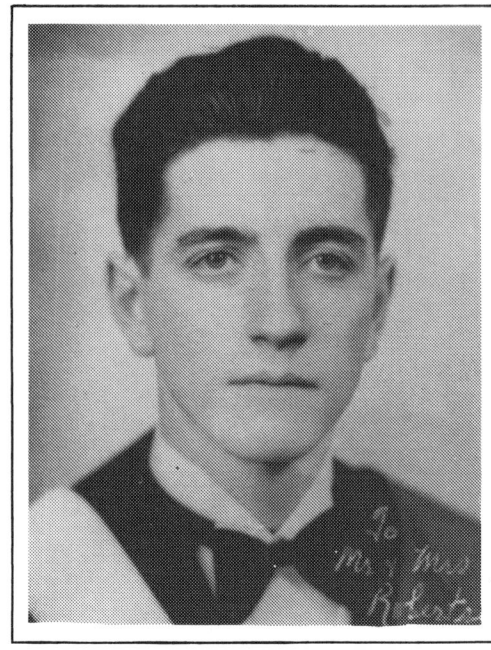
JOHN Y. GILLIS,
MacKinnon's Harbour, Iona

DANNY CAMERON,
Creignish

THE FIVE MacDONALD FIDDLERS:
DAN R. MacDONALD, JOHNNY ARCHIE MacDONALD, HUGH MacDONALD, BERNIE MacDONALD and ALLAN MacDONALD

RORY MacISAAC ("RUAIRIDH SHIM"),
Ben Eoin

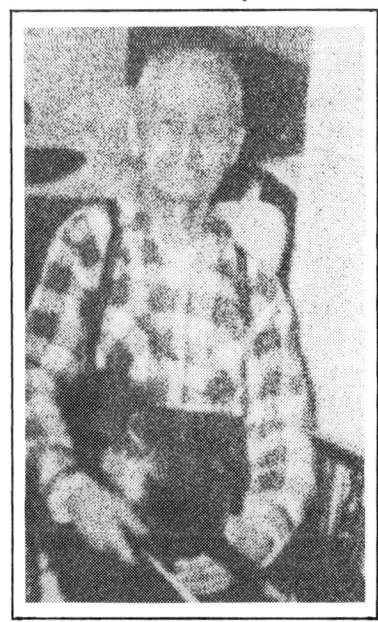

"PETIT" PLACIDE ODO,
Cheticamp

CHARLIE MacKINNON,
St. Rose

"CURLY" SANDY BEATON,
Glenville

DOUGALD MacINTYRE and
JOE SMITH (1904)

HUGHIE F. MacKENZIE,
Rear Christmas Island

J. J. MacINNIS,
Sydney

PETER MacPHEE,
Mabou

Cape Bretoners in Detroit:

This photo was taken by a Detroit Times photographer in Detroit, Michigan (4300 W. Vernor), on March 19, 1950. The occasion was a "musical entertainment party" held by a group of former Cape Bretoners, then residing in Windsor and Detroit. Back row: left to right - piano players Mrs. Johnny Archie MacDonald, Mrs. Bernie MacNeil, Mrs. Chas. MacInnis, Mrs. Neil R. MacDonald and her daughters Marion, Margaret (Mrs. Hugh MacDougall) and Joan (Boes), and piper Alex MacDonald.

Middle row: violin players Ronald Campbell, Steve MacEachern, Jimmy D. MacKay, Hugh MacDonald, Neil R. MacDonald, Dan R. MacDonald, Stanley Scotford and Ambrose Beaton.

Sitting: violin players Jackie Daigle, Bobby MacNeil, Johnny Archie MacDonald, Leo MacDonald, Bernie MacDonald, "Little" Jack MacDonald, J.D. MacKenzie (violin and guitar player), John E. Cameron, Dannie MacDonnell and Bernie MacNeil.

Pictures on the wall are of the late John W. Smith, two-term mayor of Detroit and the Honorable Frank Murphy, Chief Justice of the United States Supreme Court, both noted fiddlers of strathspeys and reels.

Ambrose Beaton   The Present

Birth: March 7, 1889 at Black River
Parents: Alexander Beaton (Alasdair Aonghais 'ic Fhionnlaidh, 1835-1923) and Anne Cameron

Ambrose learned to play at age fifteen, his earliest tunes coming from his father, one of the first note-reading violinists in that area of Inverness County. In this manner, the young Beaton, though an "ear" player himself, assembled a repertoire of "correct" pieces which he spiced with his own distinctive brand of interpretation.

Gifted with much natural ability, he was able to make music on sundry instruments such as harp, organ, piano and bagpipes. He owed his precision control of the Highland pipes to the tutoring of his famous uncle "Professor" Archie Beaton. Ambrose's fiddling, on the other hand, blossomed in the company of Dan J. and Angus Campbell, and Duncan MacQuarrie. These four men developed a bond of friendship which was solidified by their mutual love for the Cape Breton violin.

Born into a musical and religious family, Ambrose eventually left home to spend nearly ten years in a monastery in St. Louis, Missouri. After reconsidering his vocation, he departed the order in 1923 and, in time, married Margaret MacDonald and settled in Michigan. It was there that he became a valuable member of Detroit's fiddling fraternity which starred "Little" Jack MacDonald, Johnny Archie MacDonald and Leo MacDonald (of Glengarry, Ontario), among others. Though "down east" dances were rarer in Detroit than in Boston, great times were had at the countless houseparties and Sunday-afternoon gatherings.

A consummate musician, being able to tune a violin to perfect standard pitch without referring to a piano, Ambrose gravitated naturally to the realm of composition. Here, he created some clever pieces, much to the delight of his close friend, "Little" Jack.

When the first wire recorders came into existance, Ambrose wasted no time in procuring one, and proceeded to accumulate a huge collection of priceless fiddling tapes. Alas, this collection was inadvertently destroyed a few years ago.

Until the age of 83, Ambrose applied himself regularly to the violin, and could always raise a cheer with his stirring version of "Lord MacDonald's Reel". Though he occasionally manages a trip back to his beloved island, he is spending his nineties in South Rockwood, Michigan.

Donald Angus Beaton

Birth: April 20, 1912 in Mabou
Parents: Angus R. Beaton (Aonghas Raonuill) and Annie Belle Campbell

Donald Angus is the son of Angus Ronald Beaton, a blacksmith and a famous fiddler. "My Father had a good violin," Donald Angus says, "and he played at dances. He also played quite a bit around home. Sometimes, he'd do the fingering and let the children do the bowing."

The name Beaton and the violin have always been closely associated, and it is no wonder when one considers the number of quality musicians belonging to Donald Angus' family tree, people like Domhnull Iain an Taillear, John Beaton (Iain Alasdair Bhàn), Mairi Alasdair Raonuill, Danny Beaton and Johnny Ronald Beaton, to name but five. On his mother's side, Donald Angus is descended from a musical branch of the Campbell clan of Glenora Falls.

At the age of seven or eight, a curiosity about music overpowered him. "Over home," he says, "there used to be a great number of fiddlers coming to the house. A young fellow would be wishing he could play a tune or two. That's how we got so fond of music. I'd be taking the violin and trying to get a tune on it when my father was in the blacksmith shop. When he finally heard us play, he was very proud and let us use his violin. My sister Janet played the piano as well as the violin.

"My first public performance," Donald Angus remembers, "was at a picnic up in Glencoe Mills in 1924. My father and Duncan Peter Campbell (fiddler) were playing that day. They coaxed me to play, so I went up to the stage. Afterwards, they said that the set I played was O.K. - it gave me courage.

"The bowing came naturally to me, though I got some helpful hints from certain fiddlers. Dan J. Campbell, Ronald Allan 'the Baron' MacDonald and Danny Beaton were older than I was, but I played with them. Another fellow, Allan Gillis, lived near Foot Cape. He was one of the people who came to my father's house. He said to me, 'I'm going to show you the notes'. That Allan Gillis was a good teacher! I had been playing by ear before that. Then, Fr. Rory MacNeil used to send me 'starters' with a map of the fingerboard in them.

"I got a lot of traditional music from my uncle, Johnny Ronald Beaton. If you were smart enough to pick them up, you could get great tunes from a man like him.

"I went blacksmithing, with my father in 1932. He died in 1933, and I kept the business going on my own 'till 1946 when I went taxi driving." In 1940, Donald Angus married Elizabeth MacEachen, the lady who now usually accompanies him on piano.

In the years during which Donald Angus played for regular weekly dances, he attracted record crowds. Here he reminisces about that aspect of his career: "As a young fellow, I played with Sandy Donald Cameron of Mabou, though mostly I teamed up with Angus Joseph MacDonald - we did a lot of playing! There was a dance hall going in Port Hood in the forties, and I played a weekly dance there for a number of years. Then, there were the dances at Mabou and Brook Village, and we used to get a good crowd at Malcolm MacEachern's hall in Broad Cove (the Brookside Hall)." Donald Angus' accompanists, besides his wife, included the late Neil Finn and Danny MacEachen.

A composer for the Scottish violin since 1935, many of Donald Angus' original pieces enjoy great popularity, and among these are "Sandy MacIntyre's March", "The Mabou Jig", "Willie Fraser's Strathspey", "Ann MacQuarrie Reel" and "Memories of Rev. Donald Michael Rankin March". Several of the above can now be heard on a Rounder Lp (7011) entitled "The Beatons of Mabou" which presents the combined talents of Donald Angus, Elizabeth and their sons Joey and Kinnon.

The music of Donald Angus Beaton, Mabou Coal Mines influenced, has evoked the following commentary by Rev. Hugh A. MacDonald: "The 'Gaelic expression' is achieved through the highly developed employment of bow triplets (or 'cuts') and the use of 'flying spiccato' - the art of bouncing the bow to achieve several distinct notes without reversing bow directions. Donald Angus is a master of this difficult technique."

MEMORIES OF THE LATE REV. DONALD MICHAEL RANKIN

March   by Donald Angus Beaton (1971)

Kinnon Beaton

Birth: March 26, 1956 in Mabou, Inverness County
Parents: Donald Angus Beaton and Elizabeth MacEachen

The youngest in a long and impressive line of Scottish violinists, Kinnon is a left-handed player like his grandfather's brother, known as Donnie Ranald Beaton.

Kinnon says, "My father played quite a bit at home when I was young. I always wanted to play. On the day before my twelfth birthday, I heard my parents and brother (Joey) play over CJFX Radio on the twenty-fifth anniversary of the station. That same day, I went right down to George Hunt's grocery store and bought a little tin fiddle with my birthday money; it cost about two or three dollars. The next morning when I got up, my father had it strung up. I learned a tune or two on it - I think 'Donald MacLean's Farewell to Oban' was my first tune. I didn't keep it for a fiddle, though - after a while I used it for a baseball bat!

"Within a year, my brother Francis asked Ernie Burke of River Bourgeois to build me a violin, and paid twenty-five dollars for it; it was a good one to learn on, and I had it for about two years. Then, I used one of my father's fiddles, which he eventually gave me. My father encouraged me a lot. He had figured by now that no one in the family was going to play, especially since the last two boys were left-handed.

"I began to play in March, and I attended my first concert in July at Glendale; I played with my father that time. That was my first public performance as a fiddler. The next week or so, I played at Broad Cove - I was the youngest fiddler there and Ronald Smith was the oldest.

"In the beginning, I played by ear - all the tunes my father would play. There were a lot of old ones and a lot he made himself, like 'Trip to Toronto' and 'Sandy MacIntyre's March' - I like that one quite a bit!

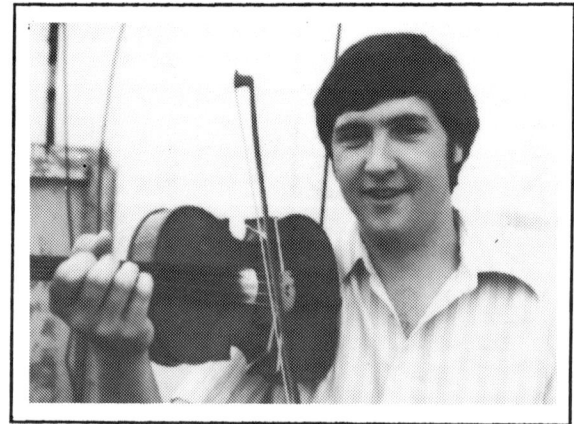

"Dan R. MacDonald taught me how to read music. He used to be over at our house often, and he showed me the basics. It helped me for learning new tunes, that's for sure! But, I still find it easy by ear, and I remember the tunes better that I've learned that way. I like the old music because that's pretty well all that I heard at home.

"John Morris Rankin was about the only one around my age playing the fiddle in Mabou - he was a little younger. We used to play a bit together on Sundays at his place. Sometimes, he'd chord for me on the piano. You'd get a lot of flak for playing the fiddle from some of the kids at school. They were into 'rock', and I hadn't a clue what they were talking about - it was pretty well all fiddle at our house!

"I don't know when I began to compose, but I was a teenager anyway. The first piece was 'Jessie's Jig', dedicated to my sister-in-law. I've made about sixty-five tunes.

"I used to play at weddings, doing the odd set for my father. I played at concerts, and once in a while made tapes for CJFX and CBI, Sydney. Later, when my father started to give up his dances, I sometimes filled in for him. My mother or my brother, Joey, would accompany me on piano. My father showed me the 'cuts' and the other styles of bowing. I try to do that 'flying spiccato' bowing that they used to do in the Mabou Coal Mines fiddling.

"When I finished school, I started playing more for dances - Scotsville, Mabou, Judique, Strathlorne. I played in Sudbury at age nineteen, and quite a bit in Boston, Detroit and Windsor. Half the time I played alone - half, with the family. In later years, there was always music at our house on Sundays, mostly among ourselves."

In August, 1977, Kinnon, Donald Angus, Elizabeth and Joey Beaton recorded an album at their home in Mabou. The record includes some of Kinnon's compositions as well as a taste of the stirring music of Cape Breton's past.

Kinnon is married to Betty Lou MacMaster, one of the Island's most tasteful piano accompanists.

BETTY LOU'S JIG

by Kinnon Beaton (1978)

Elmer Briand

Birth: June 8, 1922 at L'Ardoise, Cape Breton
Parents: George P. Briand and Nora Bona

Born into a French Acadian home in which the father was a piper and the mother a Gaelic speaker, Elmer experienced much exposure to Celtic culture. In addition, several of his neighbours were active violinists, including "Johnny" Alex Thibeau, Ned Longaphy, Willie Mombourquette, Charlie Sampson and Johnny MacDonald. "Johnny MacDonald of Salmon River Road gave me my start. Up until then, the only fiddling I had heard was that of Joe Allard of Quebec on the old Gramophone." By age 12, Elmer could play "Lord Lovat's Lament", a tune which he learned from his father's piping.

In 1936, the family moved to Halifax where Elmer became acquainted with many Inverness-style fiddlers. "I learned from such men as Charlie MacKinnon, home from the States. He was much older than me, but Charlie gave me some really good tunes! When I was seventeen, Roddy 'The Plumber' MacDonald encouraged me to read music. Then, by studying other players, I got the 'ree-drum, rah-drum, roo-drum' of the bowing - it's not in any book!" He adds, "As a teenager, I played several times with Hank Snow - so did my brother, Peter."

In 1938, Elmer joined the merchant marine and began taking his fiddle on board the boats because "the boys loved the music!" On March 30, 1942, he was torpedoed off Russia and narrowly escaped with his life. After returning to Halifax, he regained his health and formed the dance band called "Elmer Briand and his Cabot Trail Boys". His music became a familiar feature on many radio and television programs, and he was instrumental in founding the Cape Breton Club of Halifax. In the year 1962, he placed in the top ten of 129 fiddlers at the Shelburne Fiddling Contest.

As a composer, Elmer enjoys great popularity. Recently, "The Elmer Briand Collection" was published, which contains such noted selections as "Beautiful Lake Ainslie", "Johnny Wilmot's Fiddle", "The Cheticamp Jig" and "The Margaree Valley Waltz". He also now appears in a National Film Board presentation concerning the life of his friend and fellow fiddler, Don Messer.

Elmer Briand on long-playing record:
    Celtic SCX 56
    Celtic SCX 58

Reel   **JOHNNIE WILMOT'S FIDDLE**   by Elmer Briand

LOCH LOMOND STRATHSPEY   by Elmer Briand

Fr. Francis Cameron

Birth: 1934 at South West Mabou
Parents: Angus Finlay Cameron (son of "Domhnull Mór") and Sera Beaton

"My father loved music very much, and so we were always hearing it at home. In the late 1930's, our family left Mabou and the strong fiddling environment which was there. In time, we settled in Boisdale, and, to make up for the loss of the music, Papa would get all the new fiddle records as soon as they were off the press. He had an old Gramophone, a wedding gift, which was a very precious thing for our family to own. We were able to hear the 78's of players like Angus Chisholm and Angus Allan Gillis. When I was a small child, if I saw Papa put on his Sunday suit, I'd know that this was the day to hear the records!

"My father sang Gaelic songs and could play jigs and reels on the mouth organ, but one day he brought home an old fiddle from the railway - you see, he was a foreman down there. As kids, we were able to hum fiddle tunes to ourselves as we lay in bed, but I was around 12 before I actually started to play. The man who left the greatest musical impression on me at this point was Winston Fitzgerald who used to come to our house, and whom we heard often on CJCB Radio. When he'd visit, he'd ask me to play too, and I'd struggle my way through - Mama and Papa would be so proud! I soon realized that that was what I wanted to be - a fiddler, like Winston.

"There was a sort of 'hit parade' of standard tunes and I learned those first. Later on, I gathered pieces from every possible source.

"In my late teens, when Angus Chisholm or Joe MacLean would play in Boisdale, they'd ask me up on stage to play for a set; however, I played mostly at parish concerts. On these occasions, my father would arrange for fiddlers like Dan J. Campbell or Angus Allan Gillis to perform, and they'd usually come back to the house after. Though we'd be sent to bed, I'd sit at the top of the stairs to take in the music.

"One day in Boisdale, I heard a young man named Buddy MacMaster play - his music has affected me ever since.

"While I was attending St. F.X. University, we had the fiddle going on many a night at Mockler Hall. I never felt that my fiddle and my vocation were in conflict, in fact, I took the violin to the seminary with me. Later on, during parish work, the music was an asset in dealing with people. No matter where I was located, the country people were very evident, and, after performing a wedding ceremony, I'd often supply some of the entertainment.

"The environment here in Mabou is great for fiddling. I'd love now to get some of the 'old tunes' that are played here. Kenneth Joseph MacDonald and Willie Kennedy are a good team at playing that traditional style of music.

"I'm a bit of a note reader, mostly because I took piano for two years while in high school; my sister, Janet, reads too. Now I've grown to enjoy some of the 'auld country's' violin playing, especially that of Hector MacAndrew who did such a nice job on 'Niel Gow's Lament'. I also like classical violin - for the tone; it really satisfies the ear. As for myself, I can never be content with the tone I'm producing. I'll just keep trying to get the music out of that instrument which I know is in there!"

MRS. DANNY PETER MacINNIS

Pastoral Air   by J. Francis MacDonald

John Donald Cameron

Birth: November 19, 1937 at South West Mabou
Parents: Daniel L. Cameron and Katie Anne MacDonald

John Donald Cameron is noted for his ability to identify fiddle tunes and name their source. This same attention to detail is evident in the following description of his childhood and introduction to music: "In 1943, we got our first radio, and the first voice I heard was Clyde Nunn's on CJFX. He played the records of 'Little' Jack MacDonald, Angus Chisholm, Dan J. Campbell, Colin Boyd, Hugh A. MacDonald and my uncle, Dan R. MacDonald. But, we (that is, John Donald and his brother, John Allan) never heard a live fiddler till one hot summer's day our father took us by horse and wagon to 'Little' Johnny MacIsaac's at River Center; Johnny played by ear. We were thrilled and thought he was wonderful.

"I appeared in public for the first time in 1945, when I played the jew's harp in a Christmas concert. In 1951, at Easter, our father brought home a fiddle - and even a twenty-five dollar fiddle was a sacrifice in those days! But, he knew that John Allan and I were interested and had an aptitude for music. Our father had a big influence on us - he's never given enough credit.

"Our mother honed up on what she used to play, and, with practice, it came back to her. She'd play for us and we'd just listen. Shortly after that, we could both play 'The Balkin Hills', a tune which our uncle Dan R. had recorded. We longed to see Dan R., but he was in Windsor, Ontario.

"In 1952, our father came home one weekend with a guitar - for anyone who wanted to learn to play it. John Allan took a crack at it, but I stayed with the violin. Through parties, we heard the Nicholson boys, Finlay and Colie, playing guitar and fiddle together."

In the summer of 1952, the Cameron lads made a memorable journey when they accompanied fiddler John Willie Campbell to the Shrine in Quebec; they shared Scottish music all the way! "We'd occasionally hear other players in our area," John Donald says, "and they were important to us - Jimmy Nicholson, Dan Francis Moran, Willie MacIsaac and John Hughie MacEachern of Hillsdale, among others. But, it was our mother that we heard more than anyone else, and she was good!

"Our father always stressed the idea of learning to read music; 'Red' Johnny Campbell taught us in 1953. 'Red' Johnny was one of the few fiddlers around there who played by note. He taught us overnight to read the basics, and he gave us Cole's 'Thousand Tune Fiddle Book'. From then on, everything was from books. If we heard a tune we didn't know over the radio, we'd try to get the name of it and look it up.

"We went to Antigonish one day in 1953 to get my first pair of eye-glasses. A priority was to go to the music store where we picked up 'The Scottish Violinist' and 'MacQuarrie's Collection'. Then, from 1953 to '57, John Allan and I played together at school dances, concerts, house parties, bridal showers and weddings.

"In 1955, a strange car drove up to the farm where we were making hay - it was Buddy MacMaster saying that our uncle, Dan R., was at our house, a mile up the road. That was the first time we'd seen Dan R. since 1946, when he left the service. We were quite nervous about playing before him, but he encouraged us very much. He suggested that we learn two tunes from 'The Thousand Tune Fiddle Book' - 'Come to the Raffle' and 'Close to the Floor'. This impressed us because he was a legend to us. After Dan R. went back to Windsor, he bought a new fiddle and he sent us down his old one - a very good Italian violin. For us, at that age, to have a fiddle that good was a wonderful thing!

"In 1956, Dan R. gave us some old books he had brought from Scotland. They were valuable - Gow's, White's, MacKenzie's etc. After we got those, we told our friend, Angus Morris from Colindale, and he'd come to our house once a week to go through them. Today when I play, 99% is from books. I have a few tunes that aren't from any collection but have their origin in the 'auld' country. I also have some tunes by lesser-known Cape Breton composers like Donald MacLean, Vincent MacLellan and J.J. MacInnis.

"In 1957, John Allan and I played our first regular engagement at the West Bay Legion. It was a lot of fun. In August of that year, John Allan joined the seminary, and Jerry MacNeil and I carried on.

"In 1958-59, I joined the Royal Bank. In 1974, I got tired of the transfers, so I left the bank and came back to Nova Scotia. John Allan's T.V. show out of Montreal was starting in December of that year and there was an opening for another fiddler." The group which performed on this program came to be known as The Cape Breton Symphony and has recorded an album on Glencoe Records (GMI 001).

Presently, John Donald is working on an important project - the collection and publication of his uncle Dan R. MacDonald's best compositions.

John Campbell

Birth: January 23, 1929 at Glenora Falls, Inverness Co.
Parents: Dan J. Campbell and Mary Magdalen MacLellan

Born on the old Campbell homestead established in 1816 by his great-great-grandfather nicknamed "The Bear", John carries a musical torch handed down to him through three violin-playing generations of Campbells, represented by the following men: his great-grand uncle, Donald; his grandfather, John A. (1855-1919): and his famous father, Dan J. Other relatives, too numerous to mention, have been accomplished Celtic musicians.

True to family tradition, John developed a strong urge to play the fiddle around age nine, and, by Dan J.'s insistence, immediately emphasized precise note reading as well as the mastery of the unprinted pieces. In an old shack they had built in the woods, he and his brothers Donald and Alex diligently worked away on the ancient strathspeys and reels they had heard their father expertly coax from a violin on Sunday afternoons after Mass.

In the years to come, John took further inspiration from the playing of two other men. The first was Winston "Scotty" Fitzgerald whom he often enjoyed on CJCB radio. "I thought he was a genius in his own way!" The second was Buddy MacMaster whom John heard at a memorial picnic in Judique in 1949. "His music was so clean and smooth!"

Following his initial public appearance at a wedding at Black River in 1947, John established himself as an accomplished dance player in the Mabou area. "In the beginning, I only wanted to play for dancing - to make a dollar!" 1956 found him in Hamilton, Ontario where he organized dances at the Jockey Club during a four-year stay. After returning to Cape Breton, he married in 1962 and one year later settled in Watertown, Massachusetts. The fiddling scene in the Boston area was exciting at this point in time with three dance halls featuring Cape Breton music weekly: the Orange Hall in Brookline, the French Club in Waltham, and Bill Lamey's regular gathering at Rose Croix. Parties were a key social event and could boast the talents of players such as Angus Chisholm, Joe Cormier, Joe Beaton, Rannie Graham, Alcide Aucoin and Alex Gillis. "I could always stay busy down there and had as much work as I could handle. I often travelled out of state to Detroit, Washington and the like." It is important to note that John has always done his utmost to encourage the survival of Scottish fiddling in America.

Once, in Amesbury, John came upon what must be considered one of the greatest bargains of all time. He purchased 42 violins and their cases for a total of $630.00. ''I couldn't believe my eyes! I just backed my truck up and filled it with fiddles!'' More recently, in December of 1979, he obtained a handsome German instrument crafted by Ottoman Hausmann, the famous violin builder.

John Campbell is a successful composer of Scottish fiddle tunes. Among his most popular originals are ''Doug MacPhee's Strathspey'', ''Dan J. Campbell's Reel'', ''Salute to the Clans Strathspey'' and, the Cape Breton classic, ''Sandy MacIntyre's Trip to Boston''. Of the latter he says, ''I wanted to write a tune with a lot of 'gimp' to it. I composed it in Halifax while performing on 'Ceilidh', and I named it for my friend, Sandy. Buddy MacMaster was the first to play it publicly.'' John estimates that he has written over 450 tunes.

John's first album, produced by Rounder Records, was long awaited and heartily welcomed. It featured his own compositions as well as what he calls the old ''Mabou tunes''. The great success of this record warranted three additional releases.

Every summer, John Campbell returns to Cape Breton to fill dance halls to capacity.

SANDY MacINTYRE'S TRIP TO BOSTON

Reel   by John Campbell

John Willie Campbell

Birth: 1928, in Glencoe, Inverness County
Parents: Tom Campbell and Mary Kate MacEachern

As a child of six or seven years of age, John Willie carved a violin shape out of a shingle and then pretended to play it. His father, after viewing this curious sight, decided to give the boy a genuine fiddle.

During the twenty-five years that John Willie lived at home, he continued to acquire by ear a large selection of tunes from older players, be they neighbours or relatives. At this time in his musical development, he was assisted by various violinists in the area, for example John Joe MacInnis, Robert MacLeod, Donald Angus MacLean, Archie Campbell and John Hughie MacEachern.

The occasions for which he first provided music included house parties, school dances, church picnics and "box socials". In the 1930's and 40's at the dances in Glencoe, John Willie would play unaccompanied, often employing a scordatura tuning called "high bass" to create more volume. He now has nearly thirty tunes in that mode, and he plays them with a rhythm and timing that encourages good stepdancing. His version of the Cape Breton favourite, "Christy Campbell", can be heard on a recently-released album which features a variety of Island players.

Around 1953, John Willie left home to work in Sydney and then set his course for Toronto. While in Ontario, he befriended fiddler, Johnny Wilmot, with whom he played, and together they made many journeys home to Cape Breton. In time, John Willie decided to return to Sydney, where he became employed at the Isle Royale Hotel. During his spare time, he continued to entertain with his violin, both in person and on radio stations CJCB and CJFX.

Though he originally learned to play by ear. John Willie now reads music and has also done some composing of late. However, the music that moves him most is still the ancient variety - Gaelic-flavoured rousers such as "King George the Fourth Strathspey".

Relatives of John Willie's who have played the fiddle include: his paternal grandfather; his father, Tom; uncles Angus and Dan Campbell; uncle John Hughie MacEachern; brothers Joe, Dugald and Alex; and cousin, Archie Campbell.

A TRADITIONAL STRATHSPEY AND REEL

"The first tune - from the playing of Ranald Kennedy, Mary MacDonald and my father (Alex Dan MacIsaac) - is a great old strathspey which I don't know the name of. The second tune is one which Dad learned from his mother; there must be Gaelic words, and I don't know the title to this one either. Anyway, they're both great pieces. They seem like the type of tunes which may have been popular around the turn of the century."

April, 1981
David MacIsaac

Winnie Chafe

Birth: December 25, 1936 in Glace Bay
Parents: Rod MacMullin and Christine MacDonald

Winnie's great-great-grandfather (MacMullin) settled in Beaver Cove, near Boisdale, around the 1840's. At that time, he wrote a letter back home, making mention of a "newly-made fiddle" which he had carved from a Cape Breton tree; this man's sons and grandsons carried on the fiddling tradition. Winnie's father, Rod, was an "old-time player" and she remembers, "I got my first appreciation of music at my father's knee." Growing up in Sydney Mines, Winnie heard the playing of Bill Lamey, Angus Chisholm, Joe Confiant and Johnny Wilmot who often visited her maternal grandfather's home.

Winnie recalls an introduction at the age of nine that was to mold her future: "My father said that if I really wanted to learn violin, I must do it correctly. He took me to meet Professor James MacDonald who told me how important it was to have good pitch and asked if I could sing. I remember it so well; I sang him 'White Christmas' - it was the middle of summer!" She then began taking lessons from Professor Jimmy, and, when the MacMullin family moved to Glace Bay, Winnie and her father travelled by tram car to North Sydney every Sunday for five years to continue with her training.

An even more arduous excursion took place when she was twelve years old. "My parents and I made a trip from Glace Bay to St. Ann's by boat so that I could compete in a violin class at the Gaelic College. When we arrived there was no competition so they asked me to be a guest. That was my first time on the concert stage."

When Sister Louise Frances Reardon, a classical violinist and pianist, came to St. John's Parish, Winnie began to study with her, and says of this period, "I feel there are great parallels between classical and Scottish music, particularly in technique and style. Marshall's slow airs have the same keys and same bowing techniques as classical music. Skinner perfected this type of air by utilizing third position and advanced bowing. I believe my love for slow airs comes from my classical training." This affection matured to a virtuosity in interpreting these plaintive melodies, and combined with Winnie's professionalism, gained her the respect of her peers.

At sixteen, Winnie performed with the Cape Breton Orchestra as first violinist and, at this time, she received high marks from adjudicator, Boris Berlin, at the Kiwanis Music Festival.

After attending Teachers' College, Winnie returned home to teach, but marriage to Mike Chafe led her to travel extensively. These nomadic years saw her play with a symphony orchestra in California, appear on national television out of New York and have the distinction of being the first woman to win the International Old Time Fiddle Contest in Pembroke, Ontario.

Following ten years "away", the Chafes settled in Glace Bay where Winnie went back to teaching and continued to play her music. She held the position of fiddle-music arranger on CBC TV's "Ceilidh", has entertained in Scotland and recently produced a series of Scottish concerts throughout the Maritimes.

Winnie now has several violin classes and has this approach to teaching: "At the first class I say to my students, 'Give me three years; don't expect to play Scottish music in one year.' The first year is spent learning proper violin posture, basic writing and reading, etc. The second year we start into Scottish music - easy marches, songs, waltzes and a few jigs. The third year is spent building a repertoire of Scottish music. There is more emphasis on tempo. Now the fourth year you teach interpretation, importance of grace notes and other musical ornamentation. My skills as a classroom teacher are very necessary in teaching violin. It helps in recognizing a student's limitations and capabilities. During these four years together, I would like to see each fiddler develop his own individuality; I don't want to see carbon copies of Winnie Chafe running around!"

Winnie's long-range goal is to organize a Scottish string orchestra. "I even have the name picked out, 'Highland Scottish Strings' - the first of its kind this side of Scotland. It will comprise mainly fiddlers from my classes as well as other note readers. The music will be scored for first and second violin, cello, bass and organ. This has been in my head for years. I'd like to see a suite written containing all Scottish music. I have given myself five years to do it. I feel at the end of this time I will have the nucleus of the group - approximately forty players; I would eventually like to see about one hundred. I will extend an invitation to anyone interested who is a note reader and can interpret music well. I want to put quality into the music!"

Solo records: Rounder 7012, and Inter Media IMS-WRC1-759.

Cameron Chisholm

Birth: January 13, 1945 in Margaree Forks, Cape Breton
Parents: Willie D. Chisholm and Annie Mae Cameron

"It's in the blood - definitely, definitely!" The preceding quotation conveys Cameron Chisholm's opinion of the music which has manifested itself in him and in his relatives, close and distant and on both sides of his family tree. Even his great-grandfather, Charlie MacKinnon from St. Rose, was considered a good fiddler in his time.

After beginning piano lessons at the age of six, Cameron shifted his interest to the violin that same year. The man who gave the earliest coaching was Johnny Stephen White, the very fellow who had first instructed Angus Chisholm, Cameron's famous uncle.

Here, Cameron discusses three of the many sources from which he heard good Scottish music as a boy:
(a) the radio: "The violin was very popular in those days; turn on CJFX and that's what you'd hear. J. Clyde Nunn, the owner of the station, played the best old-time music - all the early records of Dan J. Campbell, Angus Allan Gillis and my uncle, Angus. Only for CJFX, I don't believe there'd be as many fiddlers as there are today!"
(b) his family: "I was always hearing my sister, Maybelle, playing Scotch music on the piano, and that had a definite influence on me. She showed me tunes, and so did my father who could 'jig' them correctly. My mother taught me the scale; she could play the fiddle a bit and read music too. Then there was my uncle, Angus - God knows, he was my idol!"
(c) piper, Sandy Boyd: "Sandy stayed here during my pre-school days, and after. He had more influence on me than anyone outside the family. I remember, when I was about four, he'd play in the kitchen, walking back and forth. He'd play a lament, a march, then strathspeys and reels - great medleys about a half-hour long. In later years, I learned numerous tunes from him."

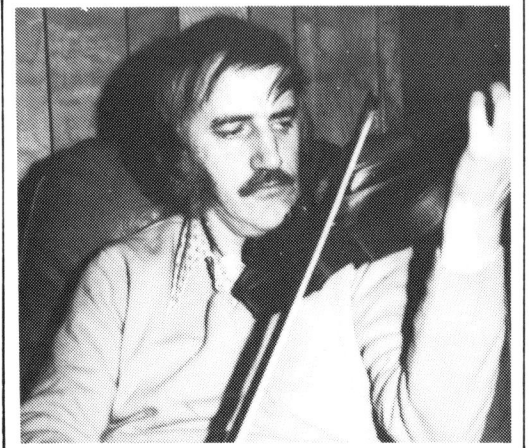

To Cameron, as a boy, life and Scottish music seemed to go hand-in-hand. "In those days," he now says, "there were concerts in all the parishes - usually one every Sunday night, and all featuring predominantly Scottish music. Here I have to give credit to the clergy for helping to promote the fiddling."

A highly-talented and ambitious youngster, Cameron began entertaining at school concerts at age eight. Three years later, he had played for his first dance, and he now describes the event: "It was at St. Rose Schoolhouse, and there was no piano so I played alone. Only adults attended."

Due to his extreme popularity, he spent the next several years maintaining a fiddling schedule which almost defies belief. "I was playing every night of the week," he recalls, "from mid-June until near Hallowe'en, all during my teens. I don't like to brag, but I was the youngest player playing every night of the week - it's true! Then, I played every weekend all winter. There was very good money in it in the late fifties and early sixties - $30.00 a night, average. In those days, $30.00 was something! Maybelle was my pianist most of the time. I played all over Inverness County, from Pleasant Bay to Creignish. Once, I played on the 'Cape Breton Ceilidh' television show from Sydney; that was a big thing for me."

Despite his age, the young Chisholm became very well travelled. "I played in a concert at the Halifax Forum at twelve. On my first trip to Boston, I played at the Rose Croix Hall for Uncle Angus; I was sixteen and in grade twelve, and I was studying for exams going down there on the plane. During my teens, I wore myself out - weddings in the day, dances in the night!"

After migrating to Toronto at nineteen, Cameron held employment as a banker and then a teacher. For a while, he worked with Johnny Wilmot at the Slovak Hall, and then entertained at the French Club for four years, usually accompanied by Daniel Aucoin. Occasionally, he made trips to Detroit, Montreal, Boston, Sudbury, Windsor and Hamilton. In the early seventies, he was seen regularly on CBC TV's "Ceilidh" from Halifax, of which program he remarks, "I loved it! The show went right to Vancouver. People right across the country were hearing Cape Breton fiddle music."

Though Cameron has a fine collection of music books, his preference is for the tunes of Cape Breton writers. "Poor Dan R. (MacDonald) used to come up from Sydney. He'd write out his tunes for me - all his compositions from 'Trip to Windsor' to 'High Bridge Jig', and all those great tunes in Bb. He was better than Scott Skinner. Pass me a book from Scotland, and I'll only like a few tunes here and there, but if all Dan R.'s tunes were in one book, I'd have to go from page to page and learn them all!"

Cameron feels that good Cape Breton violin playing is not out of danger yet, despite the recent resurgence. "There aren't as many regular concerts or dances any more, and you're not hearing the music on radio to the same extent you did when I was a kid."

Joe Cormier

Birth: March 19, 1927, a native of Cheticamp, Cape Breton
Parents: Job Cormier and Adele Deveau

Job Cormier, Joe's father, was both a left-handed fiddler and an accordion player, and he taught his sons Isidore, Sam, Daniel, Paul, and Joe to make music. Joe began to experiment on a rough, homemade violin from the time he was big enough to hold it. By age twelve, he was attending all the local get-togethers, being known as much for his stepdancing as for his violin playing. In those days, the hat would be passed for the fiddler and one dollar would be considered a good night's pay. At age sixteen, Joe was given his first real fiddle, and two years later received excellent instruction from his uncle, Professor Marcelin Cormier.

In the musical history of Cheticamp, fiddlers such as Paddy à Paul and "Petit" Placide Odo were legendary, the latter being a frequent performer at the "mi-carême" festival in each Lenten season. Joe remembers that Placide was a hero to all the budding violinists, as were Margaree fiddlers Angus Chisholm and Angus Allan Gillis.

From 1948-62, Joe resided in the Sydney area and there performed regularly with Winston Fitzgerald. Meanwhile, he could be heard occasionally on CJFX Radio, Antigonish on the show "The Cheticamp Hour".

Joe migrated to his present home, Waltham, Massachusetts in 1962, and since moving to the U.S.A. has become a very active member of the French Club where he plays weekly with fellow-countrymen Loudger LeFort and Joe Boudreau. He has also been very successful in fiddling competitions in the Boston area.

Though Joe's background is thoroughly French, his music, like that of many a Cheticamp player, is unmistakably Scottish. With a style that is both sweet and lively, Joe is highly respected throughout New England, as well as here at home.

He performs on an 1860 "François Pelement" violin, and can be heard on two deluxe Rounder records entitled "Scottish Violin Music from Cape Breton" and "The Dances Down Home".

Gordon Cote

Birth: June 20, 1938 at L'Ardoise, Cape Breton
Parents: Donald John Cote and Elizabeth Barren

St. Peters, like any Cape Breton community, has always had its own fiddlers, and a young Gordon Cote found himself fascinated with their music. As a boy, he heard Joe MacDonald, Johnny Stone, Don Martell and "Old" Dan Curry. Of the latter, Gordon says, "He'd be a first cousin to my father, and he had an old fiddle; I don't know if you'd say he played, but he made an awful racket with it!

"My father loved Scottish music, and my mother's father, Dan Barren, was supposed to have been a pretty good fiddler - I believe he learned from the Cashes of Irish Cove. Personally, I've always loved instruments. I could play the guitar when I was very young - I was always singing, playing and accompanying. My brother would come home on the weekends and bring his fiddle, and I'd play along with him on the guitar. Then, we had an old battery radio which we used before we had the lights around here. On that, I heard Dan J. Campbell over CJFX and later picked up 'Scotty' Fitzgerald's programs on CJCB in Sydney.

"My brother gave me a fiddle when I was around fourteen. I started off playing on my own, but I wanted to learn to read music. 'Old' Charlie MacKenzie near French Cove gave me the G-scale for the violin. I didn't take any instruction - I don't know too many Cape Breton fiddlers who did! I think you should play by ear in the beginning and then I think you should learn a little theory.

"Next, I went in the Army for three years - 1955 to 1958. I was piping with the Black Watch Regiment and I learned a lot more about music. I remember we'd practice as much as a month for one engagement. We had a good time, but I didn't do much fiddling there. In the band, we used a lot of tunes from The Willie Ross Collection, but Pipe Major Duncan Rankin would arrange them to suit himself - I wish I had those pieces now! I used to lean towards marches on the violin as a result of my piping experience." "The Lochty March" is one of many wonderful pipe tunes that Gordon plays well.

"After leaving the Army, I worked on ships, was a steel worker, etc. In 1970, I came home from Toronto. The interest in the violin came back again after the first Glendale Fiddling Festival in 1973."

Gordon remains active, especially in the summers, by performing with guitarist Estwood Davidson and by having frequent "sessions" with his friends Jerry Holland, Joe MacNeil and Cliffy Carter. Meanwhile, it appears that Gordon's young son, Duane, will follow in his musical footsteps.

Lee Cremo

Birth: December 30, 1938 at Barra Head
Parents: Simon Peter Cremo (1900-1964) and Annie Denny

Lee Cremo, a Micmac Indian, has been living at Eskasoni since the age of four. His vitality, sense of humour and stunning originality have earned him the admiration of musicians and audiences all across Canada and in the United States.

"I was always curious about the fiddle; I knew the tunes from my father's playing. He got the fundamentals from a parish priest in Johnstown - Fr. Saulnier; after that, he was on his own. He began playing when he was five years old, in 1905. My father travelled around selling baskets, and if he came to an area where they had no fiddler, he'd play for a dance. Sometimes I'd go with him, though I could only travel in the summertime, because of school. I could play a few chords on the guitar, so I'd accompany him. Once, we played at a picnic at Christmas Island and got $12.00; I was about ten. After, we walked home across the mountain because we had no car.

"I started to play the fiddle around seven years of age. It was on Good Friday morning, when everyone had gone to Mass. I was elected to stay home and keep the fire going. We were Catholics and no music was allowed at that time of year, but I took out the fiddle and got going on 'Pop Goes the Weasel'.

"My father never knew I played the violin until I was eighteen. I never practiced at home; I'd go to someone else's house - like Frank Paul's. One night, we played in Boisdale; I was on the guitar. My father took a stroke and had to be taken to the hospital. They were going to cancel the dance, but I said, 'If you're not too fussy, I'll play!' When my father found out, he said, 'I'll show you all my bowing techniques and how to hold the fiddle.'

"Before I was eighteen, I had figured out the best way to support the violin so that I could reach notes higher up the board. Around this time, Neil Francis MacLellan of Benacadie gave me some tips on holding the bow. Scottish and Irish music in Cape Breton require good technique, especially the bowing. I learned a lot from listening to other players like Winston Fitzgerald and Dan Hughie MacEachern. At the dances, if I had money, I'd go in; if not, I'd sit outside by the window and listen and learn.

"From age eighteen to twenty-five, I spent a lot of time in the State of Maine. I just worked in lumbercamps and played the fiddle. I didn't play for money; the best pay for me is if someone enjoys what I'm doing. I've done a lot of benefits; if I can help someone who's struggling, I will! The main thing is that we help each other; the world would be a much better place if we all did that.

"I always analyze how things are done - arm wrestling, pitching horseshoes, shooting pool - everything. I'm that kind of person, and I'm very competitive; it's the survival instinct. I have no nervousness, and I have **that** advantage over many other players; I'll tackle the hardest tune under pressure."

Lee Cremo has had phenomenal success in competition. His living room glistens with the eighty-two trophies that his Country and Scottish fiddle stylings have earned him to date. For example, he won the Maritime Oldtime Fiddling Contest in 1966, 67, and 68. He has won the major contest in Western Canada ten years in a row. In 1974, he came fifth in the North American Fiddling Championship in Nashville, Tennessee. Asked if this was his most thrilling adventure, Lee answers, "No. My most exciting moment was playing my first tune by note two years ago."

Lee is a flamboyant showman on stage, but in conversation is absolutely candid. "I'm an explorer, music-wise. If I can go beyond, I will - I'm like Christopher Columbus. I can also look at music from a non-musician's point of view. I put myself in the audience's position; they usually want something to get their hands clapping and their feet moving. At a concert, I'm an entertainer, but I prefer to play at a dance; I can relate to the people in the hall and the fact they want to have a good time. After the first forty-five minutes, my fingers are mobile and I'll try all kinds of position work. I carry four different bows with me."

Lee owns a valuable Rudolf van Merrebach violin from Amsterdam, but he loves his $150.00 Canadian fiddle just as much. It was built in Port Stanley, Ontario. Lee claims that the top is made from a coffee table, the back from a night table, and neck from a baseball bat! Whatever the case, it sounds terrific in his hands.

As for the future, he says, "Someday I'm going to start a music school in this area for the fiddle. I'll show the kids what I've learned. I wouldn't like to take it with me - I'd like to leave it here, somewhere."

Having recently met classical violinist Maurice Solway, Lee now has an appreciation for still another type of "fiddling". He admits, "If Fritz Kreisler was standing here in this room, I'd kiss his toes!"

Lee Cremo has seven long-playing records to his credit.

Winston "Scotty" Fitzgerald

Birth: February 16, 1914 at White Point, Victoria County
Parents: George Fitzgerald and Mary Paquet

"There's music in my blood," is Winston Fitzgerald's answer to the question of why he took up the violin. A product of Irish-French parentage, he was born in a small village on the northeastern tip of Cape Breton Island. "My father played, and so did my brother," Winston continues, "and there was a violin player from Sugar Loaf called Artie Gwynn who was pretty good at that time; it was him that really got me interested in music. He'd get tired up north and come down and stay a week or two at our home in the winter, and there'd be a session of music. He was about the best player up there, as far as I was concerned.

"I started fooling around with the violin at age eight. My mother would steal my brother's fiddle for me - it hung on a nail down in the living room. I'd go to the bedroom and shiver there in the cold 'till my mother would warn me that Jim was coming home.

"I started playing on my own - I just took a liking to the violin. Then came the biggest day of all, when I was about twelve. We used to have school picnics to raise money to help pay the teacher. A fellow by the name of Hector Hughie MacDonald of Bay St. Lawrence played for those picnics, but I wasn't too bad at that time. My father was secretary of the school board there and, one day after a meeting, he came home and said to me, 'You're going to play for the picnic'. I was pretty excited 'till picnic time came, and then I got nervous; but, I pulled it off. That was my big day; it was dances after that!

"There was a fellow from Dingwall named Mick Fitzgerald and he made a violin - at this time I'd be about eleven. One day when it was too windy to fish, they called me down aboard the boat to try out that violin. When I was through playing, they took up a collection - twelve cents! That was a lot of money, mister! I remember going home with those big, black coppers, thinking about all the jaw-breakers I could buy for a penny.

"I would be about eighteen when the 'Maritime Merrimakers' (a black-face minstrel show) came to our area. I played a few numbers with them between sketches. Then I travelled with them all winter through the Annapolis Valley. I went home the next spring - not too rich. I probably got my first bit of music theory with the 'Merrimakers'. I learned a lot from an organist in a church in Maitland Bridge in Annapolis.''

Like their neighbours, the Fitzgeralds fished the waters off northern Cape Breton in the summer. The boys, Winston and Bob, never failed to take the fiddle and guitar aboard their boat. Sometimes, they would engage in impromptu ceilidhs with Arthur Severance, a swordfisherman from Fourchu who played both the pipes and the guitar.

"In the 1930's, I'd fish in the summer and work at the shipyard in Halifax during the winter. I played 2½ years with Hank Snow, both on the South Shore and on the radio."

After a stint in the army, Winston settled in Sydney in 1946. "I took the U.S. School of Music course after I left the service. There were a lot of interesting bowing tips, in fact ten weeks just on bowing alone; I got a lot out of that course! In 1947, I started playing in Sydney. I formed the Radio Entertainers with Beattie Wallace and Estwood Davidson; we had standbys (eg. Professor Jim MacDonald and Chippie MacDonald) for the bigger jobs out of town.'' As Winston became more famous, he received network exposure on both "The Cliff MacKay" and "Don Messer" shows.

"As for records,'' Winston remembers, "Bernie MacIsaac of Antigonish was the first to approach. I made some 78's with him on Celtic but there was no money in it at all. Then Lloyd MacInnis at CJCB Radio asked me to make a recording and I said 'Yes'. We formed the 'Mac' label and I put on 'The North Star Hornpipe', for one. We made about a thousand records and distributed them ourselves, as far away as Halifax. I made the music and Lloyd looked after the business - we did pretty darn good! I was the only one to record on the 'Mac' label.

"It's my own style," Winston says about his unique sound. "I had a goal, and I had a hard fellow to beat - myself! I used to say, 'Today I'm going to do better than I did yesterday'. I might work on one tune for a week to get it exactly as I wanted it. I wanted to play better than everyone else and I stayed at it 'till I could. But I never looked for glory - I was trying to satisfy myself. I love all kinds of music, especially classical violin - like Perlman. I wanted to be a classical player once, but you can't be both."

Winston has always been known for his good taste when selecting his material. "I'm awful fond of 'flavour' - some tunes have it. I like tunes in the flats - Eb, Bb, F; you get a better tone on some of those keys. When I get a new book, I mark all the tunes in the flats - that's a priority.

"I've got the worst fiddle in Canada - I've got nothing more to say about it than that!" However, it is commonly believed that Winston "Scotty" Fitzgerald can draw exquisite music from any violin. A gigantic figure in Cape Breton's musical history, he is considered among the most popular and influential fiddlers in the Scottish tradition.

His Lp's include Celtic CX 17, CX 34, CX 40, and CX 44.

Mickey Gillis

Birth: February 5, 1918 at Grand Mira, Cape Breton
Parents: Stephen and Rose Gillis

Because he was the son of a good piper, as a youngster Mickey quickly became exposed to the joys of Highland Scottish music. The violin came into prominence in his life when his aunt, Cecilia Gillis, taught him a version of "Cock of the North" - Mickey was just twelve. He recalls that several players influenced his early music and among them were: his uncle, Jim; Mike MacDougall, the man for whom the MacDougall Girls Pipe Band was named; Andy MacDougall of Grand Mira; John Stephen Currie, who also built violins; and Alex Gillis of Margaree, whom Mickey often heard over a Boston radio station which could be picked up on the crystal sets in Mira.

Mickey has supplied "Scotch" music at hundreds of concerts and dances, as well as on CBC Radio and network television. In addition, each summer finds him a major contributor at the large outdoor festivals like Glendale and Big Pond. A tune which he sometimes includes in his program, and which he plays movingly, is an Elmer Briand original entitled "Beautiful Lake Ainslie".

After many years of playing by ear, Mickey began to read music in 1973. This skill has enabled him to learn new tunes very quickly, especially those in his favourite key - Bb. Having only begun to compose for the fiddle lately, one of his first efforts was inspired by a recent journey through the Canadian Rockies.

Along with his fiddle, which he obtained from John Stephen Currie, Mickey now owns a tenor banjo and intends to play Celtic instrumentals on it.

Among the enthusiastic "ceilidh" groups regularly organized by Tic Butler in the Sydney area, Mickey's is a familiar face. During a reflective moment in the evening's frivolities, in a quiet corner, the haunting strains of a tune such as "Hector the Hero" draw all ears to Mickey's violin.

He is also a member of the Sydney Scottish Violinists.

Wilfred Gillis

Birth: 1923 in Arisaig, Antigonish County, Nova Scotia
Parents: Lauchlin Gillis and Mary Ann MacDonald

Wilfred Gillis holds the opinion that the hereditary factor is of some importance in the creation of a musician, and well he might, for he himself represents the eighth generation of Gillis to be gifted with the skill of playing the violin. He says, "I think my entry into music probably came from a genuine love of it, rather than from any family-tree obligation. My father was one of the better players of his time, though perhaps not one of the best. He had a distinctive style of his own and was an accomplished note reader. He worked regularly with small ensembles, playing mostly dance music of the late nineteenth century. Most of his repertoire had a Gaelic accent, though he performed the occasional waltz and gavotte. My father had no formal musical training but my grandfather, Stephen Gillis, had, and at one time conducted a string quartet which provided the music which an organ might ordinarily have supplied in the Arisaig church. I've seen many of the arrangements they employed and discovered that some of them were extremely difficult. It's amazing to me to think that one hundred years ago in a fishing village you had people who could play this type of music.

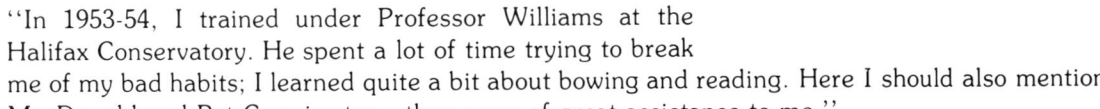

"I learned from listening to what my father played, as well as hearing Don Messer on the radio. Don was a fine musician in his own right, and Scottish fiddlers who criticize him are a little off base - just consider his precision! He was never known to make a mistake on the air during the era of 'live' radio and television programs.

"In 1953-54, I trained under Professor Williams at the Halifax Conservatory. He spent a lot of time trying to break me of my bad habits; I learned quite a bit about bowing and reading. Here I should also mention Jim MacDonald and Pat Cormier too - they were of great assistance to me."

Wilfred has received much media exposure via his Lp "Arisaig Airs" (Celtic CX 45), his work with the "Cape Breton Symphony" and his successful participation in "Canadian" fiddling championships. He adds, "I never played in Scottish music competitions - the style and interpretation are so varied that it's nearly impossible to judge a winner."

Regarding his composing he remarks, "When I feel an inspiration coming on, I write the nucleus of the tune on manuscript and develop it later." Four of his original works are very highly acclaimed: "Welcome to the Trossacks", "The Highland Centenary", "The Goldenrod Jig" and "Arisaig Mist".

Jerry Holland

Birth: February 23, 1955 in Brockton, Massachusetts
Parents: Mr. and Mrs. Jerry Holland Sr.

From the beginning Jerry Holland has been something of a prodigy. At the age of five, when most children are playing with crayons and colouring books, Jerry was beginning his romance with the violin.

"My father taught me how to hold the fiddle and the bow. He'd put my fingers on the strings one at a time. After the first two fingers, I didn't want any part of it. He put an elastic on my hand to help me hold the bow. I hated that; but after I got to play one or two tunes, I started accepting the challenge with encouragement from family and friends. For me to pick up a fiddle today is like the average person picking up a fork to eat - because I started so young."

Although Jerry was born and raised in the Boston area, he grew up hearing the music of Cape Breton first hand. His father, a former New Brunswicker and himself a fiddler, fueled the boy's excitement by exposing him to notable players. "I remember once when Winston (Fitzgerald) was at my parents' house in Halifax, Massachusetts. I was about four at the time and it was before I took up the fiddle. I fell asleep sitting at Winston's feet, staring at him and listening to every note. When I awoke in bed the next morning, I cried and cried to hear more of that fiddle music!" Eighteen or so years later Jerry was to share the spotlight with his boyhood hero as fellow member of "The Cape Breton Symphony" featured on "The John Allan Cameron Show."

Jerry's first appearance on television was to stepdance, at the age of seven, on Don Messer's Show. Shortly after this, he began his career as a dance player. "I started going to Bill Lamey's dances when I was about eight or nine. I think the first time I played publicly was for Bill at the Rose Croix Hall. I played a waltz and a reel and they had to stand me on a chair so people could see me. After I was through, Bill picked me up and hugged me. He was a great inspiration to me! I started playing the last figure of a set for him nearly every week when I was nine or ten; then I progressed to two figures and eventually to three and it became a regular thing. There was Eddy Irwin on piano and Jimmy Kelly on tenor banjo and sometimes his wife, Sally MacEachern Kelly, played piano too."

Jerry's versatility as a musician, exhibited in his picking up of the guitar and the piano, led him to an association with another of Cape Breton's illustrious fiddlers, Angus Chisholm. At the age of fourteen, and for over a two-year period, Jerry was Angus' accompanist, playing both guitar and violin, along with Bert Foley on fiddle and occasionally Lauchie MacEachern on guitar, at Tom Slavin's Club for the sum of $15.00 nightly.

There have been many television performances to Jerry's credit, with numerous appearances in Boston, as winner of a national talent contest from New York and as back-up violinist on a New England series with Irish artists, Makem and Clancy. His unique talent of playing the fiddle and stepdancing at the same time was featured on several of these shows. As a member of "The Cape Breton Symphony", he has recorded an album, as well as having a solo release.

It is quite natural, with Jerry Holland's strong sympathy for Cape Breton and its music, that he should choose the Island as his home. He plays, repairs and teaches the violin here. He has composed sixty or seventy tunes for the instrument and owns approximately fourteen violins at present. This obvious occupation with Scottish music is immediately apparent to anyone hearing the lovely lilt and tone of Jerry's playing; which playing suggests that, one day, he will be numbered among the best.

MIKE'S FANCY

Jig

by Jerry Holland

Hughie Angus Jobes

Birth: 1906, at South Side, Boularderie
Parents: Mr. and Mrs. John Charles Jobes

Hughie Angus, a life-time resident of South Side, Boularderie, has been making music on the violin since he was thirteen years of age. His father, John Charles, played, and when he passed away he left Hughie with the obligation of putting the family violin back into use. Encouraged by his mother, who could 'jig' tunes, Hughie soon acquired the skills necessary to become a good dance player. The only fiddlers in the area at that time were George MacAskill of North Side Boularderie and Stephen MacNeil, the latter being Hughie's uncle. However, using a keen ear and a strong Gaelic background for reinforcement, young Hugh A. became so accomplished that his talents were sought in the distant communities of Tarbot, North River, Munroe's Point and River Bennett.

In the earlier days of Hughie's career, a wedding was a huge social event involving an outdoor dance on a platform constructed especially for that purpose. Though the festivities usually ran until daybreak, the best a fiddler could hope to earn by the passing of a hat was $3.00 or $4.00. During the Depression years, however, these small sums were of importance to Hughie's family.

Hughie continued to play on his father's old violin until it was lost in a fire which devastated the Jobes' home in the nineteen-sixties. In consequence, he purchased another instrument from Johnny Morrison of North Sydney for fifty dollars. Recently, Hughie turned down an offer of one-thousand dollars for the same violin.

In 1971, Hughie retired from C.N. and since then has had more time to devote to the music he so loves. In 1980, he received the Buddy MacMaster Trophy for jig playing in competition. In addition, he has composed a cleverly constructed tune called "Flora's Favourite", dedicated to his wife.

Hughie Angus' son, John Hugh Charles Jobes, who passed away suddenly in 1959 at only twenty-six years of age, was both a talented violinist and guitarist. However, Scottish music still thrives in the family, notably in the person of Laurie Anne Ryan, Hughie's tiny grandchild who stepdances with great flair to her grandfather's lively fiddling.

Willie Kennedy

Birth: August 15, 1925 at Lake Ainslie
Parents: Dan Michael Kennedy and Euphemia MacLellan

"My father was very correct for an ear player. He wouldn't play a tune unless he had it perfect - the note players used to say that! I have a lot of his music. My brothers played a little bit too. My father would go out and then we'd get the fiddle.

"I got a tin fiddle around age eight - just an Eaton's toy; but I guess I really began to play at age ten. At sixteen or seventeen, I played at Kenloch for a summer with Angus Allan Gillis. It's through him that I learned a lot of the older tunes. During those years, I'd also relieve Sandy MacLean for a set now and then. The great dances they used to have! The hall is torn down now. Then, the MacLellan Hall was built in Glenville. The big boost was playing at the dances with Sandy MacLean and Angus Allan.

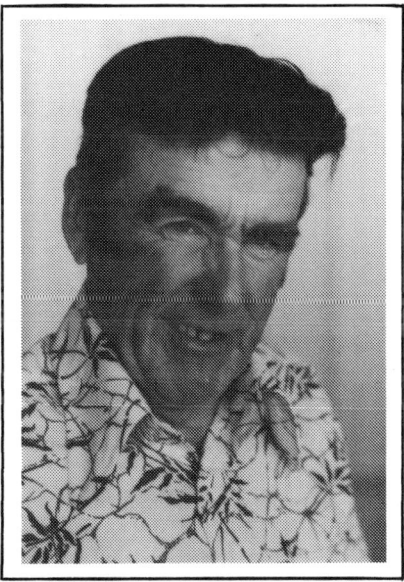

"I played mostly at school dances. We'd go in the back of a big truck - there weren't many cars then. Sometimes I'd play with John Alex MacLellan and Jack 'Malcolm' Gillis, and we'd get $5.00 each for the whole night! When I was between twenty and twenty-five years old, I was very busy playing near home. Around 1967, I moved up to Mabou, and during the last few years I've been playing quite a bit at weddings, concerts and parties."

Willie Kennedy, a man with a love for the "old time" fiddling style, is respected for his repertoire of traditional tunes. Through the years, he has befriended and performed with some of the giants of Cape Breton music, and he is generous in his praise of them all: Angus Allan Gillis, Malcolm Beaton, Charlie MacKinnon of East Lake Ainslie, and Sandy MacLean. "Sandy is about my pick - I never saw a fellow with such a bow hand!"

Lately, Willie has been dueting with his Mabou friends; they include Kenneth Joseph MacDonald, Sandy Cameron, Gregory Campbell and Father Francis Cameron, their parish priest.

"I have Dan R. MacDonald's old violin now. It's an Anton Kessel (of Breitonfeld). Dan R. said to me, 'You should have a good fiddle!' He sold it to me very cheap - I really appreciated that."

Referring to his infatuation with the ancient variety of Scottish fiddle tunes, he says, "I seem to have the old stuff in me so deep! I can't grasp the new tunes as easily."

Bill Lamey

Birth: March 9, 1914 at River Denys, Cape Breton
Parents: John H. Lamey and Margaret MacLean

Bill was born at River Denys, but 1926 found the family in Sydney Mines, and it was here that he began playing the violin at the age of eighteen, having been strongly influenced by his mother's love for Scottish music. With the musicianship of "Big" Ranald MacLellan and Gordon MacQuarrie providing additional inspiration, he immediately applied himself to the task of learning to read music. "I was never content to play tunes I already knew," he says. "I was always into the books!" After only two years of performing, he earned his own radio show on CJCB. His group at this time was known as "The Radio Entertainers" and included pianist Lila Hashem.

In 1936, Bill made yet another move, this time to Sydney, where he took on a busy schedule of dance playing at Nelga Beach, St. Theresa's Hall, Big Pond and Christmas Island. Occasionally he joined forces with his friend, Joe MacLean, to create a memorable duo. At picnics, such as those held in Frenchvale, his physical endurance would be tested as he was usually required to provide music from 11:00 o'clock a.m. to 1:00 o'clock a.m. He generally utilized a pump organ for accompaniment at such gatherings.

In 1938, Bill played at the first Gaelic Mod at St. Ann's, and ten years later he won the Premier of Nova Scotia Cup in competition there. In the 1940's and 50's, thanks to the foresight of Bernie MacIsaac of Antigonish, he made a number of 78 rpm recordings for the Celtic label. These latter featured classic performances and arrangements which are still admired and imitated.

By this time, Bill had begun accumulating what he now calls "one of the best Scottish fiddle-music collections in the world," which until recently included "The Anderson Collection". This rare and valuable book, originally obtained from John Grant's Music Store in Edinburgh, is now a showpiece at the Beaton Institute in Sydney, Cape Breton.

In 1953, Bill and his family moved to Boston. Of that migration he says, "I went for the adventure, I suppose. There were lots of fiddlers there, and I was at my peak then." A charter member of the Cape Breton Island Gaelic Foundation, which was formed at St. Ann's in 1938, Bill joined the Boston branch in 1953 and has been its president for the past fifteen years. In the company of people like Alex Gillis,

Alcide Aucoin, Agnes Campbell, Dr. Ajax Campbell and Angus Chisholm, Bill continued to pour forth his music "south of the border". He comments, "I ran dances for eighteen years in Boston, and, for ten of those, Angus Chisholm was my anchor man." Bill also had a radio program over WVOM and was responsible for sponsoring visits by many of Cape Breton's best-known violinists.

Both as a performer and an organizer, Bill Lamey has dedicated much of his life to the promotion of good Scottish fiddling in Canada and the eastern United States. In a candid comment on a controversial subject, he offers the following for consideration: "I have never joined the union - I don't believe in holding a card to play music!"

In 1966, he visited Scotland and, following a performance before three thousand people which was broadcast over the BBC, he was given a standing ovation.

Bill now possesses a beautiful "Augusta" violin and an exquisite bow crafted by Lamy of Paris. Recently, fans of his music were pleased to learn that his earlier recordings have been made available in album form on the Shanachie label.

Some 78 rpm's by W.H. [Bill] Lamey:

CELTIC 027-A (accompanied by Margaret MacDonald)
"Bog an Lochan", "Clan Ranald" and "The Nine-Pint Coggie" Reels
027-B "The Minstrel's Fancy" and "Upper Denton" Hornpipes

CELTIC 029-A (accompanied by Margaret MacDonald)
"Niel Gow's Lament for Dr. Moray", "Johnny Pringle" and "The Lassie wi' the Yellow Coatie"
029-B "MacKenzie Hay", "The Kerrie Kebuck" and "The Spey in Spate"

CELTIC 044-A (with Lila Hashem, and string bass and drums)
"Lovat Scout's" and "Marquis of Tullybardine"
044-B "Dr. Shaw's Strathspey", "The Breem Dog" and "Sandy Skinner"

Donnie LeBlanc

Birth: April 17, 1955 in Cheticamp
Parents: Joseph LeBlanc and Lucy Aucoin

Picture a large room - eager eyes watching every "cut" coaxed from sweating violins, scores of feet tapping rhythmically and ancient Highland melodies resounding from the walls; this is the scene at Cheticamp's Doryman Tavern on a Saturday afternoon. Although fiddlers Donald Angus Beaton, Alex Francis MacKay, Brenda Stubbert or Jerry Holland may be guesting on stage, the featured act for the past three and a half years has been the Acadian trio of Donnie LeBlanc, violin, first-cousin Andre LeBlanc on piano and Gelas Larade, guitar. Donnie says, "The tavern has made a big difference in getting the young people to like the music. It has a big influence."

Donnie, himself, has been involved in Scottish music since he was given a mandolin at the age of seven. He heard lots of fine fiddling at home when uncles Didace and Neil LeBlanc and second-cousin Arthur Muise came to visit, and hearing tapes and records of Angus Chisholm and Winston Fitzgerald only increased his affection for the instrument.

At the age of fifteen, Donnie switched to the violin and quickly picked up tunes by ear; but learning to read music from teacher Mederic LeFort, a few years ago, has changed the source of his repertoire. "I don't listen to tapes anymore! I go right to the books and I think I've got all the common ones on the market." He now enjoys the pieces of Skinner and Marshall, as well as those of local composers Dan Hughie MacEachern and Dan R. MacDonald.

Although Donnie is only twenty-six years old, he is already a popular fiddler and kept busy with dances in the Cheticamp area. Besides the Doryman, he has played at the Cheticamp Legion, St. Joseph du Moine Hall, the Acadian Centre, the Cheticamp Snowmobile Club and the Firemens' Club to name a few.

Donnie believes, as do many Celtic music enthusiasts, that there should be more Cape Breton fiddling on the radio. "It's a problem - the young people don't hear any local music to influence them. And, it should be **our** players on instead of overseas fiddlers! In Scotland they've never heard of our great violinists. They don't play ours over there so why should we play their fiddlers here?"

Francis MacDonald

Birth: March 7, 1932 in Inverness Town
Parents: Rory MacDonald and
Sara Anne MacLellan

Though his father's cousin, John Alex MacDonald of Port Hood, played the violin, it was from Malcolm Beaton of Strathlorne that Francis learned his first tune at the age of eighteen. Considering himself an old-time player, he says, "I got some of my bowing, especially on strathspeys, from Donald Angus MacPherson of Dunvegan, my father-in-law." He now describes some of the techniques he shares with other traditional-style Cape Breton fiddlers: "It used to seem to me to be the most natural thing in the world to use the high counter and bass, but, when amplification came in, the tuning began to die out because it was no longer necessary. But, I still play a lot of tunes with 'blending' or 'droning' - that is, sounding the 'A' or 'D' string open, along with the melody notes."

He continues, "Cape Bretoners often interpret a dotted quarter note as two notes, and we use a lot less slurring than the overseas fiddlers, especially on groups of sixteenth notes. Also, the Inverness County players use a special variation of the regular 'cut' and call it a 'shake' - it actually puts a different emphasis on the three notes of an ordinary 'cut'."

Proficient on the pipes as well as the violin, Francis once appeared with the Black Watch Regiment on "The Ed Sullivan Show", and played for both the late John F. Kennedy and the Royal Family of England. As a fiddler, he has guested on "The Ryan's Fancy Show" on the CBC TV network.

A versatile performer, Francis has also earned praise as a stepdancer, violin teacher, singer and songwriter, having composed the beautiful "Vale of Margaree". In addition, he reads music well and has written over fifty violin tunes which will soon be published along with the compositions of his talented son, Roddy, himself a fine fiddler and all-around instrumentalist.

Accompanied on the piano by his wife Corrine, Francis takes great pleasure in entertaining with his handsome Roth violin, which was presented to him in 1953 by the bandmaster of the Stadacona Band.

Margaret (Chisholm) MacDonald

Birth: July 17, 1947 in Margaree Forks, Cape Breton
Parents: Willie D. Chisholm and Annie Mae Cameron

It seems that everyone from Craig Duncan (a Nashville fiddler) to classical violinists in the Toronto area have become enthralled with the natural bowing style of Margaret Chisholm MacDonald. With no formal training, she manages to execute difficult techniques without apparent effort. "I began playing at the age of 14½, to be exact," she says. "My mother used to play the violin, and she taught me my first tune - 'Walking the Floor'; I learned it in less than an hour. I'm really an ear player. I learn a tune quickly - if I hear it twice, in twenty minutes I'll have it."

Margaret comes from a musically-renowned Cape Breton family whose most noted members are: her uncles, Archie Neil and Angus Chisholm; her brother, Cameron; and her sister, Maybelle (pianist). "My father," she continues, "was a great influence on me. He could jig any tune and correct me in any way, though he himself couldn't play the violin." Peter, Margaret's husband, adds, "Willie D. is a very proud man, and he reflects the spirit of most of his generation in Cape Breton. What really was instilled in Margaret was the dignity of playing the music - that's what she got from her father!"

When Margaret was a young girl, the Chisholm household was frequently blessed by the visits of a world-famous piper, Sandy Boyd. "Through Sandy," Margaret recalls, "I began playing the pipes, but I gave them up to concentrate on the violin. In the beginning, marches were my favourite tunes, mainly due to Sandy's playing. He was very generous with his music."

Possessing many fond memories of early encounters with other Scottish violinists, Margaret says, "At dances, Buddy MacMaster was one of the best players - his jigs were, and are, so articulate and graceful. Then, I heard Joe MacLean on record - he had such beautiful, sweet notes. And, of course, there was Donald Angus Beaton. He played at the dances at Mabou and Strathlorne - he'd get you on your feet!

"I married at age seventeen, and, in 1965, I had my first child. My children were always the most important thing to me, so, from 1966 to '73, I never touched the violin. But, in 1973, I went down to Cape Breton and, at Glendale, Father John Angus Rankin asked me to play. Actually, he had to chase me up the hill to convince me. Father John Angus supported me all the way; I don't think I would have played then without that support!

"Though he used to come to our house when I was a little girl, it was in the early seventies that I really got to hear my uncle Angus play. He was in a class of his own. I play quite a few of his tunes now. They sometimes say that I sound like Uncle Angus, but I believe I sound like Margaret Chisholm, and that's it! I play to the best of my ability and I don't copy anyone."

Though Margaret, Peter and family made their home in Toronto, Ontario, they maintained contact with the Cape Breton musicians in that area. "Around 1978," Margaret remembers, "John Allan Cameron and David MacIsaac came out here to our house and encouraged me to play. That was important to me because I had let the violin go again." Drawing upon her wonderful natural ability, Margaret was soon in top form again. "I'm really a concert player," she says. "I'm more classical in my approach; though, if I want to, I can play rough and lively. I can play in any key - hornpipes, marches, clogs, etc. One of my best-known medleys begins with 'Sheehan's Reel'. That's what I played at Glendale in 1979 because Uncle Angus had died earlier that year and that was one of **his** favourite groupings too; it was a sort of tribute." For that particular performance Margaret received an enthusiastic and extended applause.

"I find chauvinistic ways among some men, but a woman can play as good music as a man - most definitely! I can play circular bowing and staccato bowing, so I feel confident. When I make up my mind to play, nothing bothers me - not the size of the crowd or who's in the audience - nothing!

"In Toronto, it's more concert work; I don't really enjoy performing at dances. Now, I play duets with my husband who chords on the mandolin." Peter adds, "When we go up on stage, I have no idea what she's going to play. Often, when the mood hits her, she'll break into tunes I've never heard before!" The duo hopes to release an album in the mid 1980's.

In conclusion, Margaret offers these words of praise to fellow performers: "I like Sean McGuire, and, as for the younger players in Cape Breton, I enjoy the music of my brother Cameron, Arthur Muise, Jerry Holland, and Brenda Stubbert."

Mary (Beaton) MacDonald

Birth: September 7, 1897 at MacKinnon's Brook, Mabou
Parents: Alexander R. Beaton Sr. (Alasdair Raonuill) and Margaret MacIsaac

Mary MacDonald (also called "Little" Mary, Mary "Hughie" and Mairi Alasdair Raonuill) is the great-great-granddaughter of Alexander Beaton (Alasdair an Taillear), a pioneer settler of Mabou Coal Mines, having arrived in 1809. Her family tree is adorned with the names of many fine traditional fiddlers, for example: her grand-uncle, John Beaton; her uncles, Johnny Ranald, Angus Ranald, "Young" Donald and Alexander R. (Jr.) Beaton; her first cousins, Danny, Jessie, Ronald Dan, Johnny "Johnny Ranald", Janet, Ronald and Donald Angus Beaton; and her sister, Jessie.

It seems the report was true that, at one point, a fiddle existed in literally every home in Inverness County. Alexander R. Beaton, Mary's father, kept one handy, and though it could have been "off limits" to an inquisitive little girl, Mr. Beaton took a healthier, more benevolent stand: "Don't keep the fiddle from her," he used to say. "If she breaks it, I can get another one."[25] Strengthened by this vote of confidence, the tiny child proceeded to practice, though she had to rest the neck of the violin on a chair to support it.

Emphasizing the aural transmission method during her earlier years as a player, Mary absorbed the nuances of the Gaelic fiddle music which she heard in abundance. The bowing patterns and tune settings she mastered had their genesis in the Scotland of the 1700's, or earlier. One of her most influential contacts in this regard was a man named Alexander J. Beaton, who was born in 1837 in Glen Spean. During many winter visits to Alasdair Raonuill's home, he passed on his expertise in stepdancing and fiddling to Mrs. Peigi Beaton and her daughters Mary and Jessie. In the following comments, given by Mary herself to John Gibson of the Scotia Sun, she explains the important process by which she was able to capture the ancient Highland music "Old" Alex offered her: "He was wanting me to look at his fingers, but I wouldn't. My sister did, but it was the tune I was wanting."[26] In this manner, throughout the years, she assembled an enviable repertoire of old tunes, and she played them as they might have been played over two centuries ago in Scotland; her setting of "The Tullochgorum", learned from Mrs. John Angus MacArthur of Mabou Coal Mines, is a prime example.

Mary has always remained loyal to what is now a nearly extinct style of fiddling; her bowing has become her trademark. In a taped interview with Frank MacInnis of Creignish, Angus Chisholm passed on the following compliments: "I'm going to tell you this: I heard Professor Cormier of Sydney say - I heard Steve MacGillivray (of Glace Bay) say the same thing - that Mary MacDonald had the greatest touch he ever heard in this business! I remember being at Mary's one time - she and Mary Jessie (her daughter) played well together. I was lying on the chesterfield, my ear close to the violin. God, that woman took beautiful sounds out of that violin - and always the soft touch she had! She holds the bow in, I would say, an awkward way, but I never heard her making a bad cutting; she'll get those cuttings in no matter how she holds the bow! Great player!"

When no accompanist was available, Mary would often supply her own chording in a unique way: she would insert match-sticks between the appropriate keys of an organ, and then would pump it with her foot. She could thus insert a two or three-note drone behind her playing of pipe tunes on the fiddle.

Mary also became a noted stepdancer, possessing some steps which were totally unfamiliar to other local dancers. Two sources of inspiration to her in this art were the aforementioned Alexander J. Beaton and "Curly" Sandy Beaton.

After marrying Hugh MacDonald of Glencoe Mills, Mary and her husband settled in New Waterford. Here, she began joining musical forces with Mrs. Margaret MacPhee, a Scottish pianist, and together they entertained at hundreds of gatherings in private homes. Another of her close friends was composer-fiddler "Red" Gordon MacQuarrie who encouraged Mary to perform in Boston and Detroit, where she occasionally took medals in competition.

Today, the home tape recordings of "Little" Mary have become precious property to their owners, not only because of their historical significance, but on account of the sheer joy they generate.

John MacDougall

Birth: April 27, 1925 in Egypt, Inverness County, Cape Breton
Parents: George MacDougall and Margaret MacLellan

"I was born in Egypt - you know, near Gillisdale. The fiddling was right in me - I had to do it! I just picked up the violin and could play a few notes the very first time I tried. I played for about three years on one of those fifty-five cent tin fiddles. A Kennedy fellow showed me the first notes of 'Pop Goes the Weasel'; when I was leaving, he gave me the tin fiddle (John was about twelve at the time). Then I got that one on the wall. I got it from Eaton's for five dollars - bow and fiddle, and, you know, she wasn't too bad at all. You wouldn't buy her for fifty dollars today. But, I really never had a good violin until lately; the ones I had were just pieces of junk! Now I own a Hopf.

"When I was a teenager, I played at a lot of parties, and at dances in the schoolhouses. When I first started, I was going seven nights a week - Sundays were for parties. Then I played with Angus Allan Gillis at a barndance at North Lake - every week for a year. I had courage to sit beside him, for all the music I knew! But, do you think he'd try to stick you? No way - he was too nice a man; I'll always respect him for that. And, he could play circles around them all. I learned a lot from Angus Allan. I can still see that bowhand of his going!

"Around age twenty, I wanted to learn to read music, but I couldn't find anyone near who'd teach me. Then, I saw this ad in the Family Herald - thirty-five dollars for a course. Money was scarce in those days, but I sent for it and I learned. And, a barber in Inverness called Alex Glabais gave me a whole set of lesson books from the U.S. School of Music in New York. Now, I want to teach everyone I can today. You follow the instruction books and they'll put your bowing in place, but you have to figure the cuttings out in your own mind - they call it the 'Cape Breton snap', and I got it from watching others. I always watched Angus Allan; I don't think there was anyone could cut like him! He had cuts that no one else had!

"I began composing fifteen years ago. The first tune I made was 'John Charlie's Lament' in three-quarter time, written for a cousin of mine who was killed in a car crash. I suppose I've written about three hundred tunes; someday I hope to publish them. I can make two or three tunes a day. I can even make a tune between the figures of a set and then use it right away that night!''

In the early seventies, John MacDougall played a key position in aiding the resurgence of violin playing among young Cape Bretoners. ''Ron MacInnis woke everyone up with 'The Vanishing Fiddler','' says John. ''In 1971, after the film came out, Fr. Colonel MacLeod approached me to teach; he didn't want to see this music die out! I started in February, and in July I had about thirteen children playing in a concert at Broad Cove. I was the first to start this teaching business. I taught in Inverness, Broad Cove, Mabou, Judique, Creignish, Glendale, Scotsville, Margaree Forks and at the Gaelic College in St. Ann's. I must have taught about two hundred people - from age seven to seventy!''

John is very positive about the future of the music in Cape Breton. He says, ''The fiddling is going to have a great revival. It'll take a little time, but I tell those youngsters, 'When you settle down, don't forget the violin' - and they won't!''

Presently, John operates a violin and piano repair shop out of his home. He still finds time to compose and perform, however. His regular pianist is Penny Kennedy.

Dan Hughie MacEachern

Birth: 1914, at Queensville, Inverness County
Parents: Duncan MacEachern and Mary MacMillan

Dan Hughie's younger days were enriched with Scottish melodies, notably through the spirited fiddling of his older brothers, John Willie and Alex who learned their high and low bass tunings from "Big" Hughie MacMaster. Encouraged to try his hand at an old family violin which had been refurbished, Dan Hughie was soon making music. A cousin, Peter MacFarlane of Queensville, explained the art of note reading, while brother Alex showed him tunes in the key of Bb. In an old tradition, Dan Hughie's sisters (Kaye and Marcella) provided a unique rhythmic accompaniment to his earliest efforts by tapping with knitting needles on the strings of his violin while he played.

Consistently warm hospitality at Duncan MacEachern's home attracted noted violinists such as Gordon MacQuarrie, who gave Dan Hughie some bowing tips, and Dan Rory MacDonald. Further exposure to fine fiddling came in the person of "Big" Ronald MacLellan, whose musical wizardry left an indelible impression on all members of the MacEachern family.[27]

After his initial public appearance at a wedding at Lauchie MacKinnon's in South Rhodena, Dan Hughie was kept busy providing entertainment at every imaginable sort of function. For dances at the Sugar Camp schoolhouse and in Creignish, he'd team up with his brother, John Willie, occasionally utilizing a technique called "first and second violins" to add harmony (basically octaves) to certain melodies. In time, Dan Hughie became known for his repertoire of technically difficult pieces.

Inspired by the music of the Gows, Marshall and Skinner, Dan Hughie embarked upon a career of composing which resulted in the creation of many hundreds of beautiful melodies, some examples being - "Trip to Mabou Ridge", "Kennedy Street March", "The Snowplough Reel", "Jean MacKenzie's Jig" and "Lament for Archie MacLellan". Father John Angus Rankin has said, "Dan Hughie is a genius of composition. His emotions pour out into his music - I would compare him with Captain Simon Fraser for plaintiveness." In 1975, "The MacEachern Collection" was published featuring over one hundred of Dan Hughie's finest pieces. This book represented the first Cape Breton collection of tunes to be released since MacQuarrie's in 1940. Dan Hughie's music is presently among the most loved, performed and recorded of any modern Scottish composer for the violin.

On November 15, 1980, the Island honoured this talented and influential musician with a testimonial held at the College of Cape Breton.

ALEX BEATON'S STRATHSPEY

by Dan Hughie MacEachern

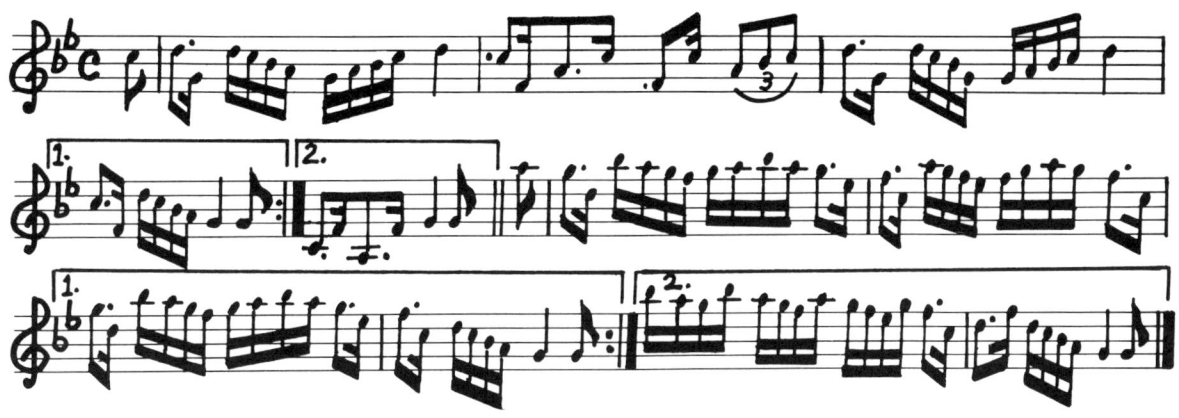

THE RED MILL

Reel

by Dan Hughie MacEachern

Dan Joe MacInnis

Birth: July 31, 1922 in Sydney, Cape Breton
Parents: Dan Peter MacInnis and Mary Campbell

Though his maternal grandfather, John Campbell, was the only close relative associated with the violin, Dan Joe began his fiddling career at the tender age of eight, with full credit going to Peter Campbell of Woodbine. "Old" Peter used to sell buttermilk and vegetables while travelling around the countryside by horse and wagon. Whenever he stopped at the MacInnis home for tea, he would reach for the violin. "He played by ear," Dan Joe remembers, "but his version of 'Christy Campbell' was unbeatable! That was the first Scottish violin music I heard."

Owing to the distracting squeaks which a novice's hands are bound to bring from a violin, Dan Joe's sisters implored him to practice in the barn. It was in that humble setting that he eventually mastered a tune on the old fiddle he had discovered in the attic, and which he had repaired with money earned by picking berries. The eager youngster made his first public appearance at the Membertou Reserve; he divided the evening's pay of twelve cents with fellow musician Steve Googoo. By the age of fourteen however, Dan Joe was playing for dances at Grand Mira, and soon operated on a regular dance circuit within a twenty mile radius of Sydney.

In 1947, encouraged by local fiddler Bill Lamey, Dan Joe learned to read music by following the instructions in the forty-five cent tutor he had purchased. Within only two weeks, he was playing a number of tunes he had learned from the written music. As years passed, he amassed a truly enviable library of rare violin books, including "The Beauties of Niel Gow", "The Oswald Collection", "The Glen Collection" (two books), "The Duncan Collection", "The Alexander MacGlashan" and an original of Simon Fraser's first book (1816).

On CJCB Radio, Dan Joe received exposure through announcer Clyde Nunn. He also played for five years on the MacDonald Tobacco Show, which was aired every Saturday evening. After recording three long-playing albums in the early sixties, he united efforts with Jack MacNeil to found the now-famous Big Pond Concert, an annual Scottish music extravaganza.

Of Dan Joe's children, four are celebrated musicians: George (pianist), Jamie (piper), Bernadette (stepdancer) and Sheldon (member of the singing group "Sons of Skye").

John Joe MacInnis

Birth: March 22, 1909 in Little Judique, Inverness County
Parents: Colin MacInnis and Annie O'Brien

"My grandfather, John O'Brien (of River Denys), raised me from the age of two. He had a brown whisker down to here. The first man I ever saw play was my grandfather - I used to steal his fiddle sometimes. He was considered a good player of both Scottish and Irish tunes, though his hands were after getting stiff when I was young. But, Gordon MacQuarrie heard him once and thought he was wonderful!

"I loved the fiddle when I was a little fellow. I used to play a shingle strung with spool-thread - I was six or seven. The first tune I got was 'One Hundred Pipers'; I got it off a MacMillan when I was twelve or thirteen. When I was practicing, my grandfather used to say, 'You're off here and you're off there!' - he knew when I was playing wrong.

"I played at dances at River Denys and around those places - the old schoolhouses, no piano or nothing! I went one night to play in Big Meadow. It started at eight o'clock and went till four in the morning. Then they said, 'We can't afford three dollars,' but I got it anyway, and I went to work in the morning at the sawmill.

"I used to get tunes from the old players, like Duncan MacDonald's father, Malcolm, from River Denys Mountain. You'd learn by listening, and try to get it as correctly as you could. You'd never just ask a fiddler to show you one of his tunes!" Besides Malcolm and Duncan MacDonald, there were other players who were a source of encouragement and inspiration: Angus MacEachern of River Denys

Station, now living in Boston; Alexander MacDonnell, a good note player from Judique; Hughie Allan MacDonald of Judique; Dan C. MacDonald of West Bay Road; Angus "the Piper" MacMaster of Judique; and John Hughie MacEachern of Hillsdale.

In 1941, John Joe joined the army, travelling to Scotland, England, France, Belgium, Holland and Germany. "I found a fiddle in a vacant house in Germany," he recalls, "but someone sat on it in the sergeants' mess and flattened it. We were stationed in Bramshot, Southern England, and we used to hear Dan R. (MacDonald) playing over the BBC. Dan R. and I had been friends since we were kids. He composed a tune for me, but I lost it."

John Joe still speaks Gaelic, the language of his childhood, but when asked if he stepdances too, he will sometimes reply, "No - one foot belongs to the Church!"

Always generous with his tunes and his time, John Joe is now a member of The Sydney Scottish Violinists. His final comment is, "I still love the music!"

Sandy MacInnis

Birth: 1919 at Skye Mountain, Inverness County
Parents: Dan MacInnis and Annie MacLellan

If music is in the blood, then Sandy MacInnis was well equipped to be a Scottish violinist. The list of his relatives who have played the fiddle includes the following: his father, Dan; uncles Archie, Jack, Jimmy, and Danny MacLellan; brothers Murdoch, George, Alex and Jimmy; sisters Margaret, Annie Florence and Johnena; and cousin Alex Cummings of Skye Glen.

Sandy says, "I guess Jimmy started playing first, and he got some music from my father and uncles. Jimmy was the oldest and he was playing before I was born. In our house, the violin was going all the time. I think there were only three violins at home, but when the uncles came to visit and brought theirs, there could be as many as four boys and two girls playing at once; some would play high and some others play low. Very seldom was there only one fiddle going.

"My brother, Murdoch Angus, used to play his fiddle at the theatre in Sydney during the time of the silent movies in the twenties. He'd play Scotch music at the intermissions.

"I don't remember learning. It seems to me that I just picked up the fiddle and started playing. My sister Florence and I used to take the fiddle down when the others were away."

By the time Sandy was fourteen, he had a fairly good grasp of violin technique, unbeknownst to the rest of his family. Then one day, some visitors to the house asked him if he was able to play, and his brothers and sisters were astonished at his reply, as Sandy explains: "I said that I could play 'The St. Ann's Reel'. My brother Alex thought that I was only kidding because that piece was so hard, considering all the cuts - but I played it!

"There were so many fiddlers in the family - seven besides my father - that I didn't follow it up at that time. At age fifteen, I bought a guitar off an Indian for five dollars. I used to chord for my brothers at the picnics at River Denys, etc. You'd play from 10:00 a.m. until daylight the next day for one dollar or fifty cents!

"I went to work in the woods when I was sixteen, and got away from the violin until 1940, when I moved to Alexandra Street in Sydney. I met Dan Joe MacInnis, 'Wishie' MacInnis, Johnny 'Washabuck' MacLean, Billy MacPhee, and Mickey Gillis - Mickey had come in from Grand Mira. Some of these were my neighbours and we'd often play together.

"In 1942, I started playing at the Carpenter's Hall," Sandy recalls. Among the musicians who shared the spotlight with him there were pianist Beattie Wallace, banjoist Ed MacGillivray and violinist Tena Campbell. "I was going five nights a week for a while there," he says, "especially in wartime; the hall was packed every night, with so many servicemen around. It was fifty cents at the door and there'd be as many as five hundred people in the hall. We were getting five dollars each, and the prompter, Tupper MacAskill, got five. In later years, the prompter was Mike MacNeil. A good prompter was 40% of your band; there were some of them you could dance to without music!

"We were at the Carpenter's Hall well into the fifties. Then, we moved to the Navy League and Winston Fitzgerald worked with us as a special guest for about two years." At one point, Sandy worked with another band called "The Ridge Runners" which featured the talents of Bernie Lee and Joe MacDougall.

"Around 1947, I started reading music. Winston had some beginner's books and he gave them to me. I learned by myself - I had no help at all. I wanted to learn the music correctly and pick up tunes faster. I got the Kerr Collection first."

Sandy composes music, plays guitar and piano, and has taught Scottish violin courses. Here he explains his approach to the right-hand technique: "Ever since I started playing I've done exercises with bowing. At home, they always talked about bowing and cuts. My mother would jig 'Devil in the Kitchen' with all the cuts, and I tried to get it that way. Now, I learn a tune the way it's written and then put in the cuts. I figure the bow hand is 75% of our music, and at a dance I really let loose."

Sandy remains active today as a dance player and as a member of the Sydney Scottish Violinists. He possesses nine violins, his favourite of which is a Georges Castagnier model made in Tournay, France at least eighty years ago.

Sandy MacIntyre

Birth: April 17, 1935 at Inverness Town, Cape Breton
Parents: Ronald MacIntyre (1896-1978) and Cassie MacIsaac (1902-1977)

Relatives of Sandy's who have played the violin: his mother and father; his brothers Francis and John R. (d. 1942); his grandfather, John Angus MacIsaac of Broad Cove Banks; uncles Johnny Archie, Dan Hughie, Alex Angus and Donald Angus MacIsaac; and aunts Mary and Flora MacIsaac. In a classic example of understatement, Sandy says, "The music was really in the MacIsaacs."

"My mother started playing at dances at age thirteen; she played with her father at the schoolhouse near Broad Cove Banks. She was a very positive thinker and it used to show in her music - she was confident and aggressive.

"I started playing the organ around age eight or nine, after watching my sister Mary Florence accompanying our mother. I remember chording for my grandfather at our home in Inverness. He played all the old traditional tunes - mostly strathspeys and reels. Boy, was he ever good! On Sundays, our house was a gathering place for fiddlers. We'd have four or five players drop in, in white shirts and ties after Mass, and they'd stay all evening - Peter MacDonnell, Dan Hector MacPhee, Malcolm Burke, Sandy MacLean; one of my sisters or myself would be on the organ. We really lived music - when you're short on everything else, you'll make it up with music!

"I guess I started playing the fiddle when I was in high school and around sixteen years of age. Our mother encouraged us all to play, but I learned very few tunes at first because I was playing the guitar and organ - I was more used to accompanying. I picked up traditional tunes by ear, mostly from my mother, up until I was twenty-one. 'Winston Fitzgerald' and 'Buddy MacMaster' were household words, and the tunes I heard them playing at dances gave me quite a mixture! I only knew music as a way of life - it was something we all did - it was a pleasure."

In high school, Sandy was a drummer with the Inverness Pipe Band. In 1955, following graduation, he headed westward to Toronto at the age of nineteen. "I found myself in the city, in a small room, on my own, starving for fiddle music. I was thinking I would have to buy a violin, but I didn't have the money. One morning, while going to work, I noticed a fiddle and a case just lying in a garbage can near my apartment - I couldn't believe it! That day, I bought a bow and strings and started playing it. I picked at it for a year and then decided to go to a music store in town and buy a book with the scale in it. Soon, I was getting tunes by note from the Kerr Collection; I chose pieces I already knew by ear. In about six months, I saw one heck of a difference in my playing! In the early sixties, Dougie MacPhee (pianist) was in Toronto and he was a great one for note reading; we'd often get into the books.''

Sandy's next violin arrived under just as amazing circumstances as his first - a Toronto Symphony member sold it to him for the amount of money Sandy had in his pocket at the time of purchase - thirty-five dollars!

In time, Sandy joined Johnny "Nel" MacDonald and Bill MacDonald in the organizing of Cape Breton-style dances in Toronto, the main locales being Liberty and St. Mary's Halls. Of the latter, he says, "It was a gathering place for Cape Bretoners, and Maritimers in general - we'd get great crowds. We'd hire special guests and keep the dances like they were down home - Winston Fitzgerald, Buddy MacMaster, Cameron Chisholm, Angus Chisholm, Johnny Wilmot, John Campbell, etc. I played at the dances myself on many Saturday nights and I found them excellent for fingering and bowing exercises.

"My first break on national television, on CBC TV's 'Ceilidh', was through Winnie Chafe - she invited me on. Confidence was one thing that really developed, playing with Buddy, Cameron, Angus and all those other good fiddlers. We became very close, and a lot of mutual respect evolved. There was total immersion in the music for a month at a time during the tapings. That show was good for Cape Breton music - it gave it a good shot in the arm!" More recently, Sandy has become a member of The Cape Breton Symphony, which had its birth on the John Allan Cameron Show.

In 1974, Sandy released a long-playing album which proved to generate a renewed interest in the recording of local fiddle music. "I encouraged the other players to record, and it opened the floodgates!" he recalls.

A composer for some years, Sandy has produced over one hundred tunes, several of which are in active circulation among Island players. In addition, he has both a fiddle and fiddle-music collection. "I own twelve violins," he says. "One is a Russian model which won a prize for workmanship in the Soviet Union. Another is an 'Alexander Galiani' (1710) which I bought for only one hundred dollars." Sandy's sensitive delivery of slow airs is enhanced by this beautiful instrument, as is his treatment of music "closer to the floor". He says, "In the old strathspeys, I like to put in the old-time bowing that my mother used. It's hard to teach - you have to grow up with it - you have to feel it! Personally, I never took any kind of lessons."

As an employee of Air Canada, Sandy uses his flying privileges to help bring Cape Breton fiddling to all the corners of the world. However, "Cape Breton is always your home. I have a long-range plan of living there again some day."

David MacIsaac

Birth: February 5, 1955 in Halifax, Nova Scotia
Parents: Alex Dan MacIsaac and Frances MacDonald

"I can remember, when I was about three or four years of age, being in a grocery store humming fiddle tunes at the top of my voice." The son of old-time fiddler Alex Dan MacIsaac of Dunvegan, David received his Cape Breton music first-hand on a daily basis throughout his childhood. "My father played for dances in Halifax in the 1950's, and Carl MacKenzie would be at our house a lot when he was studying engineering; he met my father through their common interest in the fiddle. I also heard quite a bit of music through the old 78's. When I was aged five, I remember my father getting a record of Winston (Fitzgerald) playing 'The Cabot Hornpipe' - 'The Inverness Jig Medley' was on the other side.

"When I was six, my parents got me a little tin fiddle, but I lost interest in it when I got my first guitar at age nine. I suppose it was kind of a peer thing - none of my friends were into Scottish music; however, I played the guitar with my father at parties and the like.

"I played in rock groups all through junior high. I didn't start back at the fiddle again until about 1972. Sonny Murray was living near us in Halifax. One day he put on a tape he had just made of Angus Chisholm and John Allan Cameron - taped at Roddy MacDonald's. There was another tape on the same reel of Angus playing in 1950 - a solo tape of him playing 'Mallard Clog' and 'Tullochgorum'. It blew me away! Something snapped inside my head!

"I always liked the music, and I had a great love for the fiddle. I knew lots of tunes in my head, so it didn't take me long to scratch out a few pieces by ear. On Sunday afternoons, my father and I would drive 'er with the two fiddles in the kitchen. He'd show me the bowing, the different types of cuts and the ways to accent strathspeys; he'd do it slow enough for me to see how it was done. It took me a while because my brain was going faster than my fingers. Luckily, I had the patience and love to keep it up. Through my father, I learned to love the traditional fiddling of Ronald Kennedy and Angus Allan Gillis. They played lots of tunes that you rarely hear today; I've been trying to write quite a few of them down.

"I was fortunate to hear Angus Chisholm play at one of Buddy MacMaster's dances in Halifax. Just watching him hypnotized me! I went up and asked him for some advice, and he told me to learn to read music and to become familiar with the great Scottish collections. Since then, I've been fortunate to receive a lot of music - tapes and collections - from my friend, the late Roddy MacDonald of

Halifax. Presently I have two original Captain Simon Fraser collections, various Gow collections (eg. Niel Sr., Niel Jr., Nathaniel and John), the Glen collections, Charles Duff, Robert MacIntosh and Malcolm MacDonald - all quite rare; plus, I'm glad to own a number of manuscripts by Dan R. MacDonald. I think that Dan R. was the most consistent composer of fiddle music ever! I have some of his rarer tunes such as 'Rosewood Reel' on Bb, 'The Lockwood Jig' on F, 'The Fiddler's Green Road' on A, and 'Mrs. Neil R. MacDonald Strathspey' on B minor.

"I started collecting tapes from the beginning because I love to hear all the different players. I also try to get tunes off the tapes, especially those that just aren't found in books. I really prize some of the old tape recordings I have of Mary MacDonald, Angus Chisholm and Winston Fitzgerald. It's especially great to have tapes of fiddlers who never recorded commercially. I have about six hundred cassette and reel-to-reel recordings at present. I like to trade with other collectors; I always improve the quality of the older tapes by graphically equalizing them to take out the 'hiss' and 'boom'."

Giving his book and tape collections the attention they deserve, David has now become famous for his fascinating repertoire of fiddle tunes. "I like to put together mixtures of traditional, rarely-heard tunes and book tunes. It's always nice to come out with a few surprises." In March of 1981, during a musical display of some Mary MacDonald classics at the home of Margaret MacPhee in New Waterford, David earned the praise of his hostess. On that afternoon she exclaimed, "Those wonderful, old tunes - they bring tears to my eyes, they really do! If you weren't looking at him, you'd think that David was sixty or seventy years old!"

"Jerry Holland and I have a lot of fun playing together," David says of one of his closest musical friendships. "I think his tone is sweet and impeccable, and his compositions will stand up with any. His tunes are very original and 'tasty', and it takes a certain degree of proficiency to play many of them."

Accomplished on violin, guitar, bass, mandolin, tenor banjo and mandola, David is now a professional musician and travels the world with his comrades John Allan Cameron and Allie Bennett. "It's great to meet different fiddlers and to play your Cape Breton music for people who'd otherwise not get a chance to hear it." During most of his spare time, he journeys from community to community, a veritable Pied Piper, charming the hearts of all his associates with lively music and animated conversation.

Alex Francis MacKay

Birth: 1922 at Kingsville, Inverness County
Parents: Angus MacKay and Mary MacDonald

His Family: Alex Francis is not the only MacKay to have wielded a violin in recent history. He lists the following as having played: his grandfather, John MacKay; his father, Angus; his uncles, Peter and John Willie; and his brothers, Peter and Dannie (d. 1930). In addition, there is John MacDonald, his mother's brother.

His Influences: When Alex Francis was a boy, the family violin hung on the dining room wall, just high enough so only serious players could reach it. Angus MacKay used to "scratch a few tunes at night", but Alex doesn't really remember his father's music. He does recall, however, the pioneer recordings of Angus Allan Gillis, Dan J. Campbell and Angus Chisholm which were given many a spin on the old Gramophone. More Scottish music travelled over the air waves from stations CJFX and CJCB. As for his own musical beginnings, Alex Francis says, "I was just interested. Maybe it was born in me! There were players like Gordon MacQuarrie, Ronald MacLellan and Dan R. MacDonald who'd come to our house; I guess it was in the thirties. They knew we liked music - that's why they came. Gordon was an influence on me, but Dan R. gave me the most tips." Attending the picnics also afforded a youngster the chance to hear accomplished fiddlers, and the MacKays journeyed from Glendale to Margaree to take in such events.

His Early Years: By age fourteen, Alex Francis had begun his playing career, using a violin his brother Peter had. Another brother, Jimmy, can still visualize Alex's enthusiastic response to his new-found pastime, and says, "He was very anxious to learn. When he'd come from school, he'd go directly to the violin. There was an old class of violin players in the district, and when they'd come to the house, by listening and observing, he'd pick up a lot!"

In the early 1940's, Alex Francis received some training in music theory for the violin, as he explains: "I was about eighteen or twenty before I began reading music. Jimmy Gillis from Margaree used to visit here with his brother, Ambrose. He showed me how to read."

His Performances: "When I started out first, I played for dances in the schoolhouses. I was about nineteen or twenty. You'd be glad to get a couple of dollars then. I played with Dan R., Dan Hughie MacEachern, John

Willie MacEachern. The dances were held at Princeville, Glendale, Kingsville, etc." Sometimes the condition of the roads necessitated the use of horse and buggy by travelling fiddlers. Alex Francis also provided entertainment at the parish picnics staged in Broad Cove, Judique, Port Hawkesbury, Glendale, Big Pond and Margaree.

In 1941, Alex Francis shared the fiddling honors with Peter MacPhee and Angus Chisholm during the opening of the National Park at Ingonish. This was one of Alex's first public performances as a Scottish musician. Around ten years later, he played at a concert in Judique which featured a rare appearance by "Little" Jack MacDonald who was visiting from Detroit. Farther from home, Alex played regularly at the Cape Breton Club in Windsor, Ontario during an extended stay in that city while working for the Chrysler Corporation.

His Repertoire: "The old traditional tunes," says Alex Francis, "are pretty hard to beat, but as for books, I got most of mine from Dan R.; he got them overseas. When he was finished with them, he gave them to me - Gow, Marshall, Glen, Skinner - about two dozen books in all!"

His Violin: "I bought it in a pawnshop in Ontario in 1956. It's an Italian make - a Maggini. I got it for fifteen dollars. I like it very much."

In an area which has boasted the likes of "Big" Ronald MacLellan, Gordon MacQuarrie, Archie MacLellan, Dan Hughie MacEachern and John Alex MacEachen, Alex Francis has made his mark as an important fiddler. His Glendale dances in the early seventies were very popular but, now that he has decided to enjoy a period of rest, he has this observation: "Since I quit playing regularly, they've started making big money with the fiddle!"

A few selections by Alex Francis have been included in the albums entitled "The Music of Cape Breton" (Volumes 1 and 2).

Carl MacKenzie

Birth: 1938, a native of Washabuck, Cape Breton
Parents: John Stephen MacKenzie and Mary Anne Deveaux

Carl grew up in one of the most talented families imaginable, with all his brothers and sisters being able to produce fine Scottish music on a variety of instruments. In addition, an uncle named Neil Deveaux was a popular fiddler in the Washabuck area years ago.

Recalling his boyhood, Carl says, "As a youngster, I always thought a lot of Scotty Fitzgerald - there's no question about that! I heard him often on radio and at dances. Also, Dan Hughie MacEachern came often to our place, and I was amazed at him. I tried to play the fiddle at age nine or ten, but I got so frustrated that I gave it up for a while; a few years later, I picked it up again. The first tune I learned was 'The 42nd Highlanders' - I was about age twelve. When I went to high school in Iona, I remember meeting Francis Cameron (now Fr. Francis); he could play and was very good. By age sixteen or so, I was entertaining at the Legion in Iona, with my sister Jean on the piano.

"I played the guitar for a while - I used to accompany John Y. Gillis. When John Y. got going, I'd have to strum very fast and, by the end of the night, my fingers would be raw! He was a very good player. I remember that one of his favourite tunes was 'The Bonny Lass of Head Lake' by Gordon MacQuarrie."

In the early 1960's, Carl studied civil engineering at the Nova Scotia Technical Institute. After graduating, he remained in Halifax where he regularly performed at the Cape Breton Club. Frequently he became involved in all-night music sessions when dance players such as Buddy MacMaster came to town. By now, Carl's distinctive tone and left-hand technique had won him extensive praise. "But," he is quick to assert, "you never stop learning! For instance, it took me a long time to perfect my bowing. I used to hold the bow in a more or less classical manner, but I was always intrigued by Scotty's (i.e. Winston Fitzgerald's) grip, which basically consists of supporting the bow between the thumb and index finger of the right hand." Carl mastered this local technique several years ago and admits, "It improved my cuts quite a bit and, by applying pressure with my thumb on the inside of the frog, I can get more volume when I need it. It made 'The Tullochgorum' a cinch to play!" Carl has recently released a thrilling recording of Skinner's arrangement of this latter piece. It features all the written variations, each delivered with the ease and grace universally associated with Carl's music. "I recorded it at the urging of Dougie MacPhee," he says. "I had been playing it for ten years before I put it on record. I always go for variety and for tunes that are reasonably difficult and challenging."

Along with a small contingent of Cape Breton musicians, Carl once visited and performed in Scotland. He claims that the overseas audiences were slightly bewildered: "The general impression was that our music couldn't possibly sound like anything they might have had in Scotland before J. Scott Skinner. But I say our fiddling couldn't have evolved in that short a time - that is, since the early 1800's; it's barely over one hundred-fifty years since the pioneers arrived! In Scotland, the violins and books were destroyed, but our settlers took the old music with them and it survived. We play the same music as the old pipers. Also, if Duncan MacQuarrie (a former New Waterford resident) was living, he'd be over one hundred years old. Duncan learned from his father. How could they have invented a new style of fiddling? Even in isolated sections of Cape Breton, the music has tremendous similarities; they all have fiddling that dates back hundreds of years!"

A staunch supporter of Cape Breton music, Carl has some interesting theories on the teaching of traditional-style playing: "You make a better player if you learn by ear first, and **then** start note reading later - that's the way **I** teach. We'll lose this Cape Breton style if we have too much classical instruction. It's important to have the players who play the **real** Cape Breton music showing the youngsters how to be fiddlers. And, I feel it's more important to stress the feeling in the music than how to hold the fiddle and bow. I tell my students to hold the violin in the position that's most comfortable; most of the good Cape Breton players hold it like that, though it's wrong from the classical point of view. It's easier to get the Cape Breton sound holding the violin in the method that I use; for first position playing, your fingers are right in line."

Besides the application of "cuts" with the bow, Carl feels there is another aspect of local playing which cannot be ignored: "You'll never make a very good fiddler unless you make good use of the little finger (on the left hand)!"

Carl MacKenzie continues to be an influential musician both locally and abroad. "Even in Washington," he says, "our music goes down very, very well. The head of the music department of a university in Seattle offered me a chance to teach Cape Breton music there for one year."

His albums:
"Welcome to Your Feet Again" Rounder 7005
"Tullochgorum" CLM Records CLM 1000

Hector MacKenzie

Birth: 1933 in Washabuck, Cape Breton
Parents: John Stephen MacKenzie and Mary Anne Deveaux

Iona, accessible only by ferry from most directions, boasts many a MacNeil, MacKinnon, MacLean and MacKenzie. Here, music flows as sweetly from the finger as the Scottish brogue trickles off the tongue. "In our family," says Hector, "four boys and two girls played. There was only one fiddle in the house, though; we got it from Johnny Brown who lived just across the river. My brother, Charlie, was the first of us to take up the violin. Then one winter, when I was aged twelve, I got the measles; I was recuperating when I started to play. I used only two fingers for a long time in the beginning. I learned from Charlie who in turn learned from Philip MacKinnon, Dan's son." With a touch of the wry humour that has become one of his trademarks, he adds, "After that, I never looked back!"

"Michael Anthony MacLean was the most important influence on me, though many fiddlers used to arrive at our house, usually for a party." As for the building of one's repertoire, he recalls, "You'd go to the dances and pick the tunes up by ear. The ear was well developed and you'd only have to hear a tune once or twice. I don't know if I could do that now, since I rely more on reading music. I didn't learn to read until Charlie taught me in 1947. The first books I used were 'The Cape Breton Collection', 'Kerr's' and 'The 1000 Tune Fiddle Book'.

"I also played the guitar for a while. I'd often chord for Archie MacKenzie and John Y. Gillis at the dances. I was fifteen or sixteen and was the only guitar player around at that time; there were few pianos then either."

Hector received a solid musical education, like many a Cape Breton fiddler, at the numerous household and community gatherings. "In my late teens, I was playing for dances. There were about a dozen one-room schoolhouses around here then, and each one would have a dance. At house parties and weddings, I often teamed up with Michael Anthony (MacLean)." In 1947, Hector entertained over CJFX Radio in Antigonish, as part of a music festival.

When he eventually journeyed far from home, Hector found a much different musical environment than the one in which he had grown up; however, the experience was fuel for one of his anecdotes: "From 1953-57, I was in British Columbia. I bought a fiddle out there, but I didn't play much music. In one trio I worked with, the piano player could only accompany in Bb, so we always played everything in the same key!"

In Iona, an institution has arisen whose purpose is the preservation and promotion of Celtic culture. Hector explains his association with that institution: "I've been involved with the Iona Highland Village since the beginning - twenty years. I'm usually on the entertainment committee, and I often act as master-of-ceremonies. I enjoy M.C.-ing Scottish concerts." In this latter capacity, Hector's distinctive wit is always much in evidence.

The multi-talented MacKenzie family received network television exposure in 1978 when the Irish group Ryan's Fancy produced a program featuring Hector, his mother, brothers, and sisters, and a "houseful" of other dancers, singers and players - all related! More recently, Hector has become the musical mainstay at the Iona Legion.

Hector, a fan of William Marshall's, has also delved into the realm of composition. One of his originals, "Penny Hill Jig", has been recorded by his brother, Carl; the piece was inspired by a "small hill out behind our barn". Highly ranked among Hector's favourite composers and players is Dan Hughie MacEachern. "We stay in touch with him all the time. He sends us his music, new and old. We have many of his manuscripts." It was Hector who hand-copied all the tunes for Dan Hughie's first publication of original compositions (Charlie MacKenzie is undertaking volume two).

A sample of Hector MacKenzie's fiddling style is now available for listening on a long-playing record released through the Iona Highland Village organization.

PENNY HILL JIG

H. MacKenzie

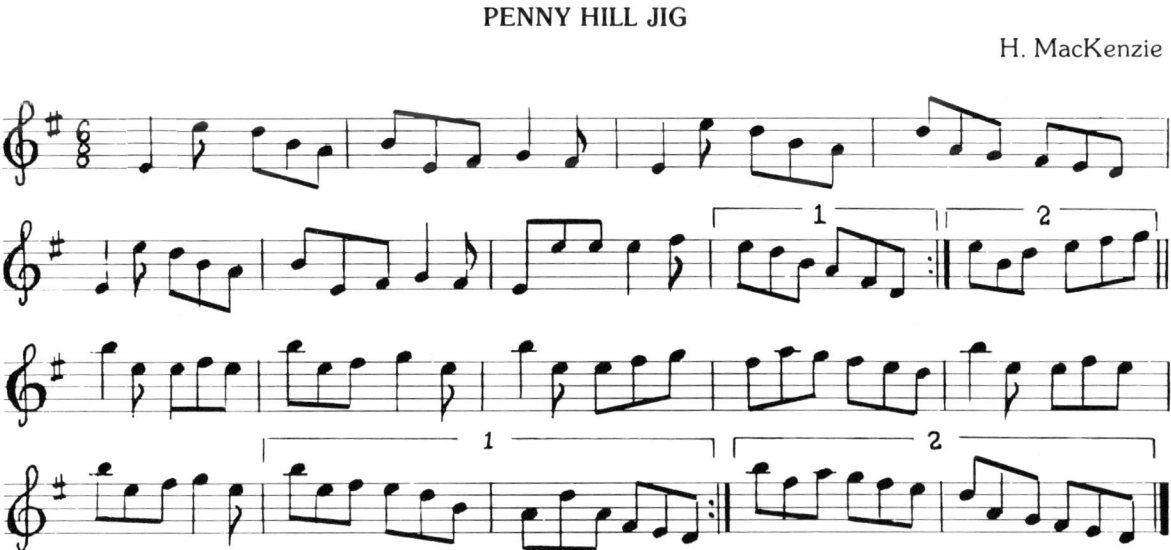

Joe MacLean

Birth: September 22, 1916 in Lower Washabuck
Parents: Vincent MacLean and Theresa MacNeil

"My father played a bit himself, and he liked us to play. We all took turns on the one fiddle. At home, you had chores to do, but you'd play in the evenings. I was around sixteen or seventeen before I had a good grasp of the violin. I played first at school dances - pretty well always unaccompanied. You didn't care whether you made money or not.

"Hector MacKinnon, Fr. Sam Campbell and others would drop into the house and play. Visitors would just come around - uninvited but always welcome. You'd pick up tunes by ear; the older people had them and would jig them in Gaelic. About the first tunes I learned were 'The Irish Washerwoman' and 'Calum Crùbach'.

"From 1934-39, I was working in Nyanza in MacRae's General Store. On Saturday nights, I'd drive over to North East Margaree to hear Angus Allan Gillis and Angus Chisholm; you could learn a lot by just looking. Usually on Friday nights, I'd play in the schoolhouses - Middle River, Bucklaw, Baddeck, all around that territory. There were no pianos; you'd just sit in the corner and eat the dust! You were good 'till two or three in the morning and then would end up getting two or three bucks."

In 1939, Joe settled in Sydney, and, after a year at the Steel Plant, joined the CNR as a trainman and conductor. He also became part of the musical community there, associating with fiddlers such as Donald MacLellan, Tena Campbell, and Bill Lamey. "I played a lot with Bill," says Joe. "He was reading music, and you realized yourself that it was the thing to do. There were a lot of good tunes and you wanted to learn them - the simplest way was to read.

"When Dan R. MacDonald came back after the war, he told me about J. Murdoch Henderson in Scotland, and I started corresponding with him. He'd write to tell me what was available and, if the price was right, I'd order the collections. I also dealt with Grant Book Sellers in Edinburgh; I got their address from Bill Lamey." Joe now possesses a fine library of rare fiddle-music books, and he makes good use of them, being known for his ability to sift the finest melodies from a publication. "It's one thing on paper, and another thing to play it. Sometimes, if you play a tune directly from a book, it might not sound that good. So, you make changes here or there, put a little flourish on it and make something of it. I often picked tunes that were good for dancing. There's music for just sitting down and listening to, but it wouldn't have the swing for dancing. I always had a preference for dance playing; I found it rewarding. It would keep you practiced in your music; you'd keep the tunes in your head **and** in your fingers.''

Joe believes that his distinctive fiddling style developed while he was performing at dances during the 1940's and 50's. At these events, a strong rhythm, accurate timing and a good 'swing' could be established. "We played at Nelga Beach, St. Theresa's and the outlying halls in Boisdale, Waterford, etc. We always loved going to New Waterford. Sometimes, we'd go to all-night affairs there, and play with Duncan MacQuarrie, Jack MacNeil, 'Little' Mary MacDonald and Johnny Archie MacIsaac. The usual pianists would be Margaret MacPhee, Mabel Beaton and Mary Jess MacDonald. At dances, I played with Lila Hashem, Beattie Wallace, Marie MacLellan and Janet Cameron."

Joe gradually built a large following of fans as he appeared in person, on radio and on records. The records blended his talents with those of Lila Hashem, Peter Dominic and a host of other accompanists, and the result was an increased demand for Joe's playing. He was now required to make personal appearances in Detroit. Toronto, and Boston. At home, his violin duets with his sister, Theresa, were highly acclaimed as well. "I played from the 1940's into the 60's," he says, "and then, I suppose, the rock 'n roll coming in changed it all. But, there seems to have been a revival in the seventies."

Soon Joe MacLean can proudly celebrate fifty years as a Cape Breton fiddler. Though his beautiful Antonio Loveri is a far cry from his very first instrument, he maintains the attitude he once had as a boy on the shores of Washabuck: "In the earlier years, if you heard something, you weren't satisfied until you learned it. You had the incentive. You loved the music!"

Among Joe MacLean's recordings are:
Rodeo RLP 107
Celtic CX 12 and CX 32
Banff-Rodeo RBS 1246
Celtic 045 (78 rpm)
Celtic 043 (78 rpm with Bill Lamey)

John Neil MacLean

Birth: April 13, 1930 at Gabarus Lake, Cape Breton
Parents: George W. MacLean and Effie MacDonald

The southeast section of Cape Breton Island has produced its share of fiddlers: "Little" Angus MacDonald and Duncan L. MacIntyre (b. 1909) of the French Road; Joe MacDonald and his son John Joe of Fiddler's Lake; "Old" Allan MacKinnon, a popular wedding player from Fourchu who died around the turn of the century; Philip MacLeod and Allison MacCormick of modern-day Fourchu; and Donald John MacKinnon, of whom John Neil says, "My father used to speak of a player called Donald John MacKinnon who used to hold dances on the old wooden bridges in the area."

John Neil's love for the violin came as naturally as his bowing style. "I heard radio programs on CJCB; I heard Tena Campbell play a lot. My family - they all liked Scotch music. Earl MacVicar, a neighbour, played a bit; he used to come up, and that helped get me started. In the beginning, I borrowed Earl's fiddle - that was the first time I got a violin in my hand; I was about twelve. I guess the first tunes I learned by ear were 'Haste to the Wedding' and 'The Crooked Stove Pipe'.

"The late Alex Ferguson of Ferguson's Lake was the schoolmaster; he taught at the little one-room schoolhouse near our place. His brother was Willie 'the Fiddler'. Alex knew a lot about music, and he boarded here at my father's house. In the evenings, we'd get the fiddles out and pick a few tunes. I was about fifteen.

"In later years, I got quite a few books - Henderson's 'The Skye', 'The Athole', etc. Once I started to read, I learned by the books; before that, I would hear a tune once and I had it! I'd listen to CJFX and get tunes off the radio - lots of tunes. That was about the only way to get them.

"At about age sixteen, I bought a violin through Simpson's catalogue. It was only a cheap one - about forty dollars. Then I sent for another one, and two fiddles came. I kept the best one and I've had it till this day.

"From age sixteen until into my twenties, I played at dances in Fourchu, Marion Bridge, Gabarus, Grand Mira. There'd be about one dance a week; in the daytime, I'd be going to school. When I started, I used guitar for accompaniment; my guitar player used to be Stewart MacLean - he drowned a few years ago. Later on, pianos and sound systems came along to help a fellow out. Then, back in the fifties, I played over CJCB quite a few times.

"I worked for seven years in town. I used to go into the Venetian Gardens when Winston Fitzgerald was playing; I guess I was in my thirties. Anywhere there was Scotch music, you'd find me there! I still enjoy every minute of it! I never miss 'Scottish Strings' on CJFX, and I really enjoy Donnie Campbell's program over CJCB FM.

"I'm a member of the Sydney Scottish Violins - I look forward to that. We get together to practice, mostly. I think there's over twenty in our group. Now, I'm going to try composing, to see if I can write a few jigs or something."

A sample of John Neil's music is now available on an album entitled "Cape Breton Scottish Fiddle"; his accompanist on that occasion was pianist Phyllis MacLeod. Besides being an avid fiddler, John Neil is a fluent Gaelic speaker. "I was brought up on it," is his comment on his control of this ancient tongue.

John Neil MacLean revels in the joy of making music in his home. "Good friends of mine often come to visit - Dougie MacPhee, John Shaw, Sonny Slade, Paul Cranford. We play together."

Johnny "Washabuck" MacLean

Birth: December 2, 1925 in Lower Washabuck
Parents: "Red" Rory and Ellen Ann MacLean

During the long winter nights of his childhood, Johnny "Washabuck" heard Highland music from his father, as well as from relatives Joe and Michael Anthony MacLean. At age nine, he was given a small, tin violin by neighbour Francis MacDonald, and it was upon this instrument that he produced his earliest music while seated on the stairs where he could tap his feet.

Though he found that some of the older players were reluctant to share their favourite tunes, Johnny gradually assembled a solid repertoire of good pieces. The music of the following three violinists had a tremendous effect on him at age fifteen: Willie Danny "Betsy" MacDonald and Willie Probert, both of Middle River, and John Alex "the Fiddler" MacNeil of Gillis Point. In time, Johnny became proficient enough to play for schoolhouse dances in Washabuck, sometimes utilizing guitar accompaniment. Later, he made appearances at the Masonic Hall in Baddeck.

In 1942, Johnny's playing was interrupted when he joined the Army. After two years and eight months with that organization, he took employment with the railroad and on the old Aspy Ferry. After another short stint in the Army, he signed up at the Sydney Steel Plant, and, while a resident of metropolitan Cape Breton, befriended Bill Lamey who drove a bread truck at that time. Bill strongly encouraged Johnny to learn to read music, stressing that a fiddler must master each tune before moving on to the next. CJCB Radio began a program which featured Johnny in combination with violinist John Willie Campbell and pianist Lawrence MacDougall.

After moving to Toronto in 1962, he continued to get media exposure with several appearances on a network radio show called "Opry North". This was followed by a regular position on CBC TV's "Ceilidh" from Halifax.

Johnny has owned his "Henning" violin for 35 years. It is an old English instrument and he has promised the previous owner that he will never part with it. Being also a very good stepdancer, he can accurately execute some ancient and difficult steps passed on to him through the family of Dan MacKinnon of Washabuck.

Both Johnny and his son, a medal-winning piper, remain musically active in Ontario.

Michael Anthony MacLean

Birth: 1911 at MacKay's Point (Washabuck), Cape Breton
Parents: Vincent MacLean and Theresa MacNeil

"My father played a number of tunes; he played them well and he taught us. The violin was in the house when we arrived on the scene; he helped us to tune it and encouraged us. Peter F. picked it up first, then Alexander, Murdoch, myself, Joe, John and Theresa - seven children out of twelve could play. When I began, I was around sixteen. We used to take shifts at the fiddle until our dad bought a new one - that eased the time limit on each player!"

Some outstanding violinists spent long hours "making the rafters ring" in Vincent MacLean's home: Dan MacKinnon, John Alex "The Fiddler" MacNeil, John Francis Campbell, Agnes Campbell, "Red" Rory MacLean and Jimmy MacInnis of Skye Glen. "They used to cross on the ice in the winter, and in the summer a ferry boat operated from Baddeck to MacKay's Point. My father was a good stepdancer and Dan MacKinnon was wonderful for dance music! As a matter of fact, Dan's son, Hector, was one of the outstanding dancers on Cape Breton Island; he had such nifty legwork!

"As for the family, we'd play together; Dad would do the dancing. Getting tunes was no problem - I was always listening. The bowing came as a sort of natural thing, though I definitely picked up things from Angus Allan Gillis by watching." Here, Michael Anthony adds a point which some experts on Cape Breton music will verify: "It seemed we had a different sound to our music (ie. in the Iona area); there's no real way to explain it."

The motivation for Michael Anthony and his family is obvious - a love of Scottish fiddling. "I'd play at weddings, house rackets and at any little ceilidh, as well as at dances in Baddeck, Whycocomagh, Iona, Washabuck - all over! If music was needed, we'd play. Mostly, it was just for entertainment. At dances, the payment was light - about $3.00, in the beginning. I played unaccompanied at first, but later had John S. MacNeil on the piano and the "Lighthouse Boys" (ie. Stephen and Joe I. MacLean) on the organ. Most recently, Jean MacKenzie accompanied me. It was my father's second violin that I used mostly then, but the one I have now I got from my brother, Joe; I think he got it in Boston."

An ardent supporter of the Fiddlers' Association, he says, "I approve of developing the music; the fiddling is in no trouble now!" He is pleased that some of his grandchildren have taken to the violin.

Sandy MacLean

Birth: 1893, a native of Foot Cape, near Strathlorne, Inverness County
Parents: Mr. and Mrs. Murdoch MacLean

"The fellow that owned the Isle of Rum got sale for it, and it was turned into a place for wild game - like a park. The MacLeans had to leave - it was rough in them days! My great-grandfather, Donald Bàn (1794-1874), got a grant of two hundred acres and settled on this quarter - Foot Cape. My grandfather, John MacLean (1823-1911), was three years of age when they left Rum in 1826. They set sail for Buenos Aires, but were warned of the cannibals there, so they shifted their course to Mulgrave.

"My grandfather played a little, and my father played fair. My uncle was a good player - Charles William MacLean. There was lots of music in the family - even the sewing machine was a Singer."

Sandy MacLean, known in "The Language of the Garden" as MacMhurchaidh Iain 'ic Dhomhnuill, began experimenting with the violin in 1905. "I played the bagpipes before I played the violin," he says, "but I got sick and never touched the pipes after 1916. I got taught on the violin by Allan Gillis, starting in 1911 - though I'd been playing six years before then. Allan was a professional dancer and a boxer - he held a championship belt for Minnesota. Then, he travelled with the circus for nine years as a dancer - you talk about a stepdancer! Allan went to school with my uncles, and he came to our house. He saw the violin on the wall and asked who was playing. When he found out it was me, he said, 'Go to McNutt's Store and get a tutoring book.' " Sandy studied theory for three years with Mr. Gillis, and then took one year of bowing. "Before I met Allan," he says in jest, "I thought the musical scale went A, B, C, D, E, F, G, H, I, J, ... !"

His brothers Kenny and Murdoch were both good fiddlers, but Sandy was destined to become one of Cape Breton's most noted Scottish musicians. His first violin, however, was not quite a Stradivarius, as he explains: "You'd see an advertisement to send for perfumed lockets. I got twenty-four and they were selling at ten cents a piece. So, the company sent me a two-dollar-and-forty-cent violin; but, my uncle bought me a good one later at McNutt's Store."

In 1912, Sandy made his first of several trips to the Boston area, where for a while he was employed at a mental hospital. In the early twenties, he worked in western Canada. "In 1928, I went back to Boston again - I'd be thirty-five then. I liked Boston alright. There was a fiddling contest there in 1929, and there were twenty-one players in it from all over; I believe it was in the Intercolonial Hall. I took first prize - twenty dollars. 'Big' Dan Hughie MacEachern got second - fifteen dollars.'' Other fiddling acquaintances Sandy made in Boston included Ranny Graham, ''Tall'' Charlie MacKinnon from Lake Ainslie and ''Curly'' Charlie MacKinnon from Antigonish. ''I pulled out in 1930,'' he says. ''It's fifty-one years since I left Boston.''

Though Sandy is very generous in his praise of the violinists with whom he has associated through the years, a few deserve special mention: ''Donald Beaton - I thought a lot of him. My uncle used to bring him up and he'd stay all night. He was the man who wrote out 'Maggie Brown's Jig' for me. Then, there was John A. MacDonald of Broad Cove Marsh.'' In addition, there was Alex Young of Foot Cape, Ned MacKinnon of Cooper's Pond, Mary Beaton MacDonald, Alex ''John Y.'' Beaton, Malcolm Beaton and, his all-time favourite, perhaps: ''You can put this down - I thought the world of 'Little' Jack MacDonald's playing. He was so accurate, and such a neat player!''

As for composing, a number of Sandy's original pieces were published in 1940 in Gordon MacQuarrie's collection. These were by name ''Sandy MacLean's Dream'', ''Lila MacIsaac's Favourite'', ''Palace Theatre Clog'' and ''Dismissal Reel''. Of the latter, he says, ''I'd play it when the movie would be winding up in the old Temple Hall - I composed it for that purpose.''

DISMISSAL REEL by Sandy MacLean

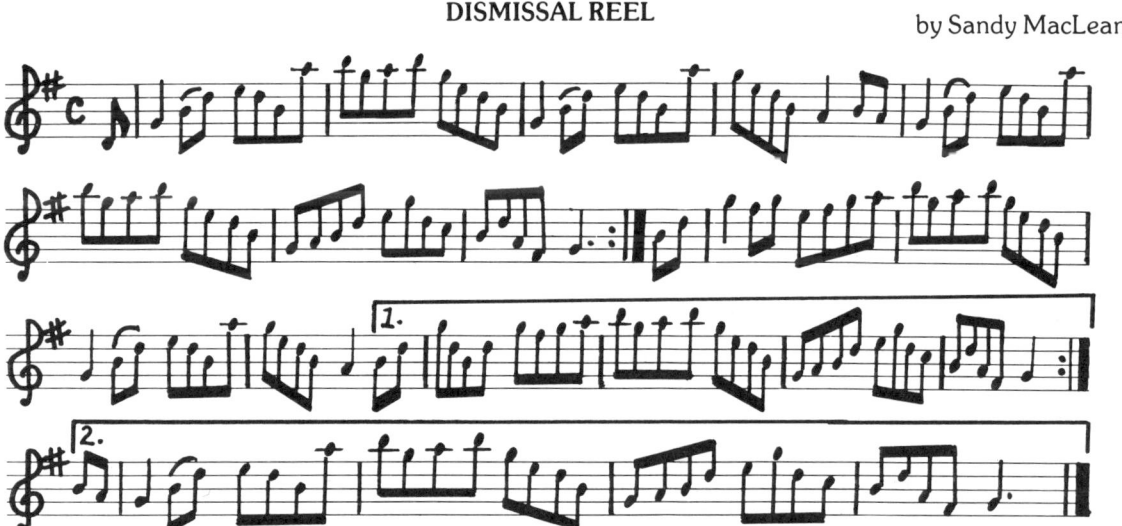

The memory of the music of Sandy MacLean's best years is deeply etched in the minds of those fortunate enough to hear him play. Seldom has a local violinist been so highly touted by so many of his fellow fiddlers. This adulation has been perpetuated for many years, as demonstrated in the words of Joseph MacInnis in the 1943-44 edition of Eilean Cheap Breatann: ''As a Scottish violinist, Mr. MacLean is considered by his contemporaries as the leading strathspey and reel player in the province. His strathspey and reel playing is inspiring and plaintive.''

Donald MacLellan

Birth: April 8, 1918 at Princeville, Cape Breton
Parents: "Big" Ronald MacLellan (d. 1935) and Mary Ann MacDonald

Legendary fiddler, "Big" Ronald MacLellan, gave Cape Breton no less than three outstanding violinists: sons Joseph and Donald, and daughter Theresa. "When did I learn to play? It's a long story, in a sense. I heard my dad play on a lot of occasions, but he used to say to me, 'You'll never make a fiddler' - that was after hearing my brother Joe play. I remember Joe's fiddling quite well; he was very good!" Donald says.

"My father was a sort of rambling person; he never stayed too long in one place. An awful lot of the time, he was away building forges in different areas across the country.

"I didn't play much at home. I moved on up with my cousin, James MacDonald of West Bay Road - they called him Jimmy Ranald. I stayed with him for a period of three and a half years, from age eleven to fourteen. I got a fiddle belonging to Mrs. Jim Lamey; it was a fiddle my dad used to play on. She brought it over to Jimmy MacDonald's one day.

"After I left Jimmy's and went back home, I took more interest in playing the violin. I was hearing tunes from my dad and brother, and I listened to the other fiddlers in our area - like Alexander MacDonald and Ernie Morrison. At age fourteen, I was playing at dances near home - sometimes there'd be organ accompaniment. We had an organ at home too.

"After my brother Joe died (1935), I started reading music. I went over to Gordon MacQuarrie's - he was the man who taught me. Gordon had taken a correspondence course himself, and he had had some tutoring from Vincent MacLellan and John Alex Gillis (of Alba), a violin maker. He drew me the scales for the violin, and he advised me to keep my eyes open, to follow the dots and practice! Scott Skinner's was about the first book I got, then Lowe's collection and Ryan's. Reading didn't change my style greatly - it was simply a matter of learning more tunes. However, I play a lot of pieces that don't have names; they were played by different fiddlers. Sometimes men working in lumbercamps would bring new tunes into an area from other parts of the Island. Then, also, I have a lot of my dad's tunes.

"I played up in Hawkesbury, Point Tupper and at the schoolhouses in Glendale, Princeville, etc. I also performed at picnics. The musicians at that time didn't get much money - they were all charitable affairs. But, I was a trapper too - muskrat, mink, otter, fox. I trapped with an Indian from Whycocomagh - we made a buck at that work!

"In 1937, I was in Halifax. In 1938, I worked with Chappell Brothers in Sydney. Bill Lamey and I played over CJCB Radio in 1940 for Eastern Bakeries, with Lila Hashem at the piano; Joe MacLean would join us the odd time. In 1942, I won a cup playing in New Glasgow - 'Championship of Eastern Nova Scotia'.

In 1943, I went in the army. I never carried the violin in the service because, if I don't have a few people around interested in fiddling, I tend not to bother with it. After the army - I was in 'till 1945 - I worked around Sydney until '47; I had a dance at the Carpenter's Hall on Friday nights.

"I came up here to Toronto in 1947. I did a heck of a lot of fiddling here. I got involved with the Gaelic Society - there were several branches and a lot of free playing. Then, I worked often with Johnny Wilmot, Johnny MacLean and Sandy MacIntyre. I bettered my reading and got a few pointers along the way, but it's hard to get professors to help you with Scottish music, though they can improve your position work.

"My records were made in the mid-fifties, I believe. They were recorded at CJCB for the Celtic label. We could use the studio after 10:00 o'clock p.m. - Robbie Robertson was the engineer. I made six 78's and one Lp by myself. The MacLellan Trio (with sisters Theresa and Marie) made two long-plays.

"I've been pretty busy in Ontario: I attended the St. Andrew's concerts at Alexandria from 1959 'till the early 60's; I've played at the Highland Games at Maxville, with Mrs. Donald MacPhee and Viola MacCuaig at the piano; I won the Mod Ontario Trophy two years running in 1976 and '77; and I played at dances at Ottawa, Sudbury, Windsor, Hamilton, Brantford and St. Catherines, as well as Boston and Detroit.

"I have some collections that are pretty rare, such as the Ellis Howe and the Peter MacMillan, and I've always picked up violins - at the moment, I have fourteen. I have an old Klotz with a beautiful tone and it answers well to the old-time music.

"As far as my repertoire, I just play the tunes that I fancy. I've made changes in many tunes - it's like figures of speech. There are many things you can do to improve tunes."

The music of Donald MacLellan is often termed dynamic and inspiring. His strathspey playing has been described as well nigh impeccable. He is certainly his father's son - physically, musically.

John Alex MacLellan

Birth: August 21, 1917 at Mount Pleasant near South West Margaree
Parents: Hughie S. MacLellan and Jessie Anne Gillis

John Alex's "people" originally settled in Mount Pleasant, but, in 1928, his family moved to S.W. Margaree. Many of his relatives were fine musicians: "I had three uncles who were violinists and, from the oldest to the youngest, they were John Archie, Alex and Ranald Gillis. Ranald was particularly good, and was a great composer; I used to know all of his compositions. He wrote a lot in Bb - mostly strathspeys and reels with the old flavour!" In addition, John Alex's maternal grandmother played, as did a distant relative named Ronald MacDougall, and even his mother could get a tune or two out of the violin.

"I started playing when I was around 12 years of age. My mother encouraged me and, with the help of those uncles I mentioned, I learned to read music by age 14. Uncle Ranald helped me more than the others because he visited us more. He had a few good books of music then.

"The first collection I borrowed was 'The Scottish Violinist' by Scott Skinner, which I got from Angus Allan Gillis when I was 16 or 17. Another fiddler, Fr. Rory MacNeil, had a library of music and, luckily for me, he was very willing to share those books as long as I looked after them."

John Alex made his first public appearance at a concert in S.W. Margaree's old red schoolhouse. In time, he realized that there was a great deal to be learned by observing the established fiddlers. He recalls, "I always watched the older players, although I was reading music. In 'dancing strathspeys' in particular, they often changed the endings to suit the dancer. Knowing the music well, I'd spot those changes right away! Stepdancing and fiddling went hand-in-hand in the old days. The player had to have his 'time' right to suit the individual dancer; for instance, some dancers preferred 'The King George Strathspey', or 'the old backstringers', as we used to call them. With these, the first turn was usually played on the back strings, while the second turn was played on the front.

"I began playing for dances at different halls with different players. Sometimes I'd team up with Archie Neil Chisholm, Angus Allan Gillis, John Grant MacFarlane, John Alex 'the Big Fiddler' MacDonald, or Archie Kennedy, Ronald's son."

One of John Alex's all time favourite listening experiences involved another of Ronald Kennedy's sons: "When I was 28, I heard Joe Kennedy put on a performance I'll never forget. We were gathered at Hughie Dan MacDonnell's in Deepdale, and I had gone to bed early, but I could hear the music coming up from downstairs and it was terrific! Joe played and played and I just sat up there and listened!

"At my first dances I got $5.00 a night - good money at that time! Besides fiddling, I was doing some farming, and we had a sawmill on our place. I made a few extra dollars with the fiddle, but it wouldn't pay you to depend on it, even though gasoline was only 19¢ a gallon when I was getting $5.00 a night.

"All the lancers were hard - they've been out for years. In the Saratoga, there were three slow figures and three fast - six in all. It was hard on the fiddler and hard on the dancers. Each figure would take roughly seven minutes, and the dancers would get a break for a few minutes between them while the fiddler was resting. We used jigs for the slow figure and reels and hornpipes for the fast. Then there was the plain lancer.

"A prompter could buy a call-book from Eaton's at one time. Tony MacDonald from Port Hawkesbury could sing the calls right out! He called at St. Patrick's Hall in Margaree from about 1938 to '41."

Not all fiddling is for accompanying dancing. "I play some tunes that I call 'parlor airs'. These are at a slower pace and are just for listening. In 'The Skye Collection', there's one called 'John of Badenyon' on Bb, which is sometimes played as a reel, but it sounds much better played slowly."

Through the years, John Alex has spent many memorable hours in the company of great fiddlers, men such as Sandy MacLean, Gordon MacQuarrie, Angus Chisholm and Malcolm H. Gillis. As for the distinct flavour of Cape Breton music, John Alex feels that "all the changes our master players made in the tunes from Scotland were generally for the best!

"In the last few years, I haven't played as much, though I still love the music; you see, I injured one of my fingers. Anyway, I think television did away with all the 'ceilidh-ing'."

Of his children, Rannie and Dougald play the fiddle, while Ann and Mary Jessie play the piano, following in their mother's footsteps.

Theresa MacLellan

Birth: Riverside, Inverness County
Parents: "Big" Ronald MacLellan and Mary Ann MacDonald

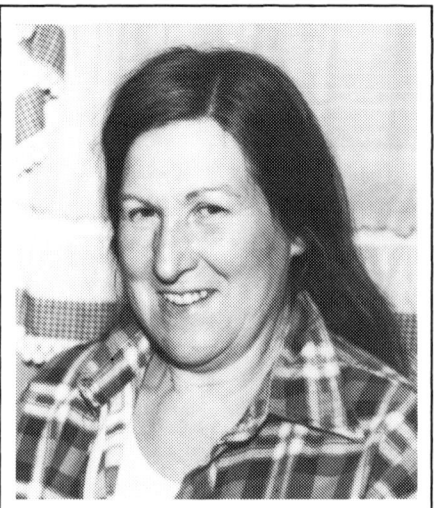

This MacLellan family has produced a remarkable number of first-class Scottish musicians. Theresa's father, "Big" Ronald, is remembered by most as a fiddling as well as physical giant, and his genius for Cape Breton music has been inherited by his children: the late "Baby" Joe, violinist; Marie, pianist; Donald F., violinist, and Theresa.

In Theresa's words, "I was eight when I started, but I was very interested in the violin before that. When I was four or five, I used to fall asleep in the chair listening to my brother (Donald), Dan R. MacDonald and Gordon MacQuarrie. Gordon used to say, 'Watch - that girl'll be a violinist some day!'

"When my brother was playing, he'd offer me the violin because I was watching so much. One day, he promised he'd get me a wristwatch if I'd take the violin and try it. I played a tune called 'Cock of the North' the very first day! From then on, Donald was the coach. Everyone would come to the house to hear me, but I'd run off into the fields because I was shy."

Theresa's brother, John A., vividly remembers her first days of playing, and he says, "You'd almost have to support the fiddle for her; her little hands would barely make the fingerboard!"

As for reading music, Theresa recalls, "One day Donald wrote out the scale for me. After he went to Sydney to work at about seventeen, Mama took over. She really made me go at it! I was playing dances when I was nine years of age - Grand Anse, Port Hawkesbury, and places like that. Marie (her sister) used to play the Hawaiian guitar then - there weren't many pianos.

"The first place I ever played was at a two-day picnic at West Bay Road - I was nine. My mother took me up and I played with all the older fiddlers, like Dan C. MacDonald, Kitchener MacDonald and Bernie MacDonald. Mama said that I gave Dan C. a queer look when he played a few off-notes in one of the tunes."

Some of Theresa's early instruction came from a very talented organist and violinist whose specialty, however, was music for Catholic Church services. "Marie and I joined the choir in Princeville. Steve

MacGillivray was the director. Steve showed me more notes and music. On cold nights, he used to say, 'Look at that poor little girl!' - I guess I was very thin then. He'd feel sorry for me and give me all his cough drops.

"Marie and I played for all kinds of dances, and we entertained a lot of people at home. The first concert I played at 'under the stars' was at the Antigonish Highland Games; I went up on the train, and I've been going up quite regularly ever since. Once, you used to be able to meet all the fiddlers there. Sometimes, you'd play with fourteen or fifteen violinists - all fantastic players!

"In the 40's, we made a 78 rpm in Sydney as The MacLellan Trio (ie. Theresa, Marie, and Donald) - Peter Dominic played the drums with us. I was fifteen or sixteen at the time. It's about twenty years since we made an Lp in Halifax; George Taylor set that up." (Celtic nos. CX 13 and 22).

In MacLellan family tradition, Theresa excells at pipe marches, and has earned many a resounding applause at Scottish concerts for her powerful delivery of the same. "I like marches and waltzes very much - and hornpipes too! Proper timing and proper bowing are important when you're playing marches; if you play them too fast or too slow, they don't sound right. The timing grew with me, and I never took any bowing studies - it came natural to me; though, people sometimes ask me where I took lessons. Once a woman said to me, 'The violin doesn't control **you** - **you** control the violin!' "

Though Theresa plays the piano and a little bit of guitar, it has been with her violin that she has earned many trips abroad. She numbers among her favourite experiences playing at the Montreal Olympics, being part of the cast of CBC TV's "Ceilidh", and entertaining the Queen. Locally, Theresa and Marie have established themselves as a popular dance-playing team. "At a dance, you're at your best! Once you get going, you're relaxed. Another thing that turns you on is if other violinists are listening in.

"The men are strong players. You've gotta get in there with them, follow them and drive 'er with them! I was the only woman playing with those men for a long time. If you have the quality, there's no disadvantage being a woman!"

Theresa on record: "A Trip to Mabou Ridge", Rounder 7006.

Buddy MacMaster

Birth: October 18, 1924 in Timmons, Ontario
Parents: John Duncan MacMaster and
Sarah Anne MacDonald of Judique

Though they were Cape Bretoners by birth, Mr. & Mrs. John Duncan MacMaster were residing in Timmons, Ontario when their son Hugh "Buddy" was born. Recalling his childhood, Buddy says, "My mother loved music. It was **her** interest, more than anything else, that created an interest in me. I used to 'jig' tunes every morning in bed and would pretend I was tuning the violin for 'Lord MacDonald's Reel'. I fell right in love with the music! I got a tin fiddle from my parents at age three or four, but it didn't last long. Being a little boy, I took it apart to see what was on the inside; but, just before that, I can remember Johnny Fortune playing a tune on it." In Ontario, Buddy heard plenty of fiddling; his father played, as did certain friends of the family, such as Angus "the Piper" MacMaster and the aforementioned Johnny Fortune.

By 1929, the year the MacMasters moved back to a farm in Cape Breton, their little son had developed a "fierce" desire for the music of his Celtic ancestors. "At age five, a relative of mine carved a fiddle and bow out of two shingles for me," he remembers. However, it was his third instrument which was to determine his musical future once and for all, as he explains: "At age eleven or twelve, I got my father's fiddle; he had gone back to Ontario for a few years. I went upstairs and found the violin in a trunk. I took it down and got a part of a tune on it - 'Rocky Valley Jig'. My first public performance was at an 'amateur hour' in Port Hood; I was about twelve, I think. I played two Angus Chisholm tunes on the key of C. Someone, who still remembers being there, has told me since that I was 'going right to town on them'.

"After that, I began playing at weddings - receptions in the home. The first dance I got paid for was in the Troy schoolhouse; I was about fifteen. There was no accompaniment and I played with Vincent MacMaster, a nephew to Angus 'the Piper'. I got $4.00 and paid my own way up on the bus and back on the train next day, which left me with $3.00 clear. On the way home, I met Dan R. MacDonald and Kitchener MacDonald on the old Judique Flyer. Dan R. told me regarding my pay, 'You did well!' "

Buddy was now on his way to a distinguished playing career. Dan Hughie MacEachern encouraged him to read music, and eventually he did. "At eighteen, I went to work on the railway in Pictou and Colchester counties. Naturally, I had my violin with me. In 1948, at age 24, I moved to Antigonish, and Mrs. Len Leadbeater there gave me the scale. I got one lesson; that's all the training I had! Now I have boxes of books and a lot of what Dan R. MacDonald composed. My first time on the radio was in Antigonish in 1948, after I learned to read music. I played tunes from 'The Scottish Violinist'. I came down to Mabou in January, 1949, and I've been going steady ever since."

Buddy MacMaster is an extremely popular dance player, owing to his good timing, exciting "lift", rich tone and a superb repertoire of tunes extracted from a wide array of sources - written and oral, ancient and new. His medleys of jigs reflect a special brilliance and have earned him countless ovations. His dance circuit takes in Glendale, Broad Cove, Scotsville, South West Margaree and Glencoe Mills, among other locales. Especially busy in the summer, he has been known to play nearly every night, for weeks on end. He admits, "It makes me feel good to see people having a good time at a dance, and I think it's good practice for me."

His other appearances have been many and varied. He has played at the old Antigonish television station, on CJCB TV from Sydney and on the CBC television network as regular on "Ceilidh" and "The John Allan Cameron Show".

To date, Buddy has made four trips to Scotland, one of which has resulted in a performance on the BBC network. He also recalls another highlight of overseas travel: "I once heard Hector MacAndrew at Edinburgh Castle. He was an outstanding player!"

The violin Buddy uses now is a Roth which he ordered from Montreal in 1959, and, using this instrument, he will soon record his long-awaited first album, a guaranteed best seller!

Kyle MacNeil

Birth: 1963 in Sydney Mines, Cape Breton
Parents: John C. MacNeil and Jean MacKenzie

Following an earlier interest in the guitar, Kyle switched his affections to the violin at the age of nine. Exposure to Scottish music came, not only from his many talented relatives, but from Lauchie and Robert Stubbert of Point Aconi who were frequent visitors to the house. In addition, while the children were still small, the MacNeil family spent a great deal of time in Iona where music sessions were commonplace and where any one of the following fiddlers might be heard performing at a house party: Joe and Michael Anthony MacLean, and Carl and Hector MacKenzie - all of Washabuck. Occasionally Dan Hughie MacEachern of Queensville took part in the festivities, contributing such showstoppers as J. Scott Skinner's version of "Reel o' Tulloch".

At the age of ten, Kyle began studying the violin under Professor James MacDonald of North Sydney. "He helped me with position playing and with the Scott Skinner tunes," says Kyle. One year later, the amazing youth played for his first "set" at the seasonal closing of a stepdancing class which his mother was teaching; a nine year old brother, Stewart, accompanied him on the piano.

After working diligently, Kyle, though still a teenager, has now blossomed into an exciting dance player. In league with his brothers Seamus and Stewart, he performs every summer weekend. "It keeps you in trim if you're playing for four hours," he says of these latter engagements. Besides radio and television exposure on programs such as "Canadian Express", "Show Case" and "Archie Neil's Cape Breton", Kyle makes scores of concert appearances each year. "When I'm picking out selections for a concert," he says, "I try to choose tunes no one else plays - I get them mostly from books and a few old tapes."

One indication of Kyle's remarkable talent is the fact that he already teaches classes for Scottish violin music.

Cape Breton culture thrives in Sydney Mines, partially due to the attitude of local priest, Fr. J.J. Mac Donald. Kyle MacNeil is a credit to that strong Celtic community.

Other violinists in his family include his mother, Jean; his brother, Seamus; his sister, Lucy; and his uncles Carl, Hector, Charlie, and Simon MacKenzie.

Billy MacPhee

Birth: September 16, 1915 in Lower River Inhabitants
Parents: Louis MacPhee and Mary DeCoste

Billy MacPhee has ties with two cultures, dating back to the time when his great-grandfather arrived in Cape Breton from Scotland and married a French girl.

The southwest corner of the Island has had its share of Scottish musicians, and Billy's neighbours included such violinists as "Baby" Joe and Donald MacLellan of Riverside, Joe MacCormack from Cleveland, and Patrick Cogswell of Lower River Inhabitants. Though his father, Louis, was an accordion player, Billy and his brothers Henry, Leo, and Peter all became enamoured with the violin - like their uncle, Amos MacPhee. Billy says, "Henry bought his fiddle from a MacEwan in St. Peters. He was the first one to start - then Peter and Leo. I always heard my older brothers playing; and, Joe MacCormack came to the house a lot. Joe would usually have his own violin; if not, he'd grab ours off the wall. Many's the time I was dying to get hold of that fiddle to see what I'd be able to get out of it!

"When I was around thirteen, my mother died. A year after that, I started playing. I learned tunes just by listening to the other guys. After I got 'Cock of the North' down, I got 'A Cold Winter's Night' - a song. Then I tackled 'King George the Fourth Reel' - Leo showed me the high turn. After that, I started feeling my way along.

"When Leo and Paddy Cogswell were teaming up at the schoolhouse dances, they'd let me play a set - I was about sixteen. It was just the fiddle alone and, by God, they could hear it all over the hall! It wouldn't work today because people are too spoiled with p.a. systems. And, you wouldn't have a square set without a prompter; he wouldn't get paid because there were all kinds of them fellows around. We wouldn't get paid half the time either - we'd do it for the fun. In 1940, I'd play regularly once a week down in the parish hall in Lower River, using a cheap, old violin and with Danny MacCormack strumming on the guitar.

"I came to Sydney in 1941. After the war, I met Winston Fitzgerald. I had heard him play and was dying to meet him. I never performed down here till I met 'Scotty'. When he couldn't go himself to play for dances, he'd send me in his place - Big Pond, Glace Bay, Millville, Waterford. Sometimes I'd use Marie MacLellan, Beattie Wallace or 'Chippie' MacDonald on piano. You'd usually play for a percentage, and then pay your accompanist. Some nights you'd hardly make anything - depending on the size of the hall. Waterford was, and still is, a dandy place to put on a dance. For dancing, you play different - a little rougher; you try to put more life in it. The people in Sydney, North Sydney, Inverness - they all danced a different set."

In metropolitan Cape Breton, square dancing has undergone periods of popularity and decline. "The 1940's and 50's were pretty good," Billy recalls. "In the 60's, though, I didn't touch the violin. The square dancing kind of went on the rocks for a while. Before 'The Vanishing Fiddler' and the Glendale Festival, I wasn't playing anywhere - there were very, very few dances. What put the fiddle out of commission was those televisions! Without this revival, I might not even own a fiddle today! I'll stay with it now."

Throughout the years, Billy MacPhee has been very generous, supplying music at senior citizens homes, at the CNIB and wherever Cape Breton fiddling is appreciated. "I entertain at all the Gaelic Societies, and at concerts, ceilidhs and dances. You meet all your old friends; it kinda makes you feel younger!"

KING GEORGE IV STRATHSPEY

traditional

Father Angus Morris

Birth: December 17, 1936 in Colindale, Inverness County
Parents: Patrick Morris and Florence MacDonald

"The violin always fascinated me - the music was so pretty. I guess I first heard it on the radio. There was a program on Sunday night from P.E.I. - 'Kelly and MacInnis'; they were both fiddlers. They played in the Messer style with some Scottish flavour. The first local players I heard were my father's first cousins: Alex, Jim and John 'Lewis' MacDonald. Then there was John Alex 'The Big Fiddler' MacDonald - high bass and long fingers! Next I heard Donald Angus (Beaton), Buddy (MacMaster) and Winston (Fitzgerald) who played at dances locally.

"I started the violin at 15 or 16; I guess it was sort of a challenge. I enjoyed music and there was music in my people. In those days, every home had a violin and a drink saved for visiting musicians. Jim 'Lewis' helped me tune our fiddle and provided a little instruction on note reading. When there was a square dance, four or five players went and would 'spell' the main fiddler. Although at 18 I didn't think I was good enough to play for dances with the likes of Buddy MacMaster around, I'd always 'spell' the fiddler to give him a chance to rest or dance. Anyway, I loved dancing and didn't want to be tied down for the night. I often played for my brother, Eugene, when he was learning new steps.

"I worked in the mines after high school and didn't start University until I was 22. The last year at St. F.X. I decided to try the priesthood - you never know if it's going to work out for you personally.

"Although I played a lot in the seminary, it wasn't until I was ordained and went to New Waterford in 1966 that I became aware of the 'Mabou' style of playing - that's when I heard Mary MacDonald. Her music was so deep - there was so much to it! She was always in good form and it was a thrill just to hear her tuning her violin. She played pieces I knew in a different way, accenting some notes very strongly, though she was only a small woman. She was so confident and enjoyed her own music so much; you could tell just by watching her. This Scottish music really moved me - the style and the tunes. There was something so stirring! It was like beginning over again; I was like a kid and I started trying harder myself."

Father Angus spent the years 1969 through 1976 far away from the home of his beloved music. He was stationed in Honduras and his work there kept him so busy that he scarcely had time to touch the old fiddle he had purchased upon arriving. Whenever he had a spare moment, he listened to his records and tapes and they were a balm to his nostalgia. In time, Father Angus became proficient in Spanish and before he left the country, he wrote a Spanish catechism.

In 1976 Father Angus came to Sydney Mines, Cape Breton. "I got back into the music rather quickly. I'd see Joe MacLean, John and Alex MacDougall, Billy MacPhee and others on a regular basis just to keep the music going, but I had lost some ground as a fiddler during those seven years in Honduras. It was a difficult transition getting back into the swing of things in Cape Breton." Fans of his music, however, insist that, driven by the strong feeling he has for the ancient traditional melodies which he handles so skillfully, Fr. Angus has regained his old form and then some!

Today Father Angus is parish priest in Eskasoni and continues to play the old tunes he specializes in. "The fiddle has been a real consolation for me. These are pretty big houses at times, eh, but you can always converse with your violin when you are alone; it can be a companion. I play whatever music suits my disposition. If I've had a rough day, there is a certain kind of tune I'll play that night. I express myself through my music; that's why I cannot criticize another fiddler - it all comes from the heart.

"It's difficult to separate our faith and culture, and music is a part of that. Look what our fiddlers have done at charitable affairs over the years - playing to support their church and faith. Their music is part of their religion and yet it is not used in church! We have distinctly Scottish parishes in Cape Breton and the violin music and Gaelic songs these people are so familiar with should be adapted into the liturgy. I'd like to utilize local musicians and have them play a lengthy piece - a slow air, march or something meditative - at the communion."

With his strong spiritual beliefs and his abiding appreciation of Scottish fiddling, Father Angus Morris seems to be the living embodiment of the motto which hangs in his living-room - "If you love music you are a believer".

Theresa (MacLean) Morrison

Birth: July 12, 1919 at MacKay's Point, Washabuck
Parents: Vincent MacLean and Theresa MacNeil

Although it was not uncommon for a child raised in rural Cape Breton to be lulled to sleep by a mother's soft Gaelic melodies, it was this singing that led young Theresa MacLean to the violin. Music was a way of life in Washabuck at that time, with all twelve MacLean children exhibiting an inclination towards it and seven of them vying to play their father's fiddle. Vincent was himself a Scottish violinist, and the area boasted two other prominent families of players: (1) Dan MacKinnon and his children of Washabuck, and (2) Hector MacLean and his brothers of Gillis Point, known locally as "the lighthouse boys".

Since education as well as music was stressed in the MacLean home, Theresa wasted no time in studying notation for the violin, and she learned a tune or two on the guitar and banjo along the way. While in her late teens, she became enthralled with the remarkable playing of Angus Chisholm of Margaree, whose music became an additional source of inspiration for her. She recalls that there was no prejudice whatsoever against a female fiddler; so, in time, her services were requested for the numerous dances, picnics and concerts in her locality.

After moving to Sydney, Theresa appeared frequently on local radio, one of the programs having been organized by A.W.R. MacKenzie of the Gaelic College in St. Anns. On occasion, she performed with her brother, Joe MacLean, in a duo which had its beginnings in 1935.

Over the years, Theresa has developed a taste for the laments and airs of Scotland, especially the compositions of J. Scott Skinner and the playing of the late Hector MacAndrew. Always thorough in her approach to mastering a new piece, she often searches out the history of a tune in an attempt to interpret it authentically. As for Cape Breton composers, she speaks highly of the works of Dan R. MacDonald; but, whatever her choice, Theresa's material experiences rich reproduction on her fine violin, a family heirloom with a deep, sonorous tone.

Theresa is married to Peter Morrison, an outstanding piper, and their children play both bagpipes and piano.

Arthur Muise

Birth: 1950 at Cheticamp Island, Inverness County
Parents: Simon Muise and Maggie Camus

Arthur Muise was born into a French-speaking family in a richly Acadian community. Interestingly enough, Scottish music had taken root there, and Arthur was only five or six years old when he and his brother Lionel stepdanced at the Highland Games in Antigonish. He also recalls that at summer picnics in Cheticamp his pockets would be jingling with the coins he had acquired for crowd-pleasing performances of fancy footwork.

Under his father's close supervision, Arthur began playing the violin at eight years of age; "La Queue de Mon Chat" ("My Cat's Tail") was the first tune he mastered. At first he used Simon's fiddle but found it too awkward, so, he obtained an inexpensive metal one for temporary use. Soon, however, his father remedied the situation by presenting the boy with a small violin he had built himself. During the earliest years of his playing career, Arthur kept a low profile, and although he made the occasional appearance at concerts in Cheticamp, he was known more as a stepdancer than as a fiddler.[28]

Arthur has nurtured a strong love for the strathspey and reel, always managing to deliver them with bowing flourishes that are quite remarkable and thoroughly entertaining. The fiddlers whom he has always admired are also known for their gifted bow hands - Angus Chisholm and Cameron Chisholm of Margaree.

While maintaining his livelihood as a fisherman, Arthur performs every summer at festivals throughout Cape Breton. He also makes frequent appearances with his friend Donnie LeBlanc at the lively Doryman Tavern in Cheticamp, and tape recordings of these sessions are proving to be great treasures.

It is only a matter of time before Arthur Muise's name becomes a household word for all Scottish fiddle-music lovers in Nova Scotia. Armed with a keen ear and a driving dance-music technique, he is gradually familiarizing all corners of the province with his breath-taking bowing exhibitions. Transcending the barriers of language and culture, his music brings joy to all.

Percy Peters

Birth: August 2, 1911 at Mira Road, Cape Breton County
Parents: Charles Peters and Gertrude O'Grady

Percy's earliest encounters with Scottish music include hearing J. Scott Skinner on cylinder record. Then, when confined indoors with a sore throat at nine years of age, he reached up and took the family violin off the wall, all with the encouragement of his father, his cousin Jimmy and Cape North fiddler "Red" John MacKinnon. Percy's own first fiddle, a gift from his father, was originally purchased by John Bernard at the old Menzies' Music Store in Sydney.

In the beginning, Percy and his brother, Dick, played for dances without either accompaniment or public address systems. Crowds would come by horse and buggy to the schools to dance the plain lancer, the Saratoga and the Caledonia figures. In 1926-27, the boys were entertaining at Spain's Hall

in Mira Ferry, and later at Gabarus, Belfry, Sydney River and Dominion. In Sydney at that time, the main dance halls were The Cabin, The Ritz and The L.O.C., and each would be filled to capacity when "Scotch" music, complete with a prompter, was the provided entertainment. "The prompter," Percy says, "would control the dancing, which was very graceful, with no galloping around - in fact, it would be more like a drill. If anyone was being too boisterous and was drowning out the fiddler, the prompter would stop the dancing and reprimand him."

Reminiscing about performing during the wintery times of the year, Percy says, "The walk or horse ride to the hall could be a cold one for the fiddler on those days. The first thing the player would do when he entered the hall would be warm his hands at the potbellied stove. When the dancers arrived, they'd pay a fifteen to twenty-five cent admission to the hall." At the end of the night, the musicians would make the long trek home with their two-dollar pay. During the Depression, Percy and his wife, Helen, teamed up for dance playing; she still supplies a piano backing for his fiddling at home.

Percy claims that his group, "The Peters' Square Dance Orchestra", was probably the first to play Cape Breton music on CJCB Radio. They also appeared regularly at the East Bay parish picnic, an event for which Fr. MacCormack would recruit such additional talent as Tena Campbell, "Queen of the Bow".

In earlier times, Sydney was the scene of a thriving Scottish-music community, and Percy remembers all the participating members, such as Danny White of Cheticamp, Mick MacInnis of Glengarry, Hughie MacVarish of East Bay, Albert Boutilier of Coxheath, Jimmy Fraser of Point Edward, Angus

Ferguson of Hardwood Hill, Angus "Mossy" MacKinnon of Meat Cove, Danny Angus Neil Lamond of Trout Brook, Harry Bagnell, Harry Duffell, Ranald Dan MacDonald of Mabou, Alex MacNeil of Boisdale, John MacIntyre of Frenchvale, Alex Boutilier of Blackett's Lake, V.J. MacGillivray of Glace Bay and John MacKinnon of Meat Cove.

Except for the six months he spent in California working on the ranch of singing star Guy Mitchell, Percy has lived near the family home at Mira Road where he raises teams of work horses. He maintains his interest in the Cape Breton Fiddler's Association and, during the summer of 1980, he attended the large rally at Rollo Bay in Prince Edward Island. Always a welcome contributor at Scottish gatherings, Percy is ever willing to swap a "yarn" or a tune whenever the opportunity presents itself.

Among his relatives who play, or played, the violin are: his father, Charles; uncles Austin and Pierce; brothers Dick, John and Barney; and cousins Joe and Jimmy Peters.

SPACE AVAILABLE MARCH

By Marcel Doucet

Wilfred Prosper

Birth: 1927 in Barra Head
Parents: Peter Prosper and Clara Young

Wilfred's maternal grandfather and great-grandfather were musical - the former was a pennywhistler and the latter, a violin player. Clara Young Prosper could herself "jig a few clogs", having been heavily exposed to Scottish music by all the neighbours in her former home - Antigonish.

Wilfred didn't have musical instruments of his own when he was a youngster, so he made use of the ones his friends owned. "I loved the guitar! I used to spend all night at the neighbours' in Barra Head; I must have been twelve or thirteen at the time. We had one neighbour, John Joe, who had a violin. I used to drop in there, but he must have felt like throwing me out; I'd play 'You Are My Sunshine' over and over - it was like the 'Tullochgorum' to me! I'd drop in after school or after skating parties, and I'd sit on a bench beside the stove and saw away at that tune.

"I had my own guitar at sixteen or seventeen; I got it in Halifax during the War. Every spare moment I played it. My parents must have been getting tired of it because one day they came home with a $36.00-fiddle from Simpson's. Perhaps they thought I had some potential, though the guitar was still my favourite instrument at that time. You know, that fiddle had a darn good ring to it! I had it until 1960, when I broke it accidentally.

"The first real player I heard was Tena Campbell. She played over the radio in the '40's and she had great marches. Later, I heard 'Scotty' Fitzgerald and Angus Chisholm - that changed everything for me; they were both great!" Wilfred also admired Bill Lamey and "Little" Jack MacDonald. Of the latter, he says, "I grew to love the slow airs of 'Little' Jack; I'll fight anyone who'll say anything against his playing!

"Dances were held around Barra Head and Soldiers Cove (called Salmon River and Big Cove by the Indians then); we'd go in and just listen. The house parties on the reserve had Simon Cremo, and I'd make darn sure I was there, crouched under the window. Then there was Frank Paul - he wasn't stingy with his Scottish tunes. He was an ear player but he was correct, though he lacked some polish.

"When I was about eighteen, I didn't know what 'A' was, but a man from Pictou called George MacKenzie began showing me what the 'keys' of tunes meant; he taught a lot of Barra Head players.

"In the beginning, all I played was a few Don Messer tunes. When I was around twenty, we moved to Eskasoni - I was still immersed in the Messer style. Joe Googoo used to say, 'You're playing the Scottish tunes too fast!'; he knew Scottish music. Messer's stuff was all straight bowing, but the Scottish music presented a challenge; it was more complicated. There was such variety in Scottish - jigs, reels, strathspeys, hornpipes, clogs, etc. - that's what really turned me on! My father used to say, 'You'll never get tired of fish - you can cook it so many different ways'; that applies to Scottish music too!

"I never played for that many dances; there were lots of other fiddlers to play. I played more at house parties. I loved Scottish music, though most of the other Indians didn't really go for it. I'd work a full shift cutting pulp, then play all night.

"When the choir was started here, I wasn't really interested, but I was coaxed to go and I gave in. The sister was patient and a good teacher. She'd point out crescendos, quarter notes, half notes, etc., but I couldn't understand how a person could read music. It never dawned on me then that someday I'd learn to read. She gave me a small book of 'Wayne King Waltzes'. I took it out one day and, by God, I could make sense out of it! I could understand what I was playing! I went to McKnight's Music Store in Sydney and bought the '1000 Tune Fiddle Book'. Then came the break-away point - hearing Angus Chisholm. I'd listen to his tunes, then I'd look at the music. Because he played the tunes so correctly, I could figure out the notation.

"Next I bought the 'Scottish Violinist'. It nearly drove me crazy at first, but eventually I went through the whole darn book; it's tricky stuff, though. Now I can take any fiddle book and play most of the tunes. Father Angus Morris just loaned me a 'Capt. Simon Fraser Collection'. Other parish priests stationed on the reserve, like Fr. Raymond MacDonald, gave me tips on music.

"I really like the music of the Cape Breton composers, especially young Roddy MacDonald of Margaree. In the last few years, I've done some composing myself; the Fiddlers' Association has published some of my tunes in the newsletter.

"The fiddle I have now is one of the best sounding fiddles in Cape Breton. I got it from Matty Morris for $3.50; it was in his attic for years.

"Music imparts some sort of message; I hope the Scottish people think I'm doing it right." Wilfred Prosper has the music of Cape Breton in his heart and in his hands. He's the envy of many a Scot.

John Morris Rankin

Birth: April 28, 1959 at Mabou, Inverness County
Parents: Alex J. ("Buddy") Rankin and Kathleen Wright

"There were twelve kids in the family," says John Morris. "We used to sing songs at home - about ten out of the twelve kids could sing. I started on the piano at age eight; we got the piano from our neighbour, Katie Ann Cameron. A few weeks later, I played with members of my family at a John Allan Cameron concert in Whycocomagh.

"My father had tapes going in the house all the time - ever since I can remember. The tapes were of Dan Hughie MacEachern, Theresa MacLellan, Cameron Chisholm, etc. At around age nine, I started at the fiddle. A lot of the tunes I played I heard from Donald Angus Beaton, who played regular dances for years in the hall here in Mabou. I was too young to go, but that's my bedroom window right there (pointing), and I could hear the music all night!

"Dan R. MacDonald was one of my biggest influences. I used to chord to him on the piano. He'd get you warmed up, then play the tricky stuff in the flats!"

John Morris "fooled around" with many musical instruments, but he began to take his fiddling quite seriously as a teenager. With Dan R., Donald Angus, Buddy MacMaster, Peter MacPhee and Willie Kennedy to inspire him, he worked hard and learned well. He played an important part in the Ron MacInnis film, "The Vanishing Cape Breton Fiddler", produced in the early 70's. John Morris became a symbol for those who believed that the fiddling would **not** "vanish"!

"I wanted to learn to read music when I was in grade nine," he recalls. "I went to John MacDougall's classes for about half a year - but I still learn tunes mostly by ear." On radio, his playing received plenty of exposure, thanks to the CJFX programs hosted by Gus MacKinnon, Frank MacInnis and Joey Beaton. In 1976, John Morris and eight other fiddlers were transported to Montreal to entertain the Olympic athletes. That same year, as part of a Cape Breton contingent, he played for the Queen in Halifax. In 1978, he and neighbour Joey Beaton (pianist) displayed their combined talents in musical workshops held in New York. In addition, John Morris has been heard over the CBC Radio network, courtesy of the folk music program "Touch the Earth".

For the last nine years, John Morris has been closely involved with "The Rankin Family Band". "I find the young people are getting more into traditional music now," he says of his schoolmates.

John Morris Rankin has come a long way from the $5.00-violin he began on; he now plays a Klotz which he received from his grand-aunt, Sister Bessie Rankin, herself a former violinist.

Brenda Stubbert

Birth: July 15, 1959 at Point Aconi
Parents: Robert Stubbert and
Regina Roland

Speaking with Brenda, one is immediately struck by the importance of Scottish music in her life. Although she originally began playing piano with the help of her sister Alice and neighbour Jack Beaton, her attention was soon focused on the violin and has been there ever since. When asked why she began to play, she answers simply, "I just loved it, that's all!" and, hearing of the ceilidhs held in the Stubbert home, it is easy to understand why. Her father and a number of her uncles are good fiddlers, and among her brothers and sisters there is not a one who cannot play a tune or "do a step".

At the age of nine, Brenda made her first public appearance and won a trophy for her piano playing. It was approximately a year later that she experienced her fiddling debut at Highland Village Day in Iona. A young Brenda spent the entire time in the tuning room, just listening. This intent listening to and remembering of tunes was with her throughout her teenage years. "When you're lying down in bed, that's when the tunes come to you - one right after the other; when you get up in the morning, they're still going around in your head! I used to sit in school and jig tunes instead of listening to the teacher." The fact that fiddling and Scottish music were not popular with her peers at school did not dampen Brenda's determination to learn or her desire to play. "After school," she recalls, "the first thing I made for was the fiddle. You know, I often thought it must be an awful thing for a person not to know that music; there are some people who don't understand!"

Brenda has a deep love for the "old-fashioned tunes" and she admires Buddy MacMaster and Donald Angus Beaton because they play them. Winston Fitzgerald, who was a frequent visitor to the Stubbert home when Brenda was growing up, also inspired her. Her repertoire now includes rare old pieces she learned from her father who, in turn, learned them from Johnny Walker and John R. Fraser, both of whom lived in Point Aconi. She also performs her own as well as her father's compositions.

In 1976, Brenda had the honour of being among the fiddlers chosen to play for the Queen's visit to Halifax. More recently, she has been a frequent contributor at the regular Saturday afternoon "sessions" at the Doryman Tavern in Cheticamp, sharing the spotlight with local fiddlers Arthur Muise and Donnie LeBlanc.

Robert Stubbert

Birth: March 29, 1923 at Point Aconi, Cape Breton
Parents: Peter Stubbert and Margaret MacQueen

Robert Stubbert has a good memory of what times were like a few years ago: "A violin and a prompter were all you'd see back then - never a piano or a guitar." It was during this period that he grew up. Although there wasn't much music in the Point Aconi area then, both of his parents played, and it was from his father, Peter, that Robert learned. "I remember when the violin was never in the case - it was always in the front room hanging on the wall; and, you didn't dare touch it! When my father went away, I'd take it down, and as soon as I heard tell he was coming, I'd put it back - until he caught me; I was about seven at the time. When he knew I was really going to learn, he was glad that at least one of us was going to be a player!" Eventually, however, several of Robert's brothers **did** turn to music, and Lauchie, for one, became an exceptional Cape Breton fiddler.

Robert was also influenced by two other violinists in his community, Jack Walker and John R. Fraser. The latter, a former Meat Cove resident, was still able to handle the violin at age one hundred and five, and Robert says of him, "I've heard fiddlers all over Cape Breton and I've never heard the tunes he played!" Not only does Robert still perform the ancient melodies he learned from these two men, but he has, in turn, handed them down to his daughter, violinist Brenda Stubbert. Both Robert and Brenda have a good memory for tunes, and he says, "I could hear a tune one night, and the next day it would come right back to me."

Of his youth, Robert recollects, "Things were different in the old days. They'd have 'pound parties' where everyone would bring a pound of something - soap, tea, butter - and there would be a fiddler sitting in the corner, usually an old man; I was the first young fellow to play around here. After the lunch, they'd pass a cap around to take a collection for the fiddler." Robert, himself, has been playing for dances since the amazing age of ten.

A friendship with Joe Confiant, a noted fiddler from North Sydney, introduced Robert to the Irish jigs and reels he plays with such dexterity. Joe passed on to Robert his wealth of tunes, as well as the bowing technique necessary to play them.

These days at the Stubbert home, there is music every day of the week.

Johnny Wilmot

Birth: 1916 at Centerville, Cape Breton
Parents: Mr. and Mrs. John Alex Wilmot

"Old" Henry Fortune passed on a very distinctive style of fiddling to his three nephews George, Jack and Joe Confiant, and these men are Johnny Wilmot's uncles. Joe, a champion fiddler who could "cut coming up and down", had a very positive influence on Johnny's playing.

It was at age seventeen that Johnny began his fiddling career. One year later, equipped with an instruction manual from MacLeod's Bookstore, he proceeded to gain a basic understanding of note reading after only three days of study. "I was about nineteen when I played my first picnic in Frenchvale with Joe Confiant," says Johnny. "I made five dollars. John Willie Morrison from Sydney Mines played the piano - he was about the best around! Shortly after, I began playing at Boisdale, Johnstown, etc. Then, I formed a band with Sonny Slade, Elizabeth Fennel and Roy Romeo."

In 1936, Johnny moved to Glace Bay. Having established his unique sound, a rich blend of the Scottish and the Irish, he recorded three 78 rpm's and a number of long-playing albums, all which were met with great enthusiasm. He became a regular member of the cast of a weekly CJCB Radio program called "The Irish Serenaders", one of the longest running shows of its time. Farther from home, he performed over Boston's WMEX and Charlottetown's CFCY. In 1952, Johnny displayed his versatile talents at Joe MacPherson's Irish Tavern in Roxbury, Massachusetts and was a hit. Regarding the fiddlers from Éire, he is quick to announce, "My favourite of all Irish players was Michael Coleman!"

1959 found Johnny in Toronto. "From the time I landed," he remembers, "I was playing regularly. The place was full of Cape Bretoners!" His violin at that time was a beautiful Hopf which he had obtained originally from Alex MacDonald in Dominion for one hundred dollars.

Like many faithful Maritimers, Johnny moved back home in 1976. His undying love for Celtic music is evidenced by the large reel-to-reel tape collection which continues to occupy the bulk of his listening time.

LAUCHIE STUBBERT,
Point Aconi

WALTER MacISAAC,
Codroy Valley, Nfld.

JOE A. KENNEDY,
Inverside

ARCHIE NEIL CHISHOLM,
Margaree Forks

JOHNNY STEELE,
Sydney

BILL MATHESON,
River Denys

DIDACE LeBLANC,
Grand Etang

ARCHIE MacKENZIE,
Sydney River

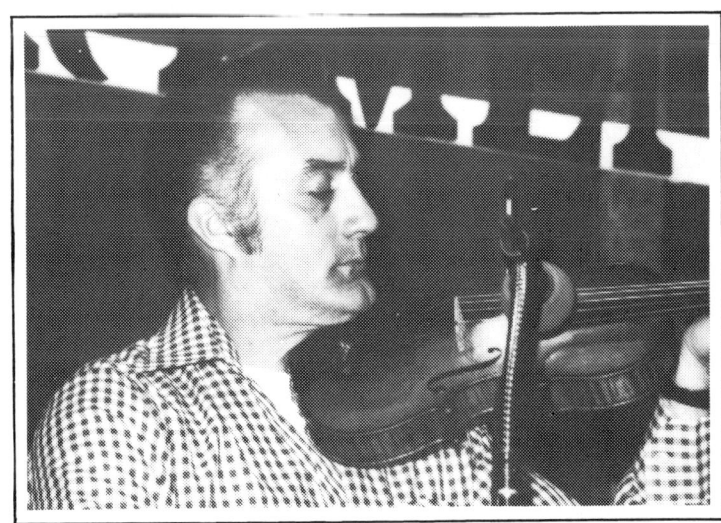
ALEX URQUHART,
Pleasant Bay

JOHN FERGUSON,
Halifax

ALEX DAN MacISAAC,
Halifax

JOHNNY STEPHEN WHITE
Margaree Forks

MIKE MacLEAN,
Big Pond

BOBBY JOBES,
Cape North

ALLIE BENNETT,
Sydney Mines

RODDIE MacDONALD,
Inverness Town

GREG SMITH, Port Hawkesbury

JOHN ALLAN CAMERON, Toronto

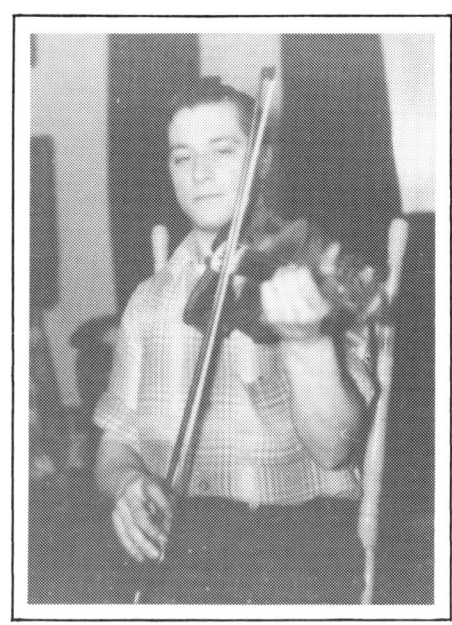

HARTWELL PINKERTON,
Boston

NEIL DAN MacINNIS,
Glenville

NEIL ARCHIE BEATON,
Strathlorne

DONNIE "DOUGALD" MacDONALD,
Queensville

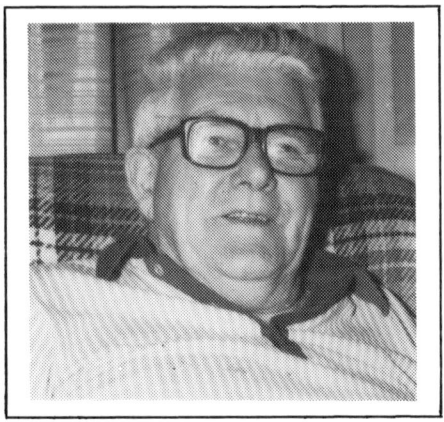

MALCOLM CAMPBELL,
Sydney

JOHN DAN MacNEIL,
Sydney

STAN CHAPMAN,
Stellarton

"The Vanishing Cape Breton Fiddler"

In the spring of 1971, the CBC Television program entitled "The Vanishing Cape Breton Fiddler" aroused many people in its audience resulting in the formation of The Cape Breton Fiddlers' Association, which group was instrumental in organizing the first Glendale Festival of Scottish Fiddling. The film has been credited with being the catalyst for the revival of Scottish violin music on the Island and Ron MacInnis, the producer, explains how he became absorbed in this tradition: -

"I was born and brought up in Cape Breton, but the interesting thing for me about Cape Breton music was that I never liked it as a kid. It took moving away and living in Halifax for about twelve years, and then coming back, before I really listened and found it appealed to me. It resonated with something deep down inside somewhere and I've been hooked ever since."

When Ron returned to Sydney, he began to work at CHER Radio where his job was to tape Scottish fiddlers for on-air concerts. As his interest in the culture grew, so did his dismay at the lack of public interest and activity surrounding it. He felt that the time formerly given to the music was now taken up by a new type of entertainment - television. "I think we're just beginning to unlock the story of what damage television has done to us as a people! I think it has robbed us of a lot of things, including our culture.

"I couldn't reason it out with people, and I had it out with a lot of them. These older players were dying off and there were no kids to take their place; I turned nearly every stone over on this island and I only found two!"

As a result of Ron's strong feelings on this subject, "The Vanishing Cape Breton Fiddler" was made. "I did the film as a kind of lament. I made it for the same reason that somebody would play a lament for a friend they'd lost."

The shock waves from the film were felt all over the Island. "They seem to think I've started a thing up there - maybe I did. I was a kid who was in the woods playing with matches but I think the forest floor was there, ready to kindle. I just happened to walk by with that program, and say a few things that sparked a few people and got their dander up, and the whole movement took off. It was like waving a red flag in front of a bull. Father Rankin and I, from that day on, went to war - he, sure he was going to prove to me that the fiddling wasn't dying out, and me, equally sure that it was.

"One of the highlights of my whole broadcasting life was sitting in the audience at the first Glendale concert and seeing a hundred or so fiddlers up on stage, and Father Rankin saying, 'If Ron MacInnis is in the audience, we want him to know that the fiddlers aren't vanishing at all! They're alive and well right here at Glendale!' Well, hooray! And, I got some very interesting letters - you name a position and somebody came in with that stance. The most common comment I got in later years was that the program had stirred up a lot of people."

In summation Ron says - "I think there's something very important these days about having roots and some sort of connection to our past. I think people are going to be grasping for any sort of solid foundation they can to know **who** they are and **where** they are, and Cape Breton music is a part of all that. I think it will be around for a long time to come!"

Tuning up at the Glendale Festival

The Future

KATHLEEN LeBLANC,
Grand Etang

BRIAN MacDONALD,
Westmount

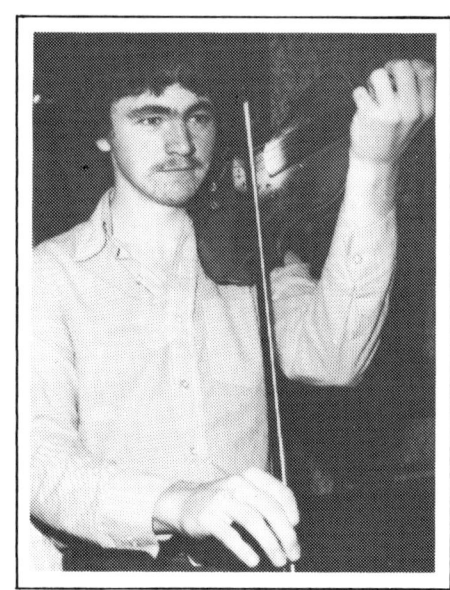

HOWIE MacDONALD,
Westmount

ELIZABETH O'BRIEN,
Mabou

DOUGIE MacDONALD,
Queensville

A Partial Directory of Cape Breton Violinists

(Including Dates, Where Possible,
and a Place-Name Commonly
Associated with Each Player)

b. = born   l. = living   d. = deceased or died

Aucoin, Alcide (d.; Boston)
Aucoin, Anthony (Cheticamp)
Aucoin, Gaston (l.; Sydney Mines)
Aucoin, Joe (Cheticamp)
Aucoin, Joseph (l.; Halifax)
Bagnell, Harry (d.; Sydney)
Beaton, Alexander J. (1837-?; Mabou)
Beaton, Alexander R., Jr. (1864-1945; Mabou)
Beaton, Alex "John Y." (d.; Inverness County)
Beaton, Ambrose (b. 1889; Michigan, U.S.A.)
Beaton, Angus "Curly Sandy" (l.; Glenville)
Beaton, Angus Ronald (1866?-1933; Mabou)
Beaton, "Curly" Sandy (d.; Glenville)
Beaton, Danny (1894-1950; Mabou)
Beaton, Donald R., Jr. (d.; Mabou)
Beaton, Donald Angus (b.; 1912; Mabou)
Beaton, Donald "The Tailor" (1856-1919; Mabou)
Beaton, Duncan Angus (Sydney)
Beaton, Janet (l.; Mabou)
Beaton, Joe (d.; Boston)
Beaton, Johnny "Johnny Ranald" (1906-1980; Mabou)
Beaton, Johnny Ranald (1862-1928; Mabou)
Beaton, Kinnon (b. 1956; Mabou)
Beaton, Malcolm (1912-1951; Strathlorne)
Beaton, Neil (l.; Judique)
Beaton, Neil Archie (l.; Strathlorne)
Beaton, Ronald (d.; Glencoe?)
Beaton, Ronald (Mabou)
Beaton, Ronald Dan (1898-1974; Mabou)
Bennett, Allie (l.; Sydney Mines)
Benoit, Jarvis (l.; Arichat)
Bourgeois, Ephrem (l.; Cheticamp)
Boutilier, Albert (d.; Coxheath)
Boutilier, Alex (d.; Blackett's Lake)
Boyd, Colin J. (1891-1975; Antigonish)
Briand, Elmer (b.; 1922; L'Ardoise)
Briand, Peter (l.; Halifax)
Burke, Ernest (l.; River Bourgeois)
Cameron, Fr. Francis (b. 1934; Boisdale)
Cameron, John Allan (b. 1938; Toronto)
Cameron, John Donald (b. 1937; Dartmouth)
Cameron, Katie Anne (l. Mabou)
Cameron, Sandy (l.; Mabou)
Cameron, Sandy Donald (d.; Mabou)
Campbell, Agnes (Boston)
Campbell, Alex (French Road)
Campbell, Alex (Glenora Falls)
Campbell, Alex (1868-1946; New Waterford)
Campbell, Alex (l.; Toronto)
Campbell, Alex (d.; Red Point)
Campbell, Alex A. (d.; Red Islands)
Campbell, Angus (d.; Glencoe)
Campbell, Angus (1892-1922; Glenora Falls)
Campbell, Angus (Glenora Falls)
Campbell, Dr. Angus (Iona)
Campbell, Angus T. (Judique)
Campbell, Anne (l.; Glenora Falls)
Campbell, Archie (d.; Woodbine)
Campbell, Dan J. (1895-1981; Glenora Falls)
Campbell, Donald (b. 1934; Glenora Falls)
Campbell, Donald "Bàn" (1789-1878; Lynch's River)
Campbell, Donald (l.; Mabou)
Campbell, Dougald (l.; Halifax)
Campbell, Dougald (l.; Sydney)
Campbell, Gregory (l.; Mabou)
Campbell, Hughie (Iona)
Campbell, James P. (1863-1942; Red Islands)
Campbell, Joe (l.; Toronto)
Campbell, John (1855-1919; Glenora Falls)

Campbell, John (b. 1929; Boston)
Campbell, John Francis (1890-1953; Iona)
Campbell, John Willie (b. 1928; Glencoe)
Campbell, Mac (l.; Port Hawkesbury)
Campbell, Malcolm (d.; Little Judique Pds.)
Campbell, Malcolm (b. 1911; Sydney)
Campbell, Michael (d.; Red Islands)
Campbell, "Old" Peter (d.; Woodbine)
Campbell, "Red" Johnny (Inverness Co.)
Campbell, Fr. Sam (l.; Sydney)
Campbell, Tena (1899-1949; Sydney)
Campbell, Tom (d.; Glencoe)
Camus, Joe (Sydney)
Carmichael, "Buckie" (l.; R. Bennett)
Carter, Cliffy (l.; Sampsonville)
Chafe, Winnie (b. 1936; Glace Bay)
Chaisson, Joe (l.; Souris, P.E.I.)
Chaisson, Joseph Luc (l.; Halifax)
Chaisson, Kenny (l.; Souris, P.E.I.)
Chaisson, Peter (l.; Souris, P.E.I.)
Chaisson, Wilfred (l.; Sydney)
Chandler, Wayne (l.; Blues Mills)
Chapman, Stan (l.; Stellarton)
Chisholm, Angus (1908-1979; Boston)
Chisholm, Archie Neil (b. 1907; Margaree Forks)
Chisholm, Cameron (b. 1945; Margaree Forks)
Christie, Kenny (l.; Englishtown)
Cogswell, Patrick (Lower River Inhabitants)
Confiant, Joe (l.; Sydney Mines)
Cordeau, Fr. Leo (l.; North Sydney)
Corkery, Jessie Beaton (1901-1972; Pittsburgh)
Cormier, Job (d.; Cheticamp)
Cormier, Joe (b. 1927; Waltham, Mass.)
Cormier, Pat (l.; Sydney)
Cormier, Paul (Cheticamp)
Cote, Daniel (l.; Halifax)
Cote, Gordon (b. 1938; Grand Greve)
Cremo, Lee (b. 1938; Eskasoni)
Cremo, Simon (1900-1964; Barra Head)
Cummings, Alex (d.; Skye Glen)
Cummings, Alexander (d.; Point Edward)
Cummings, Malcolm (Skye Glen)

Currie, John Joe (l.; Sydney Mines)
Currie, John Stephen (Mira)
Daigle, Jackie (l.; Truro)
Delaney, Chester (l.; St. Joseph du Moine)
Delaney, Joe (l.; St. Joseph du Moine)
Deveaux, Neil (l.; Gillis Point)
Dewar, Malcolm (l.; Ottawa)
Doucet, Marcel (l.; Cheticamp)
Doyle, Joey (d.; Ingonish Center)
Doyle, Sam (Glace Bay)
Duffell, Harry (d.; Mira Road)
Ellis, Raymond (l.; Little Narrows)
Ferguson, Angus (d.; Sydney)
Ferguson, John (l.; Halifax)
Ferguson, Willie "The Fiddler" (Ferguson's Lake)
Fitzgerald, Bob (l.; Dingwall)
Fitzgerald, George (d.; White Point)
Fitzgerald, Winston (b. 1914; Sydney)
Fortune, Johnny (Inverness County)
Fortune, "Old" Henry (Sydney Mines)
Fraser, Barry (l.; East Lake Ainslie)
Fraser, Dan (l.; South Bar)
Fraser, John R. (d.; Point Aconi)
Fraser, Jimmie (d.; Point Edward)
Fraser, "Little" Simon (1897-1972; Meat Cove)
Fraser, Murdoch (l.; Dingwall)
Gillis, Alex (Gillisdale)
Gillis, Alex (1900-1974; Boston)
Gillis, Allan (d.; Foot Cape)
Gillis, Ambrose (d.; S. W. Margaree)
Gillis, Angus (Glenville)
Gillis, Angus Allan (1897-1978; S.W. Margaree)
Gillis, Angus Archie (d.; Skye Glen)
Gillis, Angus Donald (Green Hill)
Gillis, Bernie (d.; Boston)
Gillis, Cecilia (Mira)
Gillis, Donnie (b. 1926; Sydney Mines)
Gillis, Hugh N. (MacKinnon's Harbour)
Gillis, Jack "Malcolm" (d.; S.W. Margaree)
Gillis, James D. (1870-1964?; Margaree)
Gillis, Jimmy "Malcolm" (d.; S.W. Margaree)
Gillis, Fr. Joe (l.; New Glasgow)
Gillis, John Archie (d.; Gillisdale)

Gillis, John Archie "Silver Dan" (l.; Inverness)
Gillis, John Y. (1921-1976; MacKinnon's Harbour)
Gillis, Malcolm H. (1856-1929; S.W. Margaree)
Gillis, Mickey (b. 1918; Prime Brook)
Gillis, Ranald (d.; Gillisdale)
Gillis, Wallace (l.; Scotsville)
Gillis, Wilfred (b. 1923; Arisaig)
Googoo, Frank (l.; Whycocomagh)
Googoo, Jimmy (l.; Whycocomagh)
Graham, Dannie (l.; Judique)
Graham, Rannie (d.; Boston)
Gwynn, Artie (d.; Aspy Bay)
Hall, John (l.; North Sydney)
Hamm, Carl (l.; Baddeck)
Hawley, Murray (d.; Ingonish Ferry)
Holland, Jerry (b. 1955; Belle Cote)
Holland, Jerry (d.; Boston)
Jackson, George (l.; Sydney)
Jackson, Hugh (d.; St. Peters)
Jobes, Bobby (l.; Cape North)
Jobes, Hughie Angus (b. 1906; Boularderie)
Jobes, John Hugh Charles (1933-1959; Boularderie)
Jobes, Johnny (d.; Cape North)
Jobes, Robert (l.; New Glasgow)
Kaizer, Ed (l.; Sydney)
Kelliher, Anna MacDonald (d.; West Lake Ainslie)
Kennedy, Angus (d.; Kenloch)
Kennedy, Archie (d.; Inverside)
Kennedy, Dan Michael (d.; Lake Ainslie)
Kennedy, Dannie (d.; Inverside)
Kennedy, Florence (l.; Inverness)
Kennedy, Joe (l.; Inverside)
Kennedy, John M. (d.; 1962; Loch Ban)
Kennedy, Joseph D. (d.; Inverness)
Kennedy, Mary Ann (Brookline, Mass.)
Kennedy, Ronald (1870-1958; Broad Cove)
Kennedy, Willie (b. 1925; Mabou)
Lamey, Bill (b. 1914; Boston)
Lamey, Rannie (l.; Sydney Mines)
Lamey, Sam (l.; Sydney Mines)

Lamond, Danny Angus Neil (d.; Trout Brook)
Landry, Dan (St. Peters)
Landry, Fred (St. Peters)
LeBlanc, Didace (l.; Grand Etang)
LeBlanc, Donnie (b. 1955; Cheticamp)
LeBlanc, Jim (East Margaree)
LeBlanc, Kathleen (l.; Grand Etang)
LeBlanc, Paddy (1923-1974; Sydney)
Lee, Bernie (d.; Sydney)
LeFort, George (l.; Toronto)
LeFort, J. Mederic (l.; Cheticamp)
LeFort, Loudger (l.; Waltham, Mass.)
Longaphie, Ned (l'Ardoise)
MacArthur, Mrs. John A. (Mabou Coal Mines)
MacAskill, George (North Side Boularderie)
MacAskill, Jim (d.; Bay St. Lawrence)
MacCormick, Allison (l.; Fourchu)
MacCormick, Joe (Cleveland)
MacCuspic, Charlie (l.; Hunter's Mtn.)
MacDonald, Alexander (l.; Halifax)
MacDonald, Alex Archie (d.; Mt. Young)
MacDonald, Alex Joe (d.; Creignish)
MacDonald, Alex "Lewis" (l., Saint John)
MacDonald, Alex Michael (d.; Port Hood)
MacDonald, Allan (l.; Detroit)
MacDonald, Allan "The Baron" (d.; Mabou)
MacDonald, Angus Archibald (1849-1939; Mount Young)
MacDonald, Angus Joseph (New Glasgow)
MacDonald, Anna (l.; Westmount)
MacDonald, Arthur (l.; North Sydney)
MacDonald, Bernie (l.; Detroit)
MacDonald, Bill (l.; Toronto)
MacDonald, Brian (b. 1964; Westmount)
MacDonald, Colin (l.; Ironville)
MacDonald, Dan C. (d.; West Bay Road)
MacDonald, Dan R. (1911-1976; Judique)
MacDonald, Dan "The Ridge" (d.; Boston)
MacDonald, Donald (d.; Little Judique)
MacDonald, Donnie (l.; Queensville)
MacDonald, Dougie (b. 1968; Queensville)
MacDonald, Duncan (l.; Judique)
MacDonald, Duncan (d.; Cleveland)

MacDonald, Fr. Faber (l.; Newfoundland)
MacDonald, Francis (b. 1932; Inverness)
MacDonald, Francis (l.; Queensville)
MacDonald, Gerald (l.; River Denys)
MacDonald, Hector (d.; Bay Road Valley)
MacDonald, Howie (b. 1965; Westmount)
MacDonald, Hugh (1920?-1965; Detroit)
MacDonald, Hughie (l.; Port Hood)
MacDonald, Hughie A. (1889-1976; Antigonish)
MacDonald, Hughie Allan (d.; Judique)
MacDonald, Hughie Angus "Lord" (Margaree Harbour)
MacDonald, Hughie Hector (Bay Road Valley)
MacDonald, Jim Dave (d.; West Lake)
MacDonald, Jim "Lewis" (l.; Port Hood)
MacDonald, John Alex (1877-1958; Port Hood)
MacDonald, John Joe (Fiddler's Lake)
MacDonald, John "Lewis" (l.; Port Hood)
MacDonald, Johnny Archie (1893?-1974; Detroit)
MacDonald, Johnny "MacVarish" (1852?-1934; Broad Cove Marsh)
MacDonald, Johnny "Nel" (l.; Toronto)
MacDonald, John R. (d.; Judique)
MacDonald, Kenneth Joseph (l.; Mabou)
MacDonald, Kitchener (Windsor, Ont.)
MacDonald, "Little" Angus (French Road)
MacDonald, "Little" Jack (1887-1969; Detroit)
MacDonald, "Little" Malcolm (d.; River Denys Mountain)
MacDonald, "Little" Rory (d.; Boston)
MacDonald, Lloyd (l.; Sydney)
MacDonald, Margaret Chisholm (b. 1947; Toronto)
MacDonald, Mary Beaton (b. 1897; New Waterford)
MacDonald, Murdoch (l.; Detroit)
MacDonald, Neil (d.; Inverness Corner)
MacDonald, Neil R. (d.; Detroit)
MacDonald, Ranald Dan (Mabou)
MacDonald, Roddie (b. 1956; Inverness)
MacDonald, Roddie "The Plumber" (d. 1980; Halifax)
MacDonald, Wilfred (l.; Truro)
MacDonald, Willie Danny "Betsy" (d.; Middle River)
MacDonnell, Alexander (1902-1970; Judique)
MacDonnell, Alexander (River Denys Road)
MacDonnell, Allan (River Denys Road)
MacDonnell, Archie (River Denys Road)
MacDonnell, Peter (d.; Deepdale)
MacDonnell, Mrs. Sarah (l.; Judique)
MacDougall, Alex (l.; North Sydney)
MacDougall, Alex (d.; Inverness Town)
MacDougall, Andy (d.; Grand Mira)
MacDougall, Angus (d.; Aspy Bay)
MacDougall, Archibald B. (d.; Christmas Island)
MacDougall, Dan Rory (d.; Ingonish)
MacDougall, Gabe (l.; Ingonish Beach)
MacDougall, George Mike (l.; Boston)
MacDougall, Hector Mike (d; Bay St. Lawrence)
MacDougall, Jack (l.; Westmount)
MacDougall, Joe (l.; Sydney)
MacDougall, John (b. 1925; Kenloch)
MacDougall, John (l.; North Sydney)
MacDougall, Mike (1928-1981; Ingonish Beach)
MacDougall, Ronald (d.; S.W. Margaree)
MacDougall, Rory (d.; Ingonish)
MacDougall, Tim (l.; Ingonish)
MacEachen, John Alex (l.; Glendale)
MacEachern, Alex (Glenville)
MacEachern, Alex (Queensville)
MacEachern, Alex D. (l.; Queensville)
MacEachern, Andrew (Sydney)
MacEachern, Angus (l.; Boston)
MacEachern, "Big" Dan Hughie (d. 1965?; Boston)
MacEachern, Dan (d.; Hillsdale)
MacEachern, Dan (d.; Victoria Bridge)
MacEachern, Dan Hughie (b. 1914; Queensville)
MacEachern, Donald (l.; Toronto)
MacEachern, Hughie (d.; Port Hastings)
MacEachern, Jimmy (d.; Glenville)

MacEachern, John Hughie (d.; Hillsdale)
MacEachern, Johnny (Glenville)
MacEachern, John R. (Glenora)
MacEachern, John Willie (d.; Queensville)
MacEachern, Lawrence (l.; Creignish)
MacEachern, Randy (l.; Judique)
MacEachern, Ronnie (l.; Sydney)
MacEachern, Steve (d.; Victoria Bridge)
MacEwan, William (l.; St. Peters)
MacFarlane, Alex D. (d.; Margaree)
MacFarlane, Allan (d.; Margaree)
MacFarlane, Joe Dougald (d.; Boston)
MacFarlane, John Grant (d.; Upper Margaree)
MacFarlane, Peter (d.; Queensville)
MacGillivray, V.J. (d.; Glace Bay)
MacInnis, Alex (Skye Mountain)
MacInnis, Annie Florence (Skye Mountain)
MacInnis, Billy (d.; Glencoe)
MacInnis, Dan (Skye Mountain)
MacInnis, Dan Joe (b. 1922; Sydney)
MacInnis, Dan Peter (d.; Sydney)
MacInnis, Gordon (d.; Boularderie)
MacInnis, Hector (d.; Glencoe)
MacInnis, Ian (l.; West Bay)
MacInnis, Jim (l.; Port Hawkesbury)
MacInnis, Jimmy (1879-1954; Glengarry-Terra Nova)
MacInnis, Jimmy (Skye Glen)
MacInnis, Joe "J.J." (1887-1944; Sydney)
MacInnis, John (pioneer; S.W. Mabou)
MacInnis, John Joe (b. 1909; Little Judique)
MacInnis, Martin (1856-1928; Glengarry - Terra Nova)
MacInnis, Mick (1870-1946; Glengarry - Terra Nova)
MacInnis, Neil (Castle Bay)
MacInnis, Neil Dan (b. 1893; Glenville)
MacInnis, Robert Hughie (d.; Judique)
MacInnis, Ron (l.; Pereau, N.S.)
MacInnis, Ronald (d.; Cape Mabou)
MacInnis, Sandy (b. 1919; Skye Mountain)
MacInnis, "Wishie" (Sydney)
MacIntosh, Kenny (d.; Chimney Corner)

MacIntosh, Paddy (Glace Bay)
MacIntyre, Alex (d.; Benacadie)
MacIntyre, Cassie MacIsaac (1902-1977; Inverness Town)
MacIntyre, Dougald (1878?-1934; New Waterford)
MacIntyre, Duncan L. (b. 1909; French Rd.)
MacIntyre, Francis (l.; Toronto)
MacIntyre, John (d.; French Vale)
MacIntyre, John (l.; Portage)
MacIntyre, John Dan (d.; Cape Mabou)
MacIntyre, John R. (d. 1942; Inverness Town)
MacIntyre, Peter (d.; Benacadie)
MacIntyre, Sandy (b. 1935; Toronto)
MacIsaac, Alex Angus (Broad Cove Banks)
MacIsaac, Alex Dan (b. 1912; Halifax)
MacIsaac, Angus (l.; Creignish)
MacIsaac, Dan (d.; Big Pond)
MacIsaac, Dan Hughie (Broad Cove Banks)
MacIsaac, David (b. 1955; Halifax)
MacIsaac, Donald Angus (Broad Cove Banks)
MacIsaac, Dougald (l.; New Waterford)
MacIsaac, Flora (Broad Cove Banks)
MacIsaac, Hughie (Dunvegan)
MacIsaac, John A. (l.; Creignish)
MacIsaac, John Angus (Broad Cove Banks)
MacIsaac, Johnny (1867?-1941; Blackstone)
MacIsaac, Johnny Archie (d. 1968; New Waterford)
MacIsaac, Mary (d.; Broad Cove Banks)
MacIsaac, Neil (d.; Big Pond)
MacIsaac, Roddy (l.; Dartmouth)
MacIsaac, Rory "Ruairidh Shim" (d.; Ben Eoin)
MacIsaac, Sandy (d.; Blackstone)
MacIsaac, Walter (b. 1909; Codroy Valley, Newfoundland)
MacKay, Angus (d.; Kingsville)
MacKay, Dannie (d. 1930; Kingsville)
MacKay, Jimmy D. (d.; Detroit)
MacKay, Peter (Kingsville)
MacKenzie, Archibald J. (1861-1939; Christmas Island)

MacKenzie, Archie (l.; Sydney River)
MacKenzie, Archie Alex (l.; Halifax)
MacKenzie, Carl (b. 1938; Sydney Forks)
MacKenzie, Charlie (l.; Washabuck)
MacKenzie, Dan Joe (Ottawa Brook)
MacKenzie, Hector (b. 1933; Washabuck)
MacKenzie, Hugh F. (1896-1971; Rear Christmas Island)
MacKenzie, Jack (Hay Cove)
MacKenzie, Maynard (l.; Baddeck)
MacKenzie, Simon (l.; Washabuck)
MacKinnon, Allie (l.; Sydney)
MacKinnon, Angus "Mossy" (d.; Meat Cove)
MacKinnon, Charlie (d.; Ainslie Glen)
MacKinnon, Charlie (long dead; St. Rose)
MacKinnon, Rev. Colin F. (l.; Toronto)
MacKinnon, Columba (1920-1973; White Horse)
MacKinnon, Dan (1864?-1949; Washabuck)
MacKinnon, Dan Joe (1916-1972; Whitehorse)
MacKinnon, Donald John (long dead; French Road)
MacKinnon, Hector (b. 1897; Washabuck)
MacKinnon, Hugh Fred (d.; Lake Ainslie)
MacKinnon, Jimmy (b. 1905; MacKinnon's Harbour)
MacKinnon, John (l.; Big Intervale)
MacKinnon, John Angus Stephen (l.; Bay St. Lawrence)
MacKinnon, John Neil (b. 1908; Hamilton, Ontario)
MacKinnon, Johnny Archie (l.; Smelt Brook)
MacKinnon, Katherine (l.; Port Hawkesbury)
MacKinnon, "Little" Fred (Lake Ainslie)
MacKinnon, Michael (d.; Castle Bay)
MacKinnon, Ned (1876-1926; Cooper's Pond)
MacKinnon, Neil F. (d.; Cooper's Pond)
MacKinnon, "Old" Allan (long dead; Fourchu)
MacKinnon, Philip (1912-1980; Windsor, Ontario)
MacKinnon, "Red" John (1870-1940; Meat Cove)
MacKinnon, Rod (1872-1969; Cooper's Pond)

MacKinnon, Roddy (1910-1972; Sydney)
MacLean, Alexander (1907-1928; Washabuck)
MacLean, Charlie Joe (l.; Frenchvale Rd.)
MacLean, Charles William (d.; Foot Cape)
MacLean, Hector (l.; Liverpool, N.S.)
MacLean, Joe (b. 1916; Lower Washabuck)
MacLean, Joe "Neil A." (Ottawa Brook)
MacLean, Joe P. (l.; Frenchvale)
MacLean, John (l.; Sydney)
MacLean, John (1823-1911; Foot Cape)
MacLean, John Neil (b. 1930; Gabarus Lake)
MacLean, Johnny "Washabuck" (b. 1925; Toronto)
MacLean, John W. (l.; Reserve Mines)
MacLean, Kathleen (l.; East Lake)
MacLean, Kenny (1896- ?; Foot Cape)
MacLean, Michael Anthony (b. 1911; Lower Washabuck)
MacLean, Mike John (l.; Iona)
MacLean, Mike (l.; Big Pond)
MacLean, Murdoch (Lower Washabuck)
MacLean, Murdoch (1910- ?; Foot Cape)
MacLean, Peter F. (b. 1899; Lower Washabuck)
MacLean, Raymond (d.; Sudbury)
MacLean, "Red" Rory (d.; Washabuck)
MacLean, Sandy (b. 1893; Foot Cape)
MacLean, Stephen (l.; Boston)
MacLean, Vincent (d.; Lower Washabuck)
MacLellan, Allan Donald (Glenville)
MacLellan, Angus "Pushie" (d.; California)
MacLellan, Archie (d.; Inverness)
MacLellan, Archie (d.; Kingsville)
MacLellan, "Baby" Joe (1915-1935; Riverside)
MacLellan, "Big" Ronald (1880?-1935; Riverside)
MacLellan, Charlie (l.; Toronto)
MacLellan, Charlie "John Donald" (d.; Dunvegan Mountain)
MacLellan, Dan Allan (1870-1946; Glenville)
MacLellan, Danny (d.; Inverness)
MacLellan, Donald F. (b. 1918; Toronto)
MacLellan, Dougald (l.; Margaree)

MacLellan, Hughie (l.; Halifax)
MacLellan, Jack (d.; Inverness)
MacLellan, Jimmy (l.; Sudbury)
MacLellan, Jimmy (d.; Inverness)
MacLellan, John Alex (b. 1917; S.W. Margaree)
MacLellan, John Alex (l.; Sudbury)
MacLellan, Johnny (1859-1951; Glenville)
MacLellan, "Little" Joe (d.; St. Rose)
MacLellan, Malcolm Allan (1876-1959; Glenville)
MacLellan, Ranald Joe (d.; St. Rose)
MacLellan, Rannie (b. 1951; S.W. Margaree)
MacLellan, "Red" Joe (d.; Deepdale)
MacLellan, Roddie (l.; Deepdale Road)
MacLellan, Ronald J. (b. 1957?; Toronto)
MacLellan, Theresa (l.; Riverside)
MacLellan, Vincent A. (1856-1935; Sydney)
MacLennan, Angus (Colorado)
MacLennan, Dr. Angus (d.; Inverness Co.)
MacLennan, Neil A. (Melford)
MacLeod, Fr. Colonel (p.p. at Creignish)
MacLeod, Daryl (l.; Harbourview)
MacLeod, Neil "Danny Kenny" (l.; North River Bridge)
MacLeod, Philip (l.; Fourchu)
MacLeod, Robert (l.; Glencoe)
MacLeod, Rory (l.; Dunvegan)
MacMaster, Angus "The Piper" (d.; Judique)
MacMaster, "Big" Hughie (d.; Queensville)
MacMaster, Buddy (b. 1924; Judique)
MacMaster, Donald Duncan (d.; Judique)
MacMaster, John Duncan (d.; Port Hood)
MacMaster, Vincent (Port Hastings)
MacMillan, Alasdair (d.; Red Islands)
MacMillan, Donald (d.; Red Islands)
MacMillan, Murdoch, (d.; Red Islands)
MacMullin, Rod (l.; Glace Bay)
MacNamara, Blair (l.; Evanston)
MacNeil, Alex (d.; Boisdale)
MacNeil, Alex (l.; Sydney)
MacNeil, Alex N. (d. 1981; Dominion)
MacNeil, Alex R. (l.; Sydney)

MacNeil, Alex "Sandi" (d.; Benacadie East)
MacNeil, Archie A. (l.; Creignish)
MacNeil, Bobby (b. 1936; Dearborn, Mich.)
MacNeil, Bernie (l.; Dearborn, Mich.)
MacNeil, Mrs. Flora Catherine Rankin (l.; Mabou Harbour)
MacNeil, Jack (d.; New Waterford)
MacNeil, Jim (l.; Sydney River)
MacNeil, Jimmy (b. 1967; Dearborn, Mich.)
MacNeil, Joe (l.; Barra Head)
MacNeil, John Alex "The Fiddler" (1889?-1957; Gillis Point)
MacNeil, John Angus (l.; Johnstown)
MacNeil, John Dan (b. 1909; Sydney)
MacNeil, Johnny (l.; Sydney River)
MacNeil, John "Og" (d.; Castle Bay)
MacNeil, John P. (l.; French Vale)
MacNeil, John "The Mason (d.; MacNeil's Vale, Iona)
MacNeil, Hector (Middle Cape)
MacNeil, Kyle (b. 1963; Sydney Mines)
MacNeil, Neil H. (Barra Glen)
MacNeil, Peter (d.; Castle Bay)
MacNeil, Fr. Rory (d.; Mabou)
MacPhail, Murdoch (l.; Boston)
MacPhee, Billy (b. 1915; Sydney)
MacPhee, Dan Hector (Inverness)
MacPhee, Henry (l.; Boston)
MacPhee, Leo (Lower River Inhabitants)
MacPhee, Michael J. (Big Pond area)
MacPhee, Peter (d.; Mabou)
MacPhee, Peter (d.; Port Hawkesbury)
MacPherson, Donald (l.; Dominion)
MacPherson, Donald Angus (1898-1967; Dunvegan)
MacQuarrie, Allan (l.; Kenloch)
MacQuarrie, Duncan (1884-1979; New Waterford)
MacQuarrie, Gordon (1897-1965; Melford)
MacQuarrie, Jack (Kenloch)
MacQuarrie, John (d.; Glenora Falls)
MacQuarrie, John Alex (1900-197?; Glenora Falls)

MacQuarrie, Morgan Gunn (b. 1946; Windsor, Ontario)
MacQuarrie, William (Orangedale)
MacVarish, Hughie J. (d.; East Bay)
MacVicar, Earl (Gabarus)
Marsh, Tom (d.; New Waterford)
Martell, Lawrence (l.; East Bay)
Martin, George (l.; Grand Greve)
Matheson, Bill (l.; River Denys)
Meagher, Donald (l.; Halifax)
Meagher, James (d. 1894; Brook Village)
Meagher, Jim (d.; Brook Village)
Meagher, John Nicholas (l.; Ontario)
Meagher, Lauchie (1881-1942; Brook Village)
Morais, Cliff (l.; Big Pond)
Morin, Kenneth (l.; North West Territories)
Morris, Albert (l.; Halifax)
Morris, Fr. Angus (b. 1936; Colindale)
Morris, Simon (Ingonish North)
Morrison, "Big" Ann (long dead; Gillis Point)
Morrison, Theresa MacLean (b. 1919; Lower Washabuck)
Muise, Arthur (b. 1950; Cheticamp I.)
Muise, Maurice (b. 1955; Halifax)
Mullins, Michael (long dead; Low Point)
Murphy, Johnny (d. 1970's; North E. Margaree)
Murray, Sonny (l.; Sydney Forks)
Nicholson, Alex Dan (Whycocomagh)
Nicholson, Alfred (Whycocomagh)
Nicholson, William (1850?-1960; N.E. Margaree)
Northern, Cosmos (l.; Little Narrows)
O'Brien, Elizabeth (b. 1960's; Mabou)
O'Brien, John (long dead; River Denys)
Odo, Placide (1875?-1956; Cheticamp)
O'Handley, Sandy (Judique)
Parks, Larry (l.; North Sydney)
Paul, George (l.; Eskasoni)
Peck, Ben (l.; Middle River)
Penny Eddy (d.; New Waterford)
Peters, Austin (d.; Mira Road)
Peters, Charles (d.; Mira Road)
Peters, Dick (d.; Mira Road)
Peters, Percy (b. 1911; Mira Road)
Petrie, Joe (l.; River Ryan)
Pinkerton, Hartwell (l.; Boston)
Poirier, Peter Henry (l.; Cheticamp)
Poirier, Wilfred (l.; Cheticamp)
Prosper, Wilfred (b. 1927; Eskasoni)
Probert, Willie (Middle River)
Rankin, Sr. Bessie (Inverness Co.)
Rankin, John Morris (b. 1959; Mabou)
Roach, Angus (Cheticamp)
Roach, Dan (Cheticamp)
Roach, Hubert (l.; Cheticamp)
Rogers, Eddy (l.; Reserve Mines)
Ross, Malcolm "Calum" (d.; Deepdale)
Sampson, Dominque (l.; Louisdale)
Sampson, Francis (l.; L'Ardoise)
Shaw, John (l.; Glendale)
Smith, Greg (l.; Port Hawkesbury)
Smith, Jim (1868-19?; Broad Cove)
Smith, Joe (1881-19?; Broad Cove)
Smith, John Alex (l.; Margaree)
Smith, John Francis (l.; Toronto)
Smith, Ronald (1876-1979; Broad Cove)
Spears, Sandra (l.; Mabou)
Steele, Johnny (b. 1912; Sydney)
Stone, James M. (l.; Halifax)
Stubbert, Brenda (b. 1959; Point Aconi)
Stubbert, Earl (l.; Point Aconi)
Stubbert, Lauchie (b. 1926?; Point Aconi)
Stubbert, Peter (Point Aconi)
Stubbert, Robert (b. 1923; Point Aconi)
Thibeau, Amos (l.; River Bourgeois)
Thibeau, "Johnny" Alex (Point Michaud)
Urquhart, Alex (l.; Pleasant Bay)
Walker, Agnes (l.; Hays River)
Walker, Alex (l.; North Sydney)
Walker, Dan Malcolm (l.; Hays River)
Walker, Dixie (l.; Port Hood)
Walker, Finlay (l.; Sudbury)
Walker, Joe (d.; Lake Ainslie)
Walker, Johnny (Point Aconi)
Walker, Vincent (l.; Hays River)
Wallace, Ambrose (l.; Heatherton)

Warner, Norman (l.; Port Hawkesbury)
Warner, Peter (l.; Port Hawkesbury)
Watson, Maurice (l.; Baddeck)
White, Danny (d.; Cheticamp)
White, Johnny Stephen (b. 1903; Margaree Forks)
Whitely, Norman (d. 1981; Cape North)
Williams, "Little" Charlie (d.; Ingonish Ferry)
Williams, Mary Jane MacLellan (d.; Glenville)
Williams, Neil (l.; Melford)
Wills, Tena (d.; Long Point, Inverness Co.)
Wilmot, Johnny (b. 1916; Sydney Mines)
Wright, Frankie (l.; Port Hawkesbury)
Wright, Freddie (l.; Mull River)
Young, Alex (d.; Foot Cape)

Some Prominent Accompanists — Past and Present

Piano: -

Anna Aucoin
Angus Beaton
Betty Lou MacMaster Beaton
Elizabeth MacEachen Beaton
Janet Beaton
Jessie Anne Cameron Beaton
Joey Beaton
Kathleen MacMaster Beaton
Katie Anne Campbell Beaton
Kay Jamieson Beaton
Mary MacDonald Beaton
Loretta Beaudry
Joan MacDonald Boes
Yvette Chaisson Bourgeois
Anne Campbell Brown
Rita Bryden
Catherine Marie Cameron
Janet Cameron
Lawrence Cameron
Helen Campbell
Margaret Campbell
Hilda Chaisson
Stan Chapman
Maybelle Chisholm
Ethel Cormier
Marion Dewar
Agnes Doyle
Margie Dunn
Florence Ellis
Elizabeth Fennell
Neil Finn
Barry Fraser
Mrs. Jean Fraser
Jack Gillis
Malcolm Gillis
Marion Gillis
Mary Jessie MacLellan Gillis
Mary MacLean Gillis
Sandra Gillis
Catherine Flora Campbell Graham
Mary Graham
Earl Gwynn
Lila Hashem
Catherine Anne Lamey Hawley
Patricia Chafe Hyde
Edward Irwin
Thelma Wilson Jessome
Sally MacEachern Kelly
Colin Kennedy
Penny Kennedy
Marg Lauzon
Mrs. Leonard MacEachern Leadbeater
Kathleen LeBlanc
Kevin MacCormick
"Chippie" MacDonald
Corrine MacPherson MacDonald
Howie MacDonald
Rev. Hugh A. MacDonald
Mary MacDonald ("Red")
Mary Jessie MacDonald
Mrs. Neil R. Beaton MacDonald
Mrs. W. J. MacDonald
Lorraine MacMaster MacDonnell
Bessie MacDougall
Lawrence MacDougall
Danny MacEachen
Anna Mae Rankin MacEachern
Susan MacEachern
Connie MacGillivray
George MacInnis
Mary Florence MacIntyre
Lila MacIsaac MacDonald
Bessie MacKinnon
Mary MacLean MacKinnon
Pauline MacKinnon
Alex MacLean
Marie Cameron MacLean
Gordon MacLean
Johanna MacDougall MacLean

Theresa MacLean
Jessie Maggie MacLellan
Lillian MacIsaac MacLellan
Marie MacLellan
Mary Ann MacDonald MacLellan
Ronald J. MacLellan
Phyllis MacLeod
Alex MacNeil
Mrs. Ann MacNeil
Catherine MacNeil
Helen MacNeil
Honey "F.X." MacNeil
Jean MacKenzie MacNeil
John S. MacNeil
Mary MacNeil
Nixie MacNeil
Seumas MacNeil
Stewart MacNeil
Doug MacPhee
Margaret MacPhee
Agnes MacPherson
Jimmy MacPherson
Roy MacQueen
Barbara MacDonald Magone
Betty Maillet
John Willie Morrison
Helen Peters
Geraldine Rankin
Fr. John Angus Rankin
John Morris Rankin
Mary Maggie Smith
Fr. R. D. Smith
Brenda Stubbert
Grace Tate

Lisa Tonnell
Beattie Wallace
Genevieve MacMaster Whalen
Barbara MacPhee White
Kay Campbell White
Gerald Wilson

Guitar: -

Allie Bennett
Edmond Boudreau
Winston Briand
John Allan Cameron
Donnie Campbell
Bernie Cormier
Estwood Davidson
Tim Donovan
Kevin Donovan
John Ferguson
Jerry Holland
Gelase Larade
John Matthews
Buddy MacDonald
Allister MacGillivray
David MacIsaac
J. D. MacKenzie
Donald MacKinnon
Stewart MacLean
Ernest MacLeod
Jerry MacNeil
Sonny Slade
Blanche Morais Sophocleous
Ralph Williams

Short Titles

Beaton and LeBlanc, "Arthur": Joey Beaton and Wayne LeBlanc, "Arthur Muise", article published by The Scotia Sun. Port Hawkesbury, June 20, 1973.

Bruford and Munro, "Fiddle": Alan Bruford and Ailie Munro, "The Fiddle in the Highlands", a pamphlet published by An Comunn Gaidhealach. Glasgow, Scotland.

Campbell, "Highland": R. J. MacKenzie Campbell, "Highland Community on the Bras d'Or". Published by Casket Printing and Publishing. Antigonish, 1978.

Dunn, "Highland": Charles W. Dunn, "Highland Settler", published by University of Toronto Press, 1953.

Gibson, "Fiddlers": John G. Gibson, "Fiddlers to the Fore" (a special paper), published by Scotia Group. Port Hawkesbury, 1975.

Gibson and Beaton, "Highland": John G. Gibson and Joey Beaton, "Highland Heritage" (a special paper). Port Hawkesbury, 1977.

Gibson, "Scotia Sun": John G. Gibson, from a series of articles on Cape Breton fiddlers in The Scotia Sun. Port Hawkesbury, 1972-73.

MacDonald and Beaton, "Tribute": Fr. Hugh A. MacDonald and Joey Beaton, "A Tribute to the Late Malcolm Beaton", Scotia Sun. February 19, 1975.

MacDonald, "Mabou": A. D. MacDonald, "Mabou Pioneers" (Volume 1), new edition by Formac Publishing Company Limited. Antigonish.

MacDougall, "History": J. L. MacDougall, "History of Inverness County", originally published in Truro, 1922.

MacInnis, "Dan Hughie": Frank MacInnis, "Dan Hughie MacEachern", article published in The Scotia Sun. Port Hawkesbury, February 21, 1973.

MacInnis, "Violin": J. J. MacInnis, "Violin Players I Have Met", from a magazine entitled "Eilean Cheap Breatann". Volumes I and II, published in early 1940's.

MacIntyre, "Souls": Linden MacIntyre, "Souls Sing in Gaelic", an article in the Halifax Chronicle Herald. July, 1975.

MacKenzie, "History": Archibald J. MacKenzie, "The History of Christmas Island and Parish". N.p., n.d.; preface dated 1926.

Shaw, Rankin and Lamey, "Cape Breton": John Shaw, Fr. John A. Rankin and William Lamey, "Cape Breton Scottish Fiddle" (a Topic Lp, including notes).

Thorn, "Looking": Dave Thorn, "Looking Back", published in "The Highlander". Sydney, November 8, 1972.

Footnotes

1. See Bruford and Munro, "Fiddle", p. 3-4.
2. MacIntyre, "Souls".
3. Dunn, "Highland", p. 73.
4. Gibson, "Scotia Sun" ("Angus Allan Gillis"), December 20, 1972.
5. See Shaw, Rankin and Lamey, "Cape Breton", p. 1.
6. See Gibson, "Fiddlers", p. 7.
7. See Gibson, "Scotia Sun" ("A Tribute to the Late Danny Beaton"), May, 2, 1973, p. 12.
8. Ibid.
9. See Gibson and Beaton, "Highland", p. 31.
10. MacInnis, "Violin", Volume I, p. 90.
11. Gibson, "Scotia Sun" ("Donald Angus Beaton"), January 10, 1973.
12. MacDonald and Beaton, "Tribute", p. 5.
13. MacInnis, "Violin", Volume I, p. 90.
14. Campbell, "Highland", p. 73.
15. Ibid., p. 70.
16. Thorn, "Looking", November 8, 1972.
17. MacInnis, "Violin", Volume II, p. 11.
18. MacDougall, "History", p. 385.
19. MacInnis, "Violin", Volume II, p. 11.
20. MacDonald, "Mabou", p. 424.
21. MacInnis, "Violin", Volume I, p. 90.
22. Ibid.
23. MacKenzie, "History", p. 133.
24. Sco Gibson, "Fiddlers", p. 8.
25. Ibid.
26. Ibid., p. 7.
27. See MacInnis, "Dan Hughie", p. 13.
28. See Beaton and LeBlanc, "Arthur", p. 1, section 2.

Photographic Credits

Consulting Personnel photos - Allister MacGillivray
Preface photo - Beverly MacGillivray

THE PAST:

All photos copied by Allister MacGillivray, except those of Dan R. MacDonald and Danny Cameron which were taken by Ron MacInnis.

The original prints of copied photos were supplied by the following:

Joey Beaton, Doug MacPhee, Colin Boyd, Betty Chisholm, Duncan Campbell, Evelyn Fraser, Mary "Jack" Gillis, Allison Gillis, Margaret Kennedy, Donnie Campbell, Winnie MacDonald, Bernie MacNeil, Angus A. MacDonnell, Winnie Muise, Archie A. MacKenzie, Jimmy MacKinnon, Alice Aucoin, Allan Albert Kennedy, Marie MacLellan, Mrs. Fred MacKinnon, Donald Meagher, Greg Smith, Willie D. Chisholm, Mrs. Owen Dan Gillis, Robbie Robertson, Marion Gillis, Cecilia Small, Rita Bryden, Frank MacInnis, Katy MacNeil, Johnny Steele, Christie MacInnis.

THE PRESENT:

All photos taken by Allister and Beverly MacGillivray, except the following:

(a) Ambrose Beaton, donated by Agnes Walker;
(b) Winnie Chafe taken by Ed Britt;
(c) Winston Fitzgerald taken by Doug MacPhee;
(d) Mary MacDonald - 1. donated by Doug MacPhee, 2. taken by Doug MacPhee;
(e) Dan Hughie MacEachern taken by Doug MacPhee;
(f) Carl MacKenzie taken by Mike Reppa;
(g) Michael Anthony MacLean donated by M. A. MacLean;
(h) Sandy MacLean donated by Mrs. Annie MacLean;
(i) Theresa Morrison donated by T. Morrison;
(j) Johnny Wilmot taken by Doug MacPhee;
(k) Walter MacIsaac donated by Mrs. W. MacIsaac;
(l) Hartwell Pinkerton taken by Doug MacPhee;
(m) Ron MacInnis donated by R. MacInnis;
(n) Mike MacLean taken by Virginia Garrison;

THE FUTURE: All photos taken by Allister MacGillivray

Art Credits

Cover - Beverly MacGillivray
Sketch of bridge dance - Beverly Brett
Sketch of Peter MacPhee - June Frank

A SPECIAL THANKS TO THE FOLLOWING:

Mary Boyd, Charlottetown; Bernie MacNeil, Dearborn, Michigan; Peggy MacLean, Baddeck; Dan Angus Beaton, Blackstone; Mr. and Mrs. Dan Malcolm Walker, Hays River; Mrs. Esther MacQuarrie, Inverness Town; Hughie "Shorty" MacDonald, Inverness Town; Msgr. M. A. MacLellan, Antigonish; Fr. Sam Campbell, Sydney; Fr. Greg MacLeod, Sydney; Dr. Bob Morgan, Sydney; Mrs. Flora Mae MacDonald, Margaree Forks; Willie D. Chisholm, Margaree Forks; Mrs. Mary "Jack" Gillis, South West Margaree; Sr. Sara Beaton, Mabou; Ms. Marie MacLellan, Sydney; John A. MacLellan, Riverside; Alex Archie MacKenzie, Halifax; Ron MacInnis, Pereau; Bernie MacIsaac, Antigonish; Robbie Robertson, Sydney; Duncan Campbell, Sydney; Muriel LeBlanc, Sydney; Margaret MacKinnon, Sydney; Angus A. MacDonnell, Judique; Mrs. Rita Bryden, Sydney; Mrs. Helen MacDougall, MacKinnon's Harbour; A.J. MacNeil, Cooper's Pond; Mr. and Mrs. Arthur Severance, Fourchu; Donald Meagher, Halifax; Theresa MacDonnell, Port Hood; Angus MacDonald, Halifax; Katy MacNeil, Iona; Bernie Gillis, South West Margaree; Annie Mae Skinner, Inverness Town; Dan Fraser, South Bar; Bob Fitzgerald, Dingwall; Annie Dixon, Broad Cove Banks; Sheldon MacInnis, Sydney; Mr. & Mrs. Cyril MacInnis, Ajax, Ontario; Hector MacLean, Liverpool, Nova Scotia; Jimmy MacKay, Kingsville; Norman MacDonald, Sydney; Mr. and Mrs. Tic Butler, Sydney; Mr. & Mrs. Donnie Campbell, Sydney; Fred White, East Bay; Ann Terry MacLellan, Sydney; Steve MacDonald, Sydney; Steve MacNeil, Sydney; Mrs. Owen Dan Gillis, Inverness Corner; Cecilia Small, Sydney; Marion Gillis, South West Margaree; Peter MacKenzie Campbell, Sydney; Alice Aucoin, New Victoria; Mrs. Winnie MacDonald, Antigonish; Dave Beaton, Broad Cove; Christy MacDonnell Gillis, Inverness Town; Jimmy MacKinnon, MacKinnon's Harbour; Greg Smith, Port Hawkesbury; Roddy MacDonald, Inverness Town; Winnie Muise, Mira Road; Mrs. Fred MacKinnon, Orangedale; Mrs. Betty Chisholm, Antigonish; Mrs. Belle Kennedy, New Waterford; Ms. Evelyn Fraser, New Victoria; Mr. & Mrs. Harold Cook, Cape North; Joe Neil MacNeil, Big Pond; Steve "John S." MacNeil, Big Pond; Mrs. Isabel MacGillivray, South Bar; Mrs. Elizabeth MacLellan, Sydney; Joe Kennedy, Inverside; Neil Archie Beaton, Strathlorne; David MacIsaac, Halifax.